KPMG Peat Marwick

With Our Compliments

David C. Potter
Partner

Certified Public Accountants

1010 Market Street
St. Louis, Missouri 63101
314 444-1400

Implementing Activity-Based Cost Management:

Moving from Analysis to Action

Implementation Experiences at Eight Companies

by

Robin Cooper

Robert S. Kaplan

Lawrence S. Maisel

Eileen Morrissey

Ronald M. Oehm

A study carried out on behalf of the
Institute of Management Accountants
Montvale, New Jersey

Research Report Publications

A Research Report Publication is defined as the product of a research effort conducted with the guidance of the Institute of Management Accountants' Committee on Research. The focus of such a document is to contribute to some segment of the body of management accounting knowledge.

Bold Step Research Series

Publications indicated as Bold Step are the end product of an ongoing major IMA program to improve management accounting by identifying state-of-the-art techniques and showing how these techniques can be adapted to changing manufacturing and service technologies. Through creative and applied research on the cutting edge of knowledge, the Institute will attempt to provide practical solutions to these emerging problems. These research findings will be directed toward real-world application by management accountants in industrial and other organizational settings. The Bold Step program initially was designed to generate a series of quality studies in cost accounting as it is currently applied in U.S. manufacturing. These studies, many of which are joint research projects initiated by the IMA, combine the strength and expertise of other leading organizations. The involvement of the Committee on Research is identical to that for a Research Report Publication.

Published by

Institute of Management Accountants
10 Paragon Drive
Montvale, NJ 07645-1760

Claire Barth, Editor

Foreword

Much has been said and written over the last several years regarding the value and the power of activity-based costing (ABC) and activity-based management (ABM). Initially, experts touted the use of ABC for improved product costing and decision making. More recently, experts have begun advocating the more universal use of ABM. But few success stories of bottom line improvement have surfaced. Is this because companies are unwilling to disclose information they feel gives them competitive advantage? Or are there real problems with the tools, the concepts, of the implementations of ABC and ABM management systems?

These circumstances prompted the Committee on Research of the Institute of Management Accountants (IMA) to sponsor research focused on understanding the realities of applying these concepts. The research objectives were to study how the financial organization can work with operating management to add value through implementing ABC/ABM, what is involved in installing either pilot systems or complete systems, and how the concepts and value of ABC/ABM can be validated. We wanted to know what was and what wasn't working and why. The desire was for real-life examples and case studies from which executive management and the management accounting community can learn. Furthermore, we wanted the researchers to analyze their findings and synthesize the study results.

Because of their acknowledged leadership, expertise, and experience with activity-based concepts, Professors Kaplan and Cooper from Harvard University and Lawrence Maisel teamed with the management consulting division of KPMG Peat Marwick to provide these new insights.

The basic conclusions from the research are that progress is being made just in having new and innovative information. Having it, however, doesn't result automatically in improvements being made. While each implementation likely will be unique to each business unit, requiring good project management skills, equally good skills are necessary for creating organizational change. For it is only when the organization takes action that insights gained through ABC analysis are converted into improved profits and enhanced competitive position.

This research contributes significantly to the emerging body of knowledge about activity-based costing/management and its place in the broader subject of management accounting for improved competitiveness.

Guidance in the preparation of the report was generously provided by the IMA Project Committee:

Robert C. Miller, *Chairman*
The Boeing Company
Seattle, Washington

Andrew D. Bailey, Jr.   Charles D. Mecimore
University of Arizona   University of North Carolina
Tucson, Arizona   Greensboro, North Carolina

W. Ron Ragland
Martin Marietta Energy Systems, Inc.
Oak Ridge, Tennessee

This report reflects the views of the researchers and not necessarily those of the Institute, the Committee on Research, or the Project Committee.

Patrick L. Romano, CMA
Director of Research
Institute of Management Accountants

Preface

During the 1980s, the field of management accounting and the business environment in North America underwent many changes, many due to the rise in global competition and use of technology. Increased competition demanded that companies improve the effectiveness of decisions concerning product and customer mix, pricing, and product design. In their search for ways to gain competitive strength, companies found they needed accurate information relating to the consumption of resources used to produce, sell, and deliver products (and services) to customers.

By the end of the 1980s, the use of activity-based costing (ABC) to obtain improved cost and profitability information had attracted a lot of attention in the financial community. Articles and seminars about ABC proliferated, and PC- based software became available to implement the process.

Yet relatively few companies throughout North America ventured and to pioneer implementation of an ABC system. Instead, organizations continued to research ABC and to ask three fundamental questions:

- What potential benefits can we expect from an ABC system?
- How do we design and implement an activity-based cost system that will allow us to gain these benefits?
- How do we ensure that we obtain these benefits?

The conceptual and technical discussions of ABC had advanced significantly over the years and broadened financial executives' conceptual awareness. Companies today want to learn *how* to implement ABC. Many are uncertain as to how to proceed and what decisions to make. They are asking:

- What are the implementation steps and issues?
- What are some of the key design decisions?
- What are the pitfalls?

At the same time, companies continue to ask *why:*

- Where's the real value of ABC?

- How can nonfinancial managers in our organization benefit by ABC?
- What is the value of ABC to our shareholders?
- What actions can be taken?

ABC success stories have only recently begun to filter out to the public. The true advantages of ABC, beyond product costing, are known only to a few who have witnessed an ABC implementation. The hard results, the changes in strategic thinking, the new ways in which organizations are beginning to look at, change, and measure themselves remain hidden from the public.

In response to this situation, the Institute of Management Accountants, KPMG Peat Marwick, Lawrence Maisel, and Professors Robert Kaplan and Robin Cooper joined to carry out a joint research project based on studies of actual companies that have implemented ABC. They focused on the many questions and concerns facing managers who have evaluated ABC alternatives. The primary objective of the project was to research, synthesize, and document key implementation issues and results, based on these companies' experiences.

Chapter 1 provides an executive summary of the findings of this research project. To assist readers in understanding ABC terminology and concepts, Chapter 2 presents an overview of activity-based costing principles and suggests key articles for further review. Chapter 3 covers the research methodology.

Eight case studies of companies that have implemented an ABC system make up the bulk of the book. The case studies, documented in Chapters 4 to 11, highlight: (1) the issues that lead management to implement ABC, (2) the implementation process and resources required in each case, (3) the results and insights gained, and (4) the actions taken. Based on the examination of the eight companies, the research team developed two synthesis chapters that summarize the form and substance of the ABC models, as well as the organizational processes required for management to sponsor, act upon, and realize the benefits from an activity-based cost system. These conclusions are presented in Chapters 12 and 13, and basic implementation steps, in the Appendix.

The material in this book was developed through observation and analysis of innovative organizations that have embarked on ABC programs. We especially appreciate the cooperation from the companies we have worked with for allowing us to describe their ABC systems and implementation experience. We were fortunate to receive permission to present these cases, sometimes undisguised.

In summary, this book represents a state-of-the-art view of the ABC principles and implementation experiences of eight companies. The findings will provide an understanding of the design decisions and pitfalls and the organizational dynamics that can directly affect the success of an ABC system. Any reader contemplating an ABC project will find this book useful in identifying good design decisions and in avoiding pitfalls. Readers who currently are considering or have embarked on an ABC study undoubtedly will identify with many of the experiences shared by these eight companies.

Acknowledgments

An endeavor such as this research project relies heavily upon the contributions of many hard-working people and their willingness to invest time and energy in the project, most often without direct compensation.

We especially recognize the efforts of our talented case writers and field researchers. These persons visited the sites, helped gather the information, described each case in detail, and, most important, remained patient during the unending review notes and revisions each case required. The researchers and writers include (alphabetically) Anik Bose, Nick Galambos, Larry Hitchcock, Marie Ireland, Joy Melton-Roberts, Eileen Morrissey, and Milan Weber, all of KPMG Peat Marwick. We also thank Jon Broduer, of KPMG Peat Marwick, for his contribution in enhancing several sections of the book.

A project of this magnitude cannot go smoothly without the dedicated effort and skills of project administration in pulling all of the chapters together and reminding each writer of deadlines and commitments. For this we are grateful to Anne Sullivan, Carl DiGiorgio, and Vickie Damore of KPMG Peat Marwick and Claire Barth, senior editor, IMA.

Our sponsors, the Institute of Management Accountants, had the foresight to see the need for this valuable research. Their support and guidance contributed greatly to this project's success.

The Project Committee, composed of Robert Miller (chairman, from the Boeing Company), Andrew Bailey (University of Arizona), Charles Mecimore (University of North Carolina), W. Ron Ragland (Martin Marietta), and Patrick Romano (IMA), provided sustained enthusiasm and irreplaceable guidance as to the content of each case and the direction of the analysis chapters.

Given the nature of this research, we feel especially appreciative of the many persons at the site companies who gave us freedom and full support to ask probing questions and view sensitive data in order to research and analyze the nature and purpose of their ABC projects. Without their efforts and candor, this project would not exist. A few of these companies and employees are described in the cases, but others have elected (for competitive reasons) to be disguised. To each and every one of you, the authors of this research extend a very special acknowledgement and our sincere gratitude for your enlightened support.

About the Authors

Robin Cooper

Robin Cooper has been a member of the Harvard Business School faculty since 1982. In September 1992, he became professor of management at the Peter Drucker Center at the Claremont Graduate School in Claremont, California. Dr. Cooper's major field of interest is management accounting. In 1990, he received the first Innovations in Accounting Education Award, presented by the American Accounting Association in recognition of his course development efforts in product costing.

Dr. Cooper's current research focuses on the design and use of activity-based cost systems. He is examining how firms can use the more accurate product costs reported by activity-based cost systems to implement more effective strategies and become more competitive. His recent book, *The Design of Cost Management Systems: Text, Cases, and Readings,* coauthored with Robert S. Kaplan, presents much of the innovative material developed during the last five years. Dr. Cooper is a regular contributor to the *Journal of Cost Management,* in which he recently published 10 articles describing the structure of cost systems. His articles include "Cost Classification in Unit-Based and Activity-Based Manufacturing Cost Systems" and a four-part series titled "Rise of Activity-Based Costing." He also has published in *Management Accounting* (U.S.), *Management Accounting* (U.K.), *Accountancy* (U.K.), and *Accounting* (Japan). He has had three articles published in the *Harvard Business Review.*

Dr. Cooper consults with many leading companies in North America and Europe on the design and implementation of advanced cost management systems. He regularly offers seminars in North America and Europe and has lectured in Japan.

Dr. Cooper received his MBA with high distinction from Harvard in 1979 and was named a Baker Scholar. A recipient of a Deloitte Haskins & Sells Foundation Fellowship and an ITT International Fellowship, he earned his DBA from the Harvard Business School in 1982. Before beginning his graduate studies, he worked as an accountant for Coopers and Lybrand in its London and Boston offices, from 1972 to 1976. A native of England, Dr. Cooper is a Fellow of the Institute of Chartered Accountants in England and Wales. He received his bachelor of science degree in chemistry with first-class honors from Manchester University in 1972.

Robert S. Kaplan

Robert S. Kaplan is the Arthur Lowes Dickinson Professor of Accounting at the Harvard Business School. Formerly, he was on the faculty of the Graduate School of Industrial Administration at Carnegie-Mellon University and served as dean of that school from 1977 to 1983. He received a B.S. and M.S. in electrical engineering from MIT and a Ph.D. in operations research from Cornell University. Author of more than 80 papers in accounting and management journals, Dr. Kaplan received the Outstanding Accounting Educator Award in 1988 from the American Accounting Association (AAA). He also received the AICPA Accounting Literature Award in 1971, the 1984 McKinsey Award for an outstanding paper in the *Harvard Business Review,* and the 1987 AICPA/AAA Notable Contributions to Accounting Literature Award for his paper, "Measuring Manufacturing Performance."

His current research focuses on developing new management accounting systems for the rapidly changing environment of manufacturing and service organizations. *Relevance Lost: The Rise and Fall of Management Accounting,* coauthored with H. Thomas Johnson and published in early 1987, was the cover story in the January 1987 issue of *Management Accounting.* It received the AAA/DH&S Wildman Medal in 1988 as the accounting publication with the greatest potential for influencing practice, as well as the first Notable Contribution to Management Accounting Literature Award from the Management Accounting Section of the AAA. *The paperback edition of Relevance Lost* was published in 1991. More recent books include *The Design of Cost Management Systems: Text, Cases, and Readings,* coauthored with Robin Cooper; *Advanced Management Accounting,* second edition, coauthored with Anthony Atkinson; *Accounting & Management: Field Study Perspectives,* coedited with William J. Bruns, Jr.; and *Measures for Manufacturing Excellence,* on performance measurement in advanced manufacturing environments.

Lawrence S. Maisel

Lawrence Maisel is the managing director of Maisel Consulting Group, a firm specializing in profit improvement, business process redesign, and performance measurements using activity-based cost management.

Prior to forming Maisel Consulting Group, he was the national director for KPMG Peat Marwick's financial management consulting practice. Mr. Maisel has considerable ABC/ABM expertise and experience as a result of implementing numerous client projects for manufacturing, distribution, and financial services organizations. These projects have enabled clients to improve profitability, redesign business processes, achieve productivity improvements, and reduce cost. In addition, he has more than 22 years of consulting experience, having performed numerous projects for senior, financial, and line management.

Mr. Maisel is editor of the *Journal of Cost Management* and consulting editor of the *Handbook of Cost Management,* has published numerous articles on related management topics, and is a frequent speaker at national conferences on ABCM. He is a CPA and member of the IMA and AICPA. Mr. Maisel is chairman of the New York State Society of CPAs Committee on Management Consulting Services and also was executive sponsor of Computer Aided Manufacturing-International (CAM-I).

He received a B.A. in economics from New York University and a MBA in corporate financial management from Pace University.

Eileen Morrissey

Eileen Morrissey, CPA, is a recognized specialist in the area of activity-based costing. She has been directly involved in many Fortune 500 and multinational ABC applications within industries such as discrete manufacturing, food processing, paper products, distribution, and financial services. Through these implementations using ABC, Ms. Morrissey has helped companies better understand true product and customer profitability, identify and implement process improvement opportunities, and make strategic decisions regarding which product can be most effectively sold to which market and how customer buying behavior drives the economics of the business.

Ms. Morrissey published articles on pricing decisions using activity-based cost management in the *Journal of Pricing Management,* Summer 1990 and Fall 1990 issues. She is a CPA in New York and Colorado. She is a member of the AICPA, IMA and New York State Society of CPAs. Ms. Morrissey is a graduate of the State University of New York at Binghamton with a Bachelor of Science degree in accounting, May 1979. She attended New York University's Master of Business Administration program with emphasis on computer application and information systems.

During the time of this research study, Ms. Morrissey worked as a senior manager in KPMG Peat Marwick's management consulting practice, where she was trained and worked with Robert Kaplan and Robin Cooper. She is currently a senior manager in Price Waterhouse's national manufacturing management consulting practice, specializing in activity-based costing.

Ronald M. Oehm

Ronald M. Oehm serves as partner-in-charge of KPMG Peat Marwick's management consulting business, serving clients in manufacturing and technology industries. He provides partnership leadership for strategic and financial management consulting (business planning, organizational analysis, marketing, and financial management). Building on 24 years of consulting experience, he is a leading proponent and practitioner in applying ABC and ABM concepts to business issues, with special emphasis on enhancing the linkage among strategy, organization structure, and performance measurement.

Mr. Oehm graduated magna cum laude from Claremont Men's College with a Bachelor of Arts degree in economics and mathematics. He received a Master of Science degree in probability and statistics from Stanford University, where, as a teaching-research assistant, he conducted classes in probability analysis. Mr. Oehm also received a Master of Business Administration degree in general management from the Harvard University Graduate School of Business Administration. Mr. Oehm has taught business policy and corporate strategy in the MBA program at Golden Gate University.

Table of Contents

Foreword   iii

Preface   v

Acknowledgments   ix

About the Authors   xi

Chapter 1: Executive Summary   1
  Case Sites and Scope   2
  Implementation Experiences   3
  Actions Taken   7

Chapter 2: Structure of ABC Systems   9
  ABC Systems Differ from Traditional Cost Systems   9
  Designing Activity-Based Cost Systems   12
  Activity Coding   19
  ABC Software   25
  Conclusion   26

Chapter 3: The Research Methodology   27
  Introduction and Background   27
  Research Approach   28

Chapter 4: Advanced Micro Devices   41
  Executive Summary   41
  Company Profile and Business Environment   42
  The Need for Improved Cost Management   43
  The Need for ABC   46
  Preparing the Organization   47
  Implementation of the Pilot Project   49
  Key Results and Findings   56
  ABC Implementation and Roll-Out Plan   60

Chapter 5: Farrall, Inc.   63
  Executive Summary   63
  Company Background   64
  Preparing the Organization   67
  System Design and Architecture   69
  Data Interpretation   73
  Management Acceptance of the ABC Study   89
  The Future of ABC at Farrall   93
  Epilogue   94

Chapter 6: Williams Brothers Metals   99
  Executive Summary   99
  Company Background   100
  Preparing the Organization   102
  System Design   104
  Implementation Process   110
  Findings and Results   111
  Management Acceptance   117
  Future of ABC at WMB   119

Chapter 7: ARCO Alaska   121
  Executive Summary   121
  Company Background   122
  Preparing for Activity-Based Analysis   124
  Model Design and Architecture   128
  ABA Results   137
  Management Acceptance and Use of ABA   146
  Future of ABA at AAI   150

Chapter 8: Monarch Mirror Door Company   153
  Executive Summary   153
  Company Profile and Business Environment   154
  The Need for ABC   158
  Preparing the Organization   160
  Implementation: System Design and Architecture   166
  Findings and Results   171
  Management Acceptance   176
  Conclusion and Next Steps   177
  Epilogue   178

Chapter 9: Steward & Company 179
Executive Summary 179
Company Profile and Background 179
The Need for ABC 181
Preparing the Organization 183
System Design and Architecture 183
Reviewing the Results 191
Management Acceptance of ABC Results 201
Where Is ABC Going at Steward? 206

Chapter 10: Slade Manufacturing, Inc.: Hudson Automotive Parts Company 209
Executive Summary 209
Company Background 210
Activity-Based Costing: Initial Motivation 213
ABC at Hudson Automotive Parts 217
ABC Model Architecture 228
Results of Activity-Based Costing at Youngstown 232

Chapter 11: KRAFT USA 237
Executive Summary 237
Company Background 239
Preparing the Organization 245
System Design and Architecture 249
Role of Consultants 256
Findings and Results 259
Management Acceptance 263
Future 270
Epilogue 271

Chapter 12: Analysis of ABC Models: Design, Structure, and Findings 273
Model Scope 273
Model Structure 277
Project Resources 295
Summary 304

Chapter 13: Organizational Issues in ABC Projects 307
Organizational Barriers 308
Management of the Change Process 309

ABC Project Management at the Case Sites   312
Change Agent in the Action Process   321
Summary: Organizational Resistance and Defensive Routines   323
Conclusion   325

Bibliography   327

Appendix: Fundamental Implementation Steps   333

Chapter 1

Executive Summary

Activity-based cost management systems have received extensive attention during the past eight years through books, articles, cases, and numerous seminars and conferences. To date, the writing and speaking on cost management systems have focused on the failings of traditional costing systems and the remedies offered by new approaches such as activity-based cost management. By 1991, the theory and conceptual framework for ABC management had been established, and numerous companies had initiated projects in an attempt to learn the applicability of the concepts in their organizations.

Little systematic evidence was available, however, as to the design of actual ABC systems, the circumstances that would lead companies to initiate an ABC project, the management of an ABC project, and the actions and benefits that resulted from the improved information produced by the ABC systems. This research project fills this knowledge gap by examining, analyzing, and synthesizing the actual experiences of eight companies that implemented activity-based cost management systems.

The research study revealed that activity-based cost models can be developed using a "generally accepted" set of practices, with a relatively modest commitment of financial, personnel, and time resources. In developing an ABC model, the project team first identifies the activities performed by the organization's resources and then estimates the costs of performing the activities. The activity costs then are linked to the organizational outputs—products, services, customers, projects, and organizational units—that benefit from the activities performed. Among the principal findings from the study are the following:

- Activity-based cost management is more than a system. It is a management process. Managers at each company understood that the ABC information enabled them to manage activities and business processes by providing a cross-functional, integrated view of the firm.

1

- ABC management benefits both strategic and operational decisions. Companies were using the information to make major decisions on product lines, market segments, and customer relationships, as well as to stimulate process improvements and activity management.
- An ABC model can supplement and coexist with traditional financial systems. Companies continued to operate their existing financial systems while developing and interpreting ABC models.
- ABC information, by itself, does not invoke actions and decisions leading to improved profits and operating performance. Management must institute a conscious process of organizational change and implementation if the organization is to receive benefits from the improved insights resulting from an ABC analysis.

Case Sites and Scope

The case sites included five manufacturing organizations, a financial services company, the finance department of a large energy company, and a distribution company. None of the eight sites developed a complete model of all organizational expenses in its initial effort. But, in aggregate, the eight sites included models of manufacturing operating expenses, marketing and selling expenses, distribution expenses, and general corporate overhead expenses. Therefore, by aggregating across the models developed in the eight sites, the study provides insight on how an enterprise-wide, organizational-activity-based model can be implemented, and on the nature of the decisions that would be supported by such a model.

All five manufacturing organizations analyzed production expenses to obtain the expenses of organizational activities and the costs of individual products. Two of the manufacturing companies also analyzed marketing and selling expenses to obtain measures of customer and market segment profitability. All the manufacturing companies emphasized the role that activity costing and activity analysis should take to stimulate operating process improvements. The companies explicitly recognized the linkage of ABC to their formal quality initiatives. The model designs typically included specific activities and activity centers to collect information on quality-related expenses.

The studies done at the financial services company and the finance department of the energy company showed how activity-based cost management can be extended to an organization's general and administrative expenses. The study at the distribution company developed an activity-based cost model of product distribution and customer service expenses.

In summary, the eight sites illustrate how activity-based cost management encompasses all aspects of a company's value-added chain: (1) purchasing and procurement, (2) operations, (3) marketing and selling, (4) distribution, and (5) general and administrative expenses.

Implementation Experiences

Activity and Business Process Analysis

The implementing companies found that the most quickly derived benefit from the ABC analysis was the restructuring and mapping of the organization's expenses from functional categories and departments into the activities and business processes performed by the organization's resources. In each study, senior managers reported that this information revealed for the first time the costs of the activities their organizational units were performing. They expected to use this information to make decisions on outsourcing activities, eliminating activities, or, most common, improving the efficiency with which activities were performed.

The general usefulness of activity and business process costs came as somewhat of a surprise to managers. Apparently these managers had believed erroneously that ABC was only a product costing system. Before conducting the ABC project, they had not appreciated the insights to be gained by identifying the activities performed by support resources and by determining the costs that were currently incurred to perform these activities.

Contributing to the insights from the activity analysis were the several types of activity classifications used by the sites. Most used some form of the activity-based cost hierarchy, in which activities are classified as unit, batch, product sustaining, or facility sustaining. Several of the sites attempted to perform a value classification for activities, but most found this process difficult and controversial.

Cost Driver Analysis

Identifying and measuring cost drivers proved to be the most difficult part of the study. One company excluded two important expense categories from the initial study because it lacked information about how individual products and services used these resources. Other companies reported that even when they used surrogate cost drivers, they had to perform extensive programming to access existing corporate databases and also considerable manual data collection. One company, however, which initially expected difficulty in collecting cost driver information, found that almost all of the desired information was accessible on machine-readable databases. A key project member recalled the cost driver analysis. He said, "When we started, we didn't know what was available in the systems. Designing cost drivers was a big deal. You really need to have good systems in place before you start an activity-based management project."

Products and Customers

All the sites drove their organizational expenses from activities to individual products, customers, or other cost objects. The manufacturing companies generally found, as expected, that low-volume, complex products tended to be much more expensive than had been calculated by the existing standard cost system. The ABC models provided a "bill of activity costs" that enabled managers to see the costs of procurement, inventory carrying and management, materials handling, inspection, shipment, and setup for individual products. This information was expected to lead to changes in the production scheduling, design, mix, and pricing for an organization's products.

The automotive division of one company started immediately to rationalize its products and customers to reduce complexity and enhance profitability. It also instituted price increases on other products that yielded $1.2 million in additional revenues. The company's controller described the impact of ABC at the division: "ABC has built our confidence during negotiations. Today we don't crumble when confronted by a customer demanding price improvements.... ABC has also made us more aggressive in pursuing new business—we're aggressive on bids for products that we believe our competitors are not pricing correctly."

The division also was using its more accurate product costing data strategically. It deliberately refused to accede to an important customer's request for a significant price reduction for the last three years of an existing contract. The division enjoyed higher prices for the period until the products were transferred away, it freed up capacity to develop and bid for profitable next-generation products that would be produced when the existing products left, and it locked a major competitor into committing a significant part of its capacity to an unprofitable contract.

The two companies that produced customer profitability reports also found the typical ABC pattern, with several customers shown to be highly profitable, most customers at or near breakeven profitability, and a few customers highly unprofitable. For example, large-volume customers with whom one company had been doing business for many years were quite profitable. Newly acquired customers or small customers, for whom generous credit terms and extensive sales and technical support were provided, were unprofitable.

The other company identified several market segments that were only marginally profitable. Mass merchandisers purchased very low-margin products and likely never could become high-profit contributors. The international and original equipment manufacturer (OEM) markets, with modest sales, were at or below breakeven. The project sponsor indicated that "since the ABC implementation, we have developed and initiated an exit strategy for the OEM market and have held off any attempt to grow our international market. The ABC data put certain decisions on the table. We now had data to support our discussions."

Similar findings occurred for the financial services company. Its product profitability model showed that only two products—equity securities and high yield securities—were profitable. The remaining securities were breakeven or showed significant losses. Based on these results, the company cut back on one product line, international, almost immediately and reorganized its product responsibilities to increase the focus on profit improvement. A second ABC model, of account executive (AE) profitability, showed that AE support costs were much higher than previously believed. The director and head of the equity department indicated:

> The ABC study revealed the average breakeven point for an AE was $325,000 in gross commissions. This was a much higher number than we had assumed. Based on these results, unprofitable AEs who do not fall into a special category [new hire, important link to other product lines, or special/unique trades] may be asked to leave. By looking at the activity expenses associated with each AE, I have better insight into the avoidable expenses if an AE leaves.

At the distribution company, the analysis indicated that the products shipped as mill direct were the most profitable. Such shipments incurred almost no inventory and materials handling costs. This finding, however, caused management to question the competitive advantage of its distribution business if the most profitable products bypassed most internal processes.

Project Resources

With one exception, each of the sites had its own project team do the bulk of the model development, which included interviews, formal and informal data collection, and running the model. Senior financial people played a critical role at all the sites. With the exception of the financial services company, where the motivation for the project came from the company CEO, the motivation and sponsorship at the other sites began and was maintained in a finance group. Most of the teams, however, drew upon people other than those from the finance group—the main contributors came from management information services (MIS) and operations. Senior management project steering committees were used at four sites, and these sites were the ones where subsequent management actions were most noticeable.

At most of the sites, outside consultants played a facilitating role:

- Providing initial training and awareness seminars and helping the project team structure the interviews;
- Transferring the hard data from the company's databases and the soft data from management interviews and estimates into a PC-based activity-based software model;
- Assisting in analyzing and preparing reports and presentations to the project sponsor and senior management.

Most of the day-to-day work, however, was performed by the internally staffed project teams.

The average time for a project was about four months, with elapsed time ranging from two months at the energy company (because of the limited scope of the project and the restricted availability of two summer interns who did the data collection and model development) to about eight months for companies at which the scope of the projects extended beyond initial expectations. The companies committed about 2.0 full-time employees (FTEs) during the project's duration, plus assistance from outside (or internal) consultants to prepare and train people in the organization and help in the tasks of analysis and report presentation.

All the sites used a PC-based software package that had been developed specifically for activity-based cost analysis. None of the companies attempted to use a mainframe computer or existing cost accounting package to develop the ABC model. Data on expenses, product characteristics, and cost drivers were derived, when available, from existing databases on the company's systems and downloaded to the PC-based ABC software package. Data not available in machine-readable form were entered manually.

No modification to existing financial systems was required, and companies continued to run all their existing systems in parallel with their new ABC models. Some observers have questioned whether managers would find credible the numbers created "outside" of the official financial reporting system. This hypothetical concern never was expressed in any of the interviews conducted at the eight sites. If anything, managers found the numbers generated from the activity-based analysis more credible and relevant than the numbers generated from the official costing system. No site considered or intended the activity-based model to be a replacement for the organization's financial transaction system, which, in all eight cases, continued to function as before and was expected to remain in the future. *The activity-based model was treated as a management information system, not as part of the accounting system.*

Actions Taken

Several of the companies already had taken action based on the insights gained from the ABC analysis. These actions included repricing, de-emphasizing, eliminating, and reorganizing certain product lines, services, or market segments. They also included process improvements to reduce the cost of key business activities and processes. But many of the companies had yet to act on the findings, even when the ABC analysis indicated that significant numbers of products, customers, or processes were much more expensive than the traditional cost accounting systems had been reporting.

In part, the delay could be attributed to the recency of the activity-based cost management approach in the chosen companies. For most of the sites, the estimation of the ABC model was not completed until mid-1991. Because of the time frame of this research study, these sites were visited while the ABC model still was undergoing final estimation or, at best, shortly after the final estimates had occurred. Senior management either had not been briefed completely on the findings or had had insufficient time to establish profit priorities for taking action. Given the radical change in thinking required by activity-based cost management, and the extended length of time for any new management decision and action to occur, the study may have captured companies at too early a stage to judge the efficacy of improved management actions from the newly gathered ABC information.

Organizational Barriers

But a more fundamental cause of the delays in taking action may have been inadequate preparation of the organization for changes in thinking and decision making. Delays like those at many of the sites, in moving from a fully estimated and analyzed ABC model to actions that improve profits, should concern corporate sponsors and finance managers who wish to have the output from their ABC models used productively. The most successful projects occurred when a specific *target* for change was identified early in the project, during the analysis stage. The target was the person or group whose decisions were expected to change as a consequence of the information revealed by the activity-based model. Also helpful was having a *sponsor* for the action stage, a senior person who wanted change to occur and who could authorize the actions to be taken by the target person or group.

Many companies do not have an explicit game plan for making the transition from generating information in the ABC analysis stage to having line managers make decisions in an action stage. The game plan should include identifying, early in the project, both the sponsor and the target for the changes that are expected in the action stage. Otherwise, companies could find that their ABC project keeps cycling within the analysis stage. In this pattern, the finance sponsor is following what could be called a field of dreams strategy: "If I build it [the ABC model], the line managers will come [and take action]." Unfortunately, the field of dreams strategy usually proceeds with the project team being asked to refine the model, re-estimate it on new data (e.g., this year's actuals, next year's budget), and develop new models for different organizational sites. The danger of this pattern is that after several years of refinement, re-estimation, and extension, but no managerial decisions or actions, the ABC project becomes viewed as a concern of the finance group only. It is not thought of as an initiative that has to be addressed, accepted, internalized, and acted upon by operating managers.

Sponsors and project managers of the analysis stage must recognize that a comprehensive ABC model is not an end in its own right. No organization ever made more money merely because it had a more accurate understanding of its economics. Only when understanding is translated into action is the potential for profit improvement unleashed. The final chapter in this book provides a framework to help managers transform an ABC project from the analysis stage to the subsequent and vitally important action stage.

Chapter 2

Structure of ABC Systems

ABC Systems Differ from Traditional Cost Systems

Traditional cost systems use a two-stage procedure to assign an organization's indirect and support expenses to outputs. Operating expenses are assigned first to cost pools and second, to the outputs of the production process (see Exhibit 2-1). These traditional two-stage assignment procedures, however, distort reported costs considerably. The traditional systems assign costs from cost pools to outputs using volume drivers such as labor and machine hours, material purchases, and units produced. Because many indirect and support resources are

Exhibit 2-1
THE TRADITIONAL TWO STAGE APPROACH

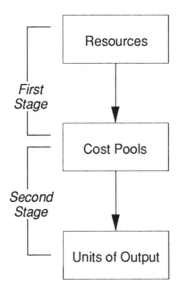

not used in proportion to the number of output units produced, these traditional systems provide highly inaccurate measures of the costs of support activities used by individual outputs.

Activity-based cost systems differ from traditional systems by modeling the usage of all organizational resources on the activities performed by these resources and then linking the cost of these activities to outputs such as products, services, customers, and projects (see Exhibit 2-2). In particular, activity-based systems measure more accurately the cost of activities not proportional to the volume of outputs produced. In manufacturing processes, four categories of activities can be identified: (1) unit-level (volume-driven) activities performed every time a unit of product is produced, (2) batch-level activities performed every time a batch of products is produced, (3) product-sustaining activities performed to support the manufacture of a given product, and (4) facility-sustaining activities performed to sustain the production of products in general. For example, ABC systems use drivers that capture characteristics of the product batch, such as the number of inspections or the number of production orders, to assign the costs of batch-level activities to products. The costs of product-sustaining activities are

Exhibit 2-2
THE ACTIVITY-BASED
TWO STAGE PROCEDURE

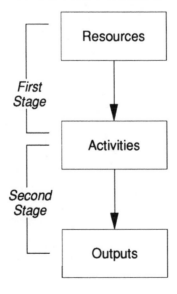

assigned to products using drivers that capture characteristics of the product itself, such as the number of components it contains or the number of engineering change orders it required.

Thus, activity-based cost systems differ from traditional systems in two ways: (1) Cost pools are defined as activities rather than as production cost centers, and (2) the cost drivers used to assign activity costs to outputs are structurally different from those used in traditional cost systems. These modifications to the two-stage procedure allow well-designed, activity-based cost systems to report more accurate costs than a traditional system because they identify clearly the costs of the different activities being performed in the organization, and they assign the costs of these activities to outputs using measures that represent the types of demands that individual outputs make on those activities.

With more accurate output costs, managers can make better decisions about their outputs and the activities that produce these outputs. Such decisions include setting prices, introducing or discontinuing products and services, and setting the levels of production, distribution, and marketing support for products and customers. Decisions about activities include learning how to perform the activities more efficiently, substituting less expensive activities for expensive ones, redesigning business processes to eliminate certain activities entirely, and designing products that make fewer demands on activities.

ABC's link to management decisions represents perhaps the major difference in thinking between traditional and activity-based cost systems. Traditional cost systems emphasize the allocation of past expenses to products, mainly for inventory valuation purposes. Activity-based cost systems measure directly the costs of resources used to perform organizational activities and then link the activity costs to the outputs (such as products, services, customers, and projects) that use or benefit from the activities. Many companies, especially in the initial estimates of ABC models, use expenses collected from their general ledger system. In more advanced applications, companies use future-oriented data such as budgeted expenses or targeted costs in which known inefficiencies are eliminated before estimating the costs attributed to outputs. An ABC system enables managers to contemplate how resource demands change as decisions get made, for example, on product and customer mix, process improvement, improved product designs, and new technology deployment. Given this fact, and despite their name, activity-based cost systems are more appropriately described as management planning, budgeting, and control systems, not costing systems. The ready acceptance and recognition of the name "activity-based costing," however, makes it difficult by now to contemplate renaming the concept more accurately.

Designing Activity-Based Cost Systems

ABC system designers make four interrelated choices: (1) identify the activities performed to produce outputs; (2) map the usage of organizational resources to these activities; (3) identify the outputs produced; and (4) link the activity costs to the outputs, via activity cost drivers. The design steps are exactly the same for service organizations as for manufacturing companies. To illustrate the design choices for a financial services company, we also will present the application of the principles to insurance organizations.

Identify Activities

In practice, one can identify a very large number of activities performed to produce outputs. For example, consider the process of setting up a machine to produce a batch of products—only one step in the production process. This process can be decomposed into numerous microactivities: identify tooling required, go to tool crib, select tool, sign out tool, bring tool to machine, insert tool into fixture, etc. Such a detailed process description, while perhaps useful for activity mapping and activity management, is rarely useful to calculate more accurate output or activity costs. If too many activities are defined, the cost of measurement for the ABC model grows disproportionately high.

Two factors drive the increase in the cost of measurement with the number of activities identified. First, the designer must specify the resources required to perform each activity and the number of times the activity is performed for each output. If the number of outputs is high, identifying numerous activities can lead to a huge data collection task. For example, a system with 200 activities and 10,000 outputs requires that up to two million activity-output relationships be specified. Second, as the number of activities identified gets larger, the activity-output relationships become more difficult and costly to measure. For example, a setup person might be able to specify quite accurately that setting up to produce a given product takes about 2.5 hours but be unable to break down the 2.5-hour elapsed time into the time required to perform 20 separate microactivities. Expensive time-monitoring systems would be needed to determine accurately the length of time required to perform each of the 20 activities product by product.

An organization's first ABC system typically is designed with 25 to 100 distinct activities. Exhibit 2-3 lists some typical activities identified in these systems. Occasionally, when management wants to focus on activity management to improve efficiency or to re-engineer operating processes, more complex systems are designed.

In an insurance company, activities are defined for each major processing step. If essentially the same process is used for all types of insurance products, then only one activity for that process needs to be defined. If, however, the process differs significantly by product or because of exceptions caused by errors or missing information, then separate activities should be identified for each differentiated process.

Assign Resource Costs to Activities

After activities have been identified, resource costs must be mapped to the activities. The steps involved for assigning resource costs to activities are identical for manufacturing and service companies. Organizational resources include indirect labor, materials and supplies, utilities, capital, equipment, and buildings. The company's general ledger is the usual starting point for information about the cost of resources deployed to perform activities. Unfortunately, most general ledger systems report the costs of the different types of resources, such as indirect labor, electricity, equipment, and supplies, but do not report the cost of activities performed. The ABC system designer must assign the financial information in the general ledger to activities. This assignment determines the cost of the resources used by each activity.

While initial ABC models usually are estimated from expenses recorded in the general ledger, subsequent models can use either budgeted expense information or targeted resource expenses from which the estimated costs of inefficient operations have been excluded. Using budgeted or forecasted expenses enables organizations to make decisions based on future activity and output costs, rather than on past costs.

The cost of the resources can be assigned to activities in three ways: direct charging, estimation, and arbitrary allocation. In direct charging, the actual usage of resources by activities is measured. For example, energy used to operate a machine can, if metered, be charged directly to that machine's operation. Data processing expenses can be charged to the organizational units using that resource, and persons performing support activities (setups, inspection, material movements) can record the time spent on each activity. Direct charging accurately captures the cost of resources used by activities but is expensive because it requires

Exhibit 2-3
TYPICAL ACTIVITIES IN MANUFACTURING SETTINGS

Procurement

Purchase Order Processing	Determine order quantities, timing issues, complete the P.O.
Contract Negotiations	Negotiate, develop, and sign vendor contracts
Inventorying Material – Receiving	Record the receipt of material, verify incoming quantities
Incoming Material Inspection	Assess the quality of incoming material
Processing Accounts Payable	Accumulate documents and provide authorization to pay

Production

Equipment, Maintenance and Repair	Maintain and repair existing production equipment
Shop Floor Control	Supervise production and production personnel
Facility Maintenance	Plant construction and facility maintenance

Production Management

Sales Forecast	Obtain a regular short-term sales forecast
Schedule Production – Normal	Schedule orders per customer request

(continued)

Exhibit 2-3 *(continued)*
TYPICAL ACTIVITIES IN MANUFACTURING SETTINGS

Production Management (continued)

Monitor Production	Collect production data at the shop floor level
Expedite	Speed up the process of production and material procurement
Inventory Material	Track material available within the factory premises
In-Process Material	Manage in-process inventories

Quality Control

Customer Complaints	Customer contact regarding complaints about quality, shipping, etc.
Product Service Testing	Testing results from customer complaints
Shop Floor Process Control	Monitor shop floor processes to ensure quality output
Quality Complaint Analysis	Determine the "root cause" of quality problems
Testing for Quality Evaluation	Perform tests required to analyze a quality problem
Final Inspection	Final inspection of finished product

measurement of the actual usage. Such direct measurement is rarely justifiable solely to improve the accuracy of an ABC system.

Lacking direct measurements, designers typically estimate the cost of resources used by each activity through surveys and interviews. Managers such as department heads and supervisors are asked to estimate the percentage of time (or effort) spent by employees on each of the identified activities. Interviews can be relatively fast and inexpensive, lasting between 30 minutes and two hours. They can be supplemented or replaced with surveys in which managers are given an activity dictionary and are asked to fill in entries that represent the percentage of time each person in the department spends on the activities performed by the department.

When no meaningful way exists to estimate the resources used by an activity, some designers resort to arbitrary allocations. For example, the cost of plant management support might be allocated to activities using headcount, even though plant management support is unlikely to be proportional to the number of persons performing a given activity. Arbitrary allocations should be minimized whenever possible, however, because they do not improve the understanding of the economics of activities.

Identify Outputs

Outputs are the cost objects for which activities are performed. Typical outputs for a cost system can include products, services, customers, projects, or business units. For example, in an insurance company, the outputs could be the individual products or services offered to customers, the customers themselves, the insurance agents, or the divisions that are receiving benefits from corporate resources.

Designers must try to identify all the outputs produced by resources whose costs are being assigned. If one or more output categories are omitted, too many costs are assigned to the remaining outputs. Some resources are used by either future or past products and should be excluded from costs assigned to currently produced products. For example, if prototypes or sample products are not identified as outputs, the cost system will assign their costs inappropriately to normal production runs. The research and development costs for future products or the costs associated with funding pensions for retired employees are not expenses of activities performed for today's products. Similarly, unused capacity costs should not be assigned to the products actually produced.

Link Activity Costs to Outputs

Activity costs can be linked to outputs in the same three ways as the cost of resources can be assigned to activities: direct charge, estimation, and arbitrary allocation. Because of the large number of different outputs in most organizations, direct charging of activities to outputs is rarely feasible. In manufacturing settings, only direct materials and labor are charged directly to products. In some service settings, almost no costs can be charged directly to outputs. In other service companies, with only a few products or product lines, direct charging of some organizational costs may be quite feasible. For example, the underwriting departments of an insurance company may be dedicated to serving a particular product or product line so that the association of the cost of this department with the product line is simple. At the other extreme from direct charging is an arbitrary allocation of costs using drivers that bear little relationship to the demands for activities by outputs. Such arbitrary allocations are inexpensive and easy to perform, but they provide no insights about the costs of producing or delivering outputs.

Therefore, designers usually must estimate the link between activity costs and outputs. Estimation is cheaper than direct charging and more meaningful than arbitrary allocation. Because of the large number of potential activity-to-output linkages, designers attempt to economize on the number of different activity cost drivers. For example, the activities—prepare production orders, schedule production runs, perform first part inspections, and move materials—all can use the same activity cost driver: number of production runs or lots produced. Exhibit 2-4 lists activity cost drivers used frequently in ABC systems.

ABC system designers use several different types of activity cost drivers. *Transaction* drivers capture the number of times an activity is performed. Transaction drivers can be used when all outputs make essentially the same demands on the activity. For example, scheduling a production run, processing a purchase order, or maintaining a unique part number may take the same time and effort independent of which product is being scheduled, which material is being purchased, or the

Duration drivers capture the length of time an activity is performed on an output. Duration drivers should be used when significant variation exists in the amount of activity required for different outputs. For example, some products may require only a simple, five-minute setup, whereas a part with extremely tight tolerances may require a six- to eight-hour setup. Examples of duration drivers include setup hours, inspection hours, and direct labor hours. Some companies estimate duration by constructing an index based on the complexity of the output being handled. For instance, in entering the data for a new insurance policy, the index would be a function of the complexity of the insurance product type, because the complexity influences the time required to enter and process the application. The choice between a duration and a transactional driver is, as always, one of economics, balancing the benefits of increased accuracy against the costs of increased measurement. Duration drivers more accurately assign activity costs to products than transaction drivers, but they are more costly to measure.

Exhibit 2-4
TYPICAL ACTIVITY COST DRIVERS USED IN MANUFACTURING SETTINGS

Internal ECNs	Number of alteration notices per product
Units Produced	Production quantity of finished products
P.O. Line Items	Number of receipts for each raw material and purchased part
Stockroom Transfers	Number of stock-to-stock transfers per part number
Direct Labor Hours	Hours of direct (standard) labor per product
Toolroom Hours	Hours of toolroom labor per part number
Sales Per Device	Dollar sales by device
Scrap Dollars	Dollars of reported scrap per product
Number of Complaints	Customer complaints per product

Occasionally, even measuring the length of time an activity is performed may not capture the activity demands required for a particular output. For example, a part may require special testing and quality procedures, or a project may require the support of specialized technicians or teams. In these cases, activity costs may be charged directly to the output, based on work orders or other records that accumulate the activity expenses incurred for that output.

Activity Coding

ABC system designers use a variety of coding schemes to classify activities along different dimensions. These coding schemes enable managers to aggregate activities to provide useful summary information. Three common coding schemes are: (1) activity centers, (2) activity hierarchies, and (3) value added.

Activity Centers

Activity centers are collections of activities that make up a significant business process. Activity centers are particularly useful in ABC systems that contain a large number of activities, because they allow summary reporting of output and business process costs. Activity centers provide enhanced visibility to a group of activities but do not affect the reported cost of either activities or outputs. For example, if the inspection department is treated as a separate activity center, attention is focused on the costs of all activities done by the inspection department. Alternatively, if activities are defined by business processes, such as receiving, production, assembly, and shipping, then the total cost of inspection activities will be dispersed among these different processes, allowing managers to see more clearly the total cost of their different business processes. Each business process could include an inspection cost component, but the total cost of inspection will not be apparent at the activity center level.

Activity centers can be designed around organizational structures such as departments or responsibility centers. For example, the assembly area might be considered as a single activity center, or three activity centers can be set up: the paint shop, assembly process, and packing, one for each of the responsibility centers in the assembly area. Alternatively, activity centers can be used to highlight the total cost of a business process. For example, by including in a single "painting" activity center: (1) all surface preparation activities, (2) the paint shop, and (3) the surface inspection and correction activities subsequent to painting, the total cost of painting, as opposed to the paint shop, can be highlighted. Finally, activity centers can be used to highlight the costs of programs that affect the entire production process. For example, by creating four quality activity centers—prevention, appraisal, internal failure, and external failure—and driving the costs of all quality-related activities to one of them, the total cost of quality and its components can be highlighted. Exhibit 2-5 illustrates typical activity centers.

Activity centers in an insurance company can be designed around actual departments such as the mailroom, underwriting, telecommunications, central files, and data entry. Nonpayroll-related expenses such as supplies, utilities, rent, and postage normally are identified easily with these activity centers, based on estimated or actually measured usage. Payroll-related activities also can be driven to these activity centers, but wages and salaries expense may be captured more informatively by business processes or business issues such as:

- Sorting: all activities performed to prepare batches of records and for separation, distribution of work, or logging and sorting;
- Filings: activities to make or cancel local, state, and federal filings;
- Redundancy: activities performed more than once, in different departments, or unnecessarily;
- Legal: activities performed for regulatory compliance;
- External failure: activities performed internally because external services provided by outside agents were not done properly.

Activity Hierarchies

Frequently, the activities performed to produce outputs can be classified into a hierarchy. For example, many manufacturing companies have found the following hierarchy useful:

- Unit-level activities: performed each time a unit is produced,
- Batch-level activities: performed each time a batch of goods is produced,
- Product-sustaining activities: performed to support the diversity of products in a plant,
- Facility-sustaining activities: performed to support a facility's general manufacturing process.

Unit-level activities (such as drilling holes, machining surfaces, and

Exhibit 2-5

TYPICAL ACTIVITY CENTERS USED IN MANUFACTURING SETTINGS

Principal Activity Centers

Production	All activities except direct labor that can be directly attributed to the production process
Customer Administration	All activities related to dealings with customers
Procurement	All activities required to provide the business with all the materials needed for operation
Production Management	All plantwide activities of scheduling, monitoring, and quality control of all production areas
Quality Control	All quality-related activities dealing with production processes, incoming material, and product service
Production Tooling	All activities relating to maintenance, repair, or replacement of existing tooling
Maintenance	All activities performed to maintain, repair, or replace existing equipment and facilities
Warehousing/ Shipping	All activities involved in the handling and distribution of finished goods from the time products are transferred from the production area

(continued)

Exhibit 2-5 *(continued)*
TYPICAL ACTIVITY CENTERS USED
IN MANUFACTURING SETTINGS

Change Related Activity Centers

Internally Generated Modifications	All activities for dealing with internal requests for product or process changes
Customer Driven Changes	All activities for dealing with product or process changes due to customer request or requirement
New Products and Processes	All activities to develop new products or processes

Support Related Activity Centers

Business Information Systems	All activities related to development of new information systems and computer systems
General Administration and Finance	All activities related to external financial reporting, general accounting, special studies, and reserves
Human Resources	All activities related to administration of employee and community services and programs, and work force maintenance
Environment and Safety	All activities performed to ensure a safe, secure work environment

inspecting every part are performed for each unit. They vary proportionately with production or sales volume. Examples of unit-level activities in an insurance company are postage cost for outgoing policies, receiving and recording incoming applications, verifying policy number for renewals, and entering data for a new policy into the system.

Batch-level activities, such as setting up a machine or ordering a group of parts, are performed for each batch produced (or ordered) but are independent of the number of units in the batch. Thus the cost of using batch-level activities is independent of the number of units processed in the batch but varies with the number of production runs or purchase requests made. Insurance company batch-level activities include logging daily totals of items processed, making the mail run twice daily, and batching new applications received.

Product-sustaining activities are performed to support different products in a company's product line. Examples of product-sustaining activities include maintaining product specifications (such as the bill of materials and routing information), performing engineering change notices, developing special testing routines, and expediting products. Examples of product-sustaining activities in an insurance company are training employees for underwriting particular (or new) product lines, developing and maintaining systems unique to particular product lines, processing systems programming requests for reports on particular product lines, and carrying out marketing and advertising programs for individual product lines.

The costs of product-sustaining activities can be assigned to individual products, but the costs are independent (that is, *fixed)* of the number of batches or number of units of each product produced. Product-level costs can be incurred even if no production (or sale) of a product occurs during a period.

Unit, batch, and product-sustaining activities can be attributed directly to individual products. Facility-sustaining activities cause costs that enable production of products or delivery of services to occur but are independent of product/service volume and mix. Examples include lighting and cleaning the facility, facility security, and plant administration and management. In an insurance company, facility-sustaining activities include general accounting, hiring and termination of agents, and general administration.

Facility-sustaining activities can be broken down further by changing the focus of analysis from the product to aggregations of products. For example, facility-sustaining activities can be split into product line-sustaining activities—the activities performed to sustain a particular product line (such as prototype development and unused capacity)—and the residual facility-sustaining activities that cannot be associated with products or product lines. Such additional analyses provide insights into the economics of producing and supporting diverse product lines or other aggregations of products.

Other hierarchies can be defined in nonmanufacturing settings. For example, a typical marketing hierarchy is customer, channel, and market (wherein a customer might be City Electric, a channel might be retail electrical distributors, and a market might be electrical suppliers). A hierarchy for product-line development and support might be: product line, product family, and product group (wherein a product line might be alternators, a product family might be electrical components, and a product group might be automotive).

Value Rankings

An ABC system identifies all the activities performed to produce and deliver the firm's outputs. This identification, however, does not guarantee that the activities are either necessary or that they are performed efficiently. Many firms rank their activities according to their value or efficiency of performance. These coding schemes can vary from simple dichotomous ones such as value added/nonvalue added or necessary/unnecessary to complex schemes using a 10-point classification.

The definition of what constitutes a value-added activity varies considerably among firms. Some common definitions for value-added include an activity that adds value in the eyes of the customer, an activity that is being performed as efficiently as possible, or an activity that supports the primary objective of producing outputs. For example, for the finance group, the activities required to produce the firm's annual report might be viewed as value added, while activities that deal with training might be considered nonvalue added. One insurance company devised a four-category value-added coding scheme:

 1. An activity required to produce the product or improve the process; the activity cannot, on a cost justification basis, be improved, simplified, or reduced in scope at this time.

 2. An activity required to produce the product or improve the process; the activity can be cost justifiably improved, simplified, or reduced in scope.

 3. An activity not required to produce the product or improve the

process; the activity can be eliminated eventually by changing a process or a company procedure.

4. An activity not required to produce the product or improve the process; the activity can be eliminated in the short run by changing a process or a company procedure.

Managers use such a value-ranking scheme to focus their cost reduction programs. Identifying activities performed inefficiently highlights opportunities for process improvements. Similarly, reducing resources devoted to performing activities that do not create value for customers lessens the risk of accidentally reducing the perceived functionality of the output. Perhaps proponents of the value-added/nonvalue-added coding scheme also implicitly believe it is easier to reduce the cost of nonvalue-added activities than of value-added ones, though the empirical support for this belief is not extensive.

Other Coding Schemes

Some firms have found other coding schemes useful as well. They include: reason codes, which provide insights into why activities are performed; purpose codes, which provide insights into whether the purpose of the activity is central or peripheral to the mission of the firm; and process codes, which identify the type of production process involved. Some ABC systems use multiple coding systems; for example, each activity is classified into an activity center, as a level in a hierarchy, and as value or nonvalue added.

ABC Software

Most activity-based cost systems have so many activities or outputs that analysts cannot use commonly available spreadsheets or database managers to calculate and revise easily the costs of activities and outputs. Because ABC developments are relatively recent, most firms have not yet adapted their existing financial systems to support ABC analysis. Consequently, the majority of ABC systems currently are implemented using specially designed stand-alone systems that run on a personal computer.

Most PC-based ABC software accepts financial information from the firm's general ledger and, through loading of resource drivers, converts resource expense data into activity costs. Frequently, the general ledger information is downloaded to the software from the firm's mainframe computer. Most ABC software allows activity driver quantities to be either entered by hand or downloaded from databases resident on other computers. Once data entry is complete, the software performs the laborious calculations required to determine activity and output costs. Some software packages compute output costs in real-time, as the data are entered, while others have special output costing runs that are performed after all relevant data are entered into the model. Most software packages contain data validation routines that allow the logic of the system design to be checked to ensure that all resource dollars are assigned to outputs. Once activity and output costs are computed, the software either allows the output to be downloaded to generic data analysis and graphics packages or produces reports and graphics with its own internal software. Typical reports include:

- Output costs, built up from activity costs or by activity drivers;
- Activity costs associated with individual drivers;
- Resource costs of any activity, output, or driver;
- Driver costs, built up from activities;
- Output profitability.

Most ABC software supports several different activity coding schemes—activity centers, activity hierarchies, and value rankings.

Conclusion

ABC analysis consists of four primary steps:

1. Identify activities,
2. Assign resource costs to activities,
3. Identify outputs, and
4. Link activity costs to outputs.

Once these four steps have been completed, the data are entered into an ABC costing system that calculates the costs of activities, activity drivers, and outputs. These costs are then validated, analyzed, and subjected to sensitivity analysis. At this point the model development and analysis stage has been completed. How managers use the insights from the ABC analysis will ultimately determine the success of the project. The eight cases described in this study provide considerable variation in the degree of management acceptance and the types of actions and decisions stimulated by the ABC information.

Chapter 3

The Research Methodology

Introduction and Background

The term "activity-based costing" began to receive special attention in the literature in 1986 in the Harvard Business School case series on the John Deere Components Works.[1] In 1988, the first articles to use the term were published in *The Journal of Cost Management*[2] and the *Harvard Business Review*.[3] By 1992, the term activity-based costing, or ABC as it often is abbreviated, had gained worldwide recognition. Companies in America, Europe, Asia, and Australia were known to be implementing ABC systems.

The worldwide acceptance of ABC appears to have been driven primarily by managers' deep dissatisfaction with their existing cost systems. ABC, with its ability to report more accurate activity, product, and customer costs, was heralded by some as a major breakthrough in cost management. For example, H. Thomas Johnson stated, "Activity-based management is the key to continuous improvement of profitability, a journey without end."[4]

In the few years since the theory of ABC was first expounded, numerous articles on the topic have been published.[5] The theory of ABC is now well developed and documented.[6]

In contrast, practical aspects such as how to implement an ABC system and how to take advantage of the insights it provides are less well understood and have been virtually undocumented. Success stories exist, but no rigorous study of the current status of ABC had been undertaken.

Objectives of the ABC Field Research Project

In the spring of 1991, the Institute of Management Accountants and KPMG Peat Marwick launched a joint research project to document the activity-based systems at eight different organizations. This activity-based costing (ABC) field research project addressed the following questions:

- What benefits did managers expect from their new ABC systems?
- How did these benefits vary from site to site?
- What were the major steps taken to implement the ABC systems?
- What were the key design decisions?
- What pitfalls were encountered?
- What roles did different managers play to help achieve the benefits?
- What conditions helped firms achieve the benefits?
- What organizational barriers stopped managers from achieving the benefits they had identified?

Research Approach

The researchers visited eight sites to collect information about: (1) the issues that led management to implement an activity-based cost system, (2) the implementation process and the resources committed to the project, (3) the insights obtained from the information reported by the ABC systems, and (4) the actions taken due to those insights. After the research team had reviewed the findings from all eight research sites, the team analyzed and synthesized the information and developed an organizational framework for understanding the issues that arose when the eight companies implemented ABC systems.

The research process consisted of five major steps: (1) forming the Project Committee and research team, (2) selecting the eight research sites, (3) visiting the eight sites, (4) writing the cases, and (5) analyzing and synthesizing the case studies.

Forming the Project Committee and Research Team

At the outset of the project, a Project Committee and research team were established to initiate and guide the project. The IMA established the *Project Committee* to oversee the entire project. Its members were:

- Robert C. Miller, chairman, Boeing Corporation;
- Andrew D. Bailey, Jr., University of Arizona;
- Charles D. Mecimore, University of North Carolina;
- W. Ron Ragland, Martin Marietta Energy Systems, Inc.;
- Patrick L. Romano, Institute of Management Accountants.

The Project Committee approved the persons selected by KPMG for the research team, identified the criteria for choosing the research sites, approved the sites chosen by the research team, reviewed and made suggestions to improve the cases and chapters as they were written, and approved the final manuscript.

KPMG Peat Marwick assembled a *research team,* with concurrence of the Project Committee. It included:

- Robin Cooper, Harvard Business School;
- Robert S. Kaplan, Harvard Business School;
- Lawrence Maisel, Maisel Consulting Group;
- Eileen Morrissey, KPMG Peat Marwick;
- Ronald Oehm, KPMG Peat Marwick.

The research team selected the research sites, visited the sites, researched the individual cases, supervised and prepared the final writing of the cases, analyzed the research findings, and prepared a synthesis of the findings. Ron Oehm and Eileen Morrissey provided overall management of the project, including the liaison with the IMA and the Project Committee.

The research team selected *field research teams* to perform on-site field research for each case. The teams visited companies to observe, analyze, and gain an understanding of the ABC system and implementation process. Each site was visited by:

- The KPMG professional(s) with primary responsibility for the initial draft of the case,
- Eileen Morrissey or Larry Maisel,
- Robin Cooper or Robert S. Kaplan.

The KPMG Peat Marwick professionals were chosen for their in-depth knowledge of the research site's ABC system, the implementation process used at the site, and their general experience with ABC.[7] Exhibit 3-1 identifies the field research team members for each case study.

Selecting the Eight Research Sites

To ensure that the sample included a broad range of ABC applications in several different industries, the research team and Project Committee established seven site selection criteria the study was to fulfill.

Exhibit 3-1

MEMBERS OF THE FIELD RESEARCH TEAM
FOR EACH CASE SITE

Company	*Research Team*
FARRALL	R. Kaplan L. Maisel E. Morrissey
AMD	R. Cooper A. Bose
WBM	R. Cooper * L. Maisel E. Morrissey
SLADE	R. Cooper L. Hitchcock N. Galambos *
ARCO	R. Cooper E. Morrissey
MONARCH	R. Cooper E. Morrissey A. Bose M. Ireland *
STEWARD	R. Kaplan E. Morrissey J. Melton-Roberts
KRAFT	R. Kaplan L. Maisel E. Morrissey M. Ireland M. Weber *

* Participated in research, but did not visit company

1. A cross section of industries (discrete manufacturing, process manufacturing, financial services, materials distribution, and energy);

2. A cross section of ABC objectives (product costing, activity management, and customer profitability);

3. Linkage to other initiatives such as total quality management (TQM), just-in-time (JIT), and performance measurement (PM) systems;

4. Linkage to existing cost management reporting systems;

5. Valuable ABC results and sound use of ABC concepts;

6. A company that had decided not to implement ABC;

7. A company with an unsuccessful implementation.

Approximately 20 companies were identified as potential research sites, through the research team's and Project Committee's professional contacts and reviews of national and regional seminar speaker lists on the topic of ABC. The final selection was based on whether each company: (1) agreed to become a research site, (2) satisfied the site selection criteria, and (3) was willing to allow the field research teams to complete the site visits within a reasonable time frame. Because of the selection method, the eight-company sample is neither random nor necessarily representative of the population of ABC-adopting companies.

The eight companies that were included in the sample are described below:

1. Advanced Micro Devices (AMD) designs, markets, and manufactures microprocessors, memory devices, programmable logic devices, and integrated circuits. Competition in the semiconductor industry had intensified in the late '80s, forcing AMD to evaluate some of its market strategies. These changes brought attention to the weaknesses of the firm's existing cost system. In response, it implemented ABC in the assembly and test operations to provide more relevant data for improving product mix, product design, and manufacturing efficiencies.

2. ARCO Alaska, Inc. (ARCO) piloted an activity-based analysis study in the controller's department that provided budgeting, financial reporting, internal auditing, and other financial services to operating oil fields and to corporate management. The pilot study was to demonstrate how operational demands affect controllership activities and costs. During the project, a head count reduction program was placed on ARCO, and then managers found themselves

using the activity data to make difficult resource utilization decisions.

3. Farrall, Inc.[8] (Farrall), a manufacturer of water filters, embarked on an ABC pilot project in two facilities that manufactured similar products but had substantially different profitabilities. One plant was located in the United States, the other in England. The pilot study was performed to identify: (a) more accurate product costs for better transfer prices and pricing decisions, (b) customer profitability, (c) cost reduction opportunities, and (d) information to assist capital investment decisions.

4. KRAFT USA (KRAFT) launched an ABC project in late 1989 following an intensive performance measurement study. Two plants that produce cream cheese were selected for the pilot in order to compare product cost between two facilities. The pilot also addressed ABC's ultimate linkage to the performance measurement system and daily production systems.

5. Monarch Mirror Door (Monarch), a privately held furniture company, implemented ABC to support strategic decision making. Growing competition and rapid growth and expansion without similar increased profits forced management to rethink its market strategy. A high-level ABC system was implemented at two plants to help address the fundamental question of which products should be delivered to which markets.

6. Slade Manufacturing, Inc.[9] (Slade), a Fortune 500 company, launched an ABC pilot in its automotive business group. Business lines included engine components, transmission components and assemblies, exterior body panels, and rubber products. Competition was increasing and customers more and more were demanding higher quality, lower price, and more reliable delivery. With sales concentrated within the Big Three auto manufacturers, ABC was piloted to address both product and customer profitability.

7. Steward & Company[10] (Steward), a broker/dealer that provides trading execution services to large institutional investors, implemented an ABC system to better understand its cost and profitability structure for both product lines and account executives (salesmen). The study focused on overhead expenses, which included general and administrative, branch, transaction processing, and data processing costs.

8. Williams Brothers Metals, Inc.[11] (WBM), a family-owned metal fabrication and distribution company, embarked on ABC to understand its costs better. ABC was piloted within a region that contained three plants and all corporate support functions. The ABC

objectives concentrated on providing product profitability and a "proof of concept" that ABC was relevant to the company's distribution business.

These eight companies chosen as the research sample satisfied five of the seven selection criteria:

1. *Criterion 1: A cross section of industries.* Four companies were discrete manufacturers (Farrall, AMD, Slade, and Monarch). One site (KRAFT) was a process manufacturer. One site (Steward) was a financial services provider. One site (WBM) was a distribution company, and one site (ARCO) was an energy company.

2. *Criterion 2: A cross section of ABC objectives.* All companies drove activity costs to the organization's outputs (products, services, projects). All the manufacturing companies also used the activity information as a link to their continuous improvement and activity management initiatives. Three companies—Farrall, Slade, and Monarch—extended their ABC model to measure customer profitability. A fourth, Steward, employed ABC for account executive (salesman) profitability.

3. *Criterion 3: Linkage to other initiatives.* Three of the companies (Farrall, AMD, and Monarch) had established TQM programs with the desire to link ABC to the TQM process. Two others (KRAFT and Steward) attempted to link ABC to their performance measurement systems.

4. *Criterion 4: Linkage to current cost management system.* Three of the companies (Monarch, Steward, and KRAFT) have or plan to develop ABC within their current cost management system.

5. *Criterion 5: Soundness of ABC concepts and value of results.* All of the eight companies perceived that they had received valuable insights or results from the ABC system. They also used ABC concepts sensibly in developing the ABC architecture.

The other two criteria ("decision not to implement" and "less than successful") were not covered by the sample of eight firms. During the selection process, it became apparent that identifying a "decision not to implement" and a "less than successful" implementation was not an easy task. In particular, it was difficult to identify at what point a decision not to implement was worth documenting. For example, a company that considered adopting ABC but, as of the time of the study, had not started any implementation process was felt not worth using up as one of the eight sites. No company could be identified that had begun serious implementation and then stopped.

Similar problems were encountered in defining a "less than successful" implementation. One possibility was to identify a company that had completed the implementation, reported its ABC findings, and subsequently scrapped the system. Again, no company could be identified that fit this description and was a willing research site. Consequently, the research team and Project Committee decided that it would be adequate to include at least one company in the sample that had implemented a system but after a reasonable time frame had not achieved any concrete benefits. As it turned out, several of the companies still are striving to achieve the concrete benefits.

After the eight research sites had been selected, letters of acceptance were sent to the contact person at each company. In several sites, members of the research team were asked to sign nondisclosure agreements with the companies.

Visiting the Sites

The field research teams interviewed both key management personnel and members of the ABC implementation team at each of the eight sites. During the interviews, the teams determined: (1) the process by which management became aware of ABC and how the project to implement the new ABC system was approved, (2) the design and implementation process, and (3) how the benefits were identified and achieved. Questions such as the following were asked by the researchers:

- What issues (competitive and market factors) led the company to implement ABC?
- What process was necessary to gain approval?
- Who was the sponsor and what role did he or she play?
- What were the key implementation steps?
- What were the implementation issues and pitfalls?
- What value have ABC findings provided across the various functions of the organization?
- How did ABC fit within the current/traditional cost management system?
- What are future applications of ABC?

Exhibit 3-2 lists the interview topics and questions. In addition to the interviews, team members typically toured the facilities at which the

Exhibit 3-2

CHECKLIST OF QUESTIONS FOR EACH CASE STUDY

Strategic Factors and Organizational Culture

How did elements such as industry, market, and competitive factors induce the need for change?

What is the organizational structure and management style of the company that shapes the change process?

What is the significance of cost information in the managerial process?

How does the company justify the resources required to improve operating and information systems?

What financial and other analytical techniques are used in evaluating these systems?

Has the company previously used any TQM or JIT approaches?

To what extent is ABC a supplement, replacement, or alternative to their other cost management approaches?

Process Factors

Who took the leadership roles in the beginning and through the development and implementation stages?

What was senior management's role?

What changes in financial accounting practices were made?

How was consensus developed across organizational units?

How was organizational resistance addressed and resolved?

How were "cost drivers" identified?

What cost factors and concepts shaped the design of the new cost accounting system?

(continued)

Exhibit 3-2 *(continued)*
CHECKLIST OF QUESTIONS FOR EACH CASE STUDY

Process Factors *(continued)*

Did management need to learn new ways of managing cost?

What lessons have been learned about implementing a complex system?

What are critical success factors and what are things to avoid?

Technical Factors

How and when were data selected and coded?

Were collection systems integrated or were interfaces used between independent systems?

What approaches were used to compile, compute, and retrieve data?

How was data integrity—both input and output—assured?

What portion of management-oriented cost information is supplied by the accounting system versus other systems and special analytical processes?

What were the significant costs to design and implement the new cost management system and how were they monitored?

Have the benefits and goals of the system been realized?

ABC systems were installed, to gain a better understanding of the production or service process and the outputs it generated. The team members also reviewed additional sources of information to complete their understanding of each company and its ABC system. These sources included the company's public financial statements; organization charts; product brochures; ABC activity, cost driver and product (and/or customer) reports; and ABC presentation materials.

The availability of KPMG professionals with an in-depth knowledge of each company and its ABC systems reduced the need to collect detailed information about the structure of the activity-based system and the implementation process during the on-site visits. This prior knowledge allowed most on-site visits to be performed in a single day.

Writing the Cases

After the on-site visit, each field research team appointed one or more members to write the initial draft of the case. Other members of the research team were designated primary and secondary editors to ensure the quality and consistency of each case. The initial case writers followed a common structure, developed by the research team, that for the most part incorporated eight major topics for each site.

1. *Executive Summary:* highlights of the case and key results.

2. *Background and Company Profile*: introduction to the company and its products. Description of competitive and business environment. Identification of issues that created the need for ABC.

3. *Planning*: how the company prepared for, created awareness of, built teams, and gained sponsorship for the ABC system. Identification of scope and objectives of the ABC system.

4. *Implementation and System Design*: description of the ABC implementation process, architecture, and key design decisions.

5. *Key Results and Findings:* interpretation of ABC results. Description of how results were shared among cross-functional groups.

6. *Actions Taken and Management Acceptance:* management's reaction to ABC data and implementation process. Identification of any actions taken based on ABC data.

7. *Future Use of ABC:* discussion of company's plans for future use.

8. *Epilogue:* when appropriate, update of the case study to include events that happened after the on-site visits.

A rigorous review and edit process was established by the research team. The process required that each case be reviewed by a primary and secondary editor from among Robert S. Kaplan, Robin Cooper, or Lawrence Maisel. The primary editor worked closely with the author(s) to ensure the coverage, quality, and consistency of the cases. The secondary editor reviewed all the cases to verify consistency in coverage and writing style.

The Project Committee reviewed each case for content and clarity and to ensure the objectives of the field research project had been met.

Each case was reviewed (sometimes several times) by the participating company. Comments were received, changes made, and revised drafts resubmitted. If necessary, competitive or sensitive information was disguised at the request of the participating company. Ultimately, each company signed a representation letter authorizing release of the final document.

At each site, management relayed to the research team its requirements for confidentiality and nondisclosure. Some companies requested that both their firm and the industry setting be disguised, others only that the firm name be disguised, and still others, only that certain information be disguised. In most cases, all data relating to ABC results have been altered. Exhibit 3-3 identifies the level of disguise in each case. Data related to the implementation process or ABC architecture (such as number of activities and cost drivers used or number and composition of ABC team members) generally were not disguised.

Exhibit 3-3
CONFIDENTIALITY OF COMPANIES

Company	*Disclosure of Information Relating to:*		
	Name	*Product*	*Data*
FARRALL	Disguised	Disguised	Disguised
AMD	–	–	Disguised
WBM	Disguised	Disguised	Disguised
SLADE	Disguised	–	Disguised
ARCO	–	–	Disguised
MONARCH	–	–	Disguised
STEWARD	Disguised	–	Disguised
KRAFT	–	–	Disguised

Analyzing and Synthesizing the Case Studies

After the field research was completed and all first drafts of the cases had been written, the research team:

- Compared and contrasted the ABC models developed at each site;
- Discussed and obtained a summary of the potential benefits identified by management at each site;
- Identified any actions contemplated or already taken based upon the ABC models;
- Identified relevant and critical organizational issues; and
- Developed conclusions.

The analysis and synthesis of the case studies are presented in Chapters 12 and 13. Chapter 12, "Analysis of ABC Models: Design, Structure, and Findings," describes the similarities and differences in design decisions and results among the eight ABC systems. Chapter 13, "Organizational Issues in ABC Projects," analyzes the organizational processes required for management to sponsor, act upon, and realize the benefits from an activity-based cost system. An appendix lists fundamental implementation steps.

Notes

[1] John Deere Component Works (A) and (B), Harvard Business School Case Numbers 9-187-107 and 9-187-108.

[2] Robin Cooper, "The Rise of Activity-Based Costing—Part One: What Is an Activity-Based Cost System?", *Journal of Cost Management*, Summer 1988, pp. 45-54; "The Rise of Activity-Based Costing—Part Two: When Do I Need an Activity-Based Cost System?", *Journal of Cost Management*, Fall 1988, pp. 41-48; "The Rise of Activity-Based Costing—Part Three: How Many Cost Drivers Do You Need, and How Do You Select Them?", *Journal of Cost Management*, Winter 1989, pp. 34-46; and "The Rise of Activity-Based Costing—Part Four: What Do Activity-Based Cost Systems Look Like?", *Journal of Cost Management*, Spring 1989, pp. 38-49.

[3] Robin Cooper and Robert S. Kaplan, "Measure Costs Right: Make the Right Decisions," *Harvard Business Review*, September-October 1988, pp. 96-103.

[4] H. Thomas Johnson, "Activity-Based Information: A Blueprint for World-Class Management," *Management Accounting*, June 1988, pp. 23-30.

[5]James P. Borden, "Review of Literature on Activity-Based Costing," *Journal of Cost Management*, Spring 1991, pp. 6-38.

[6]The bibliography at the end of the book lists selected readings on the theory and practice of ABC.

[7]Scheduling conflicts made it impossible for either Eileen Morrissey or Larry Maisel to visit two sites and for either Robin Cooper or Robert S. Kaplan to visit one site.

[8]Company name and industry are disguised.

[9]Company name is disguised.

[10]Company name is disguised.

[11]Company name and industry are disguised.

Chapter 4

Advanced Micro Devices

Executive Summary

Advanced Micro Devices (AMD), a major semiconductor manufacturer, performed its first activity-based costing project in a test and assembly facility in Penang, Malaysia. The pilot project was expected to prove the applicability of ABC methodology to a semiconductor back-end manufacturing environment and to establish the foundations for expanding ABC implementations to other manufacturing sites. The project was implemented at a time when the company was in the process of transforming itself from a "managing growth" strategy to a "managing profitable growth" strategy.

Managers recognized the need to transform the cost system to provide relevant data for decision making under the new strategy. ABC proved to be an appropriate costing methodology for setting transfer prices between manufacturing and the divisions.

The new ABC system at Penang identified significant product cost distortions (high-volume, simple products were overcosted by 20% to 30% and low-volume, complex products were undercosted by 600% to 700%). ABC provided AMD management with a more accurate basis for setting transfer prices between manufacturing and the divisions.

In addition, ABC helped close the gap between actual manufacturing practices and the way costs were reported by the firm's cost system. The existing system had not been updated to reflect recent changes that had occurred in the production process. For example, several JIT lines had been installed at the plant but AMD's traditional cost system did not report any major differences in the costs between JIT and non-JIT products.

The success of the project was underscored by the director of finance's comment. He stated, "ABC provided AMD with a cost system solution which will enable and support AMD's strategy of managing profitable growth."

Company Profile and Business Environment

Advanced Micro Devices is the fifth-largest U.S.-based manufacturer of integrated circuit devices and the 18th largest in the world. The company was founded in 1967 by Walter Jeremiah Sanders III. The firm designs, markets, and manufactures integrated circuits such as microprocessors and related peripherals, memory devices, and programmable logic devices. These products can be used in a wide range of applications, including telecommunications, office automation, and networking. In 1991, AMD had sales of more than $1.13 billion and employed approximately 12,000 people.

AMD grew rapidly between 1972 and 1984. Sales grew from $4.6 million to $1.1 billion during that period. While other firms in the industry also grew, none matched AMD's growth, which, by 1981, enabled it to become the world's sixth largest producer. Profitability in those years was assured because the company's technologically advanced products attracted premium prices. Products typically sold with 25% net margins, and the firm earned about 10% overall.

During the mid-1980s, competition in the semiconductor industry increased rapidly, both from other U.S. competitors such as Intel, Texas Instruments, and National Semiconductor and, more significantly, from Japanese competitors such as Hitachi, Toshiba, and Fujitsu, which began to dominate the industry. In 1991, the Japanese firms accounted for 50% of total industry sales, up from 33% in 1982. The intense competition eroded profitability, and AMD's return on sales fell from approximately 10% in 1983 to a mere 0.7% in 1985; net profits dropped more than 90%, from a high of $61 million to $5.6 million.

AMD's problems worsened as the industry entered a period of severe overcapacity brought on by unexpectedly slow sales growth. The years 1985 and 1986 were two of the harshest in the history of the semiconductor industry. While growth resumed in 1987, in 1989 the 200 largest electronics companies reported sales increases of just 4%, the smallest in history. The market had entered a period of maturity. Since 1989, sales growth has been about 3% a year.

Faced with a fundamental shift in competitive forces, AMD management had been forced in the mid-1980s to exit from what had become commodity chip markets, including products such as DRAMs (dynamic rapid access memory) and SRAMs (static rapid access memory). As sales growth leveled off and competition intensified in the late 1980s, profit margins on mature products such as programmable array logic (PAL) and erasable programmable read only memory

(EPROM) devices dropped to breakeven levels. Japanese competitors focused on achieving high market share for high-volume products. They exploited economies of scale to drive down product prices continuously while still making a profit.

AMD management tried to "grow themselves" out of trouble by introducing numerous new specialty and custom products. These new products were known as "liberty chips." They were expected to "liberate" AMD from its financial troubles by increasing sales and earning higher margins, thus returning the company's profitability to its previous high levels. The failure of the liberty chip program, however, led to severely reduced profitability. Management shifted from a growth-oriented strategy to one based on profitability. For the first time, divisional profitability was scrutinized heavily as management began to analyze the firm's product mix to identify the winners and losers.

The Need for Improved Cost Management

AMD's culture and organizational structure were oriented to the high growth of its early years. The firm consisted of three major groups: Sales & Marketing, Manufacturing, and the product line divisions. Sales and Product Line marketing were jointly responsible for identifying new products and deciding what products were to be designed and manufactured.

As sales growth declined and the firm shifted toward managing profitable growth as opposed to just growth, information about the cost of products became more important. The manufacturing and product groups required better product cost information to help them design products that could be manufactured more efficiently. Sales & Marketing required better cost information so that it could shift the firm's product mix toward higher margin products.

Unfortunately, AMD, like other semiconductor companies, did not perform the entire production process—from wafer fabrication to chip packaging—under one roof (see Exhibit 4-1). Instead, AMD had built specialized production facilities for each of the three major processes required for semiconductor manufacturing: wafer fabrication, assembly manufacturing, and test and mark. This manufacturing structure enabled semiconductor companies to take full advantage of economies of scale by concentrating each manufacturing step in a limited number of locations. The specialization of facilities also made rapid growth easier, because a company could add specialized plants as capacity constraints developed in any of the three production stages.

Exhibit 4-1
MANUFACTURING PROCESS OVERVIEW

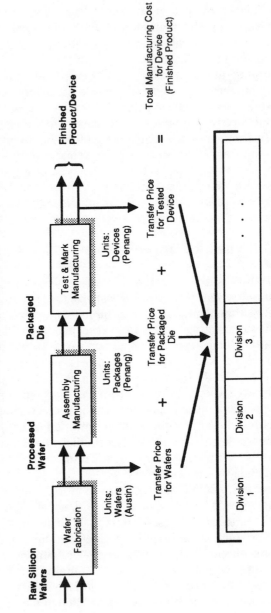

(Divisions pay transfer prices for various portions of manufacturing value added, e.g., Wafer Fab and Assembly & Test. These prices determine the division's manufacturing costs.)

The specialization of facilities, however, led to complicated product cost calculations. Each product passed through three different plants before it was completed. The typical production process began in a wafer fabrication plant where a raw wafer was processed into dies and circuit designs were etched onto each die. Next, the etched dies were sent to an assembly manufacturing plant where lead frames and packages were attached. Finally, the packages were sent to a test and mark manufacturing plant where the devices were tested, marked, and packed for sale. Product cost calculations required summing the reported costs of the three production steps, with each step performed in a different facility.

The firm's existing cost system, installed in 1969, already had been modified once when the unexpectedly slow growth rate of industry sales had led to significant excess capacity at AMD for the first time. The firm's full absorption costing system was charging the excess capacity costs to products. These higher charges distorted reported product costs and transfer prices. The distortion created difficulties in using product cost information to design more cost-effective products and to provide insights into the economics of production.

Management redesigned the system to exclude the costs of any excess capacity from reported product costs. The resulting standard cost transfer pricing (SCTP) system was introduced during 1989. This system was used to determine the transfer prices both between manufacturing facilities and between manufacturing and other parts of the firm. Thus, the standard cost transfer pricing system was used to monitor and measure the profitability of each product and product division. In the highly competitive environment of the late 1980s, profit management had become more important. Increased accuracy of transfer prices and reported product profitability was now critical.

As the emphasis on profitability and manufacturing efficiencies increased, the SCTP system began to break down. The manufacturing division was implementing a number of operational initiatives to achieve world-class manufacturing excellence in all its facilities. JIT cells were being introduced in the test and assembly facilities, and modular approaches to manufacturing management were being embraced throughout the organization. The SCTP system was using outdated labor or machine run rates. Product costs fluctuated monthly due to different capacity utilization rates. In addition, because the cost system no longer matched the current production processes, monthly and quarterly reported variances were proving impossible to explain.

AMD management began to explore the alternative costing

methodologies. Victor Lee, the finance director, rapidly identified activity-based costing as a prime candidate to improve product cost measurement. He stated, "Success at AMD is defined as profitable growth; we needed a cost methodology to support this strategy."

The Need for ABC

Three major factors drove the need for an ABC system at AMD:

1. *Improved product mix management.* During AMD's period of rapid growth, high-profit-margin products subsidized the marginal and unprofitable products. When profit margins on the more profitable products started to decrease, the firm no longer could afford to support unprofitable products. Management wanted more accurate transfer prices and product costs to help differentiate between the profitable and unprofitable products. The problem of unprofitable products had been compounded by the firm's attempt to "grow" itself out of trouble by introducing liberty chips. The product mix now contained a proliferation of low-volume products.

2. *Improved product design decisions.* AMD had many low-volume and perhaps low-margin products. Given the short life cycles of most semiconductor products, better cost information was required to help engineers design products that were less expensive to manufacture and support. Unfortunately, the SCTP system did not help engineers understand the cost consequences of different design decisions. For example, the existing system could not determine if reducing the number of insertions that devices required would be cost effective. Instead, it reported overhead as a multiple of direct labor hours.

3. *Increased manufacturing efficiencies.* Better cost information was required to help assess the impact of alternative manufacturing strategies and technologies, such as JIT cells for manufacturing high-volume devices versus non-JIT cells for manufacturing low-volume military and complex devices.

Obstacle to Full ABC Implementation

Each wafer fabrication plant supplied dies to all of the assembly manufacturing plants. Each assembly manufacturing plant, in turn, supplied all of the test and mark plants. Therefore complete product costs could not be calculated for a significant share of AMD's products unless ABC systems were implemented at virtually every plant.

The need to implement multiple ABC systems in order to report meaningful activity-based product costs was a barrier for management acceptance and authorization of an ABC project. The multiple systems would require both a long time and high development costs before the benefits of more accurate product costs could be obtained. Also, a company-wide implementation would require widespread support for ABC to justify a project that would affect so many plants.

Anticipating resistance, Victor Lee thought it best to implement ABC at a single plant, use the pilot study to prove the applicability of the ABC concept, and then attempt to use this experience to gain the widespread support required to roll out ABC across the entire organization. The key objective for the first implementation became to "prove the concept."

Preparing the Organization

Before the ABC pilot implementation could be undertaken, several steps were required. First, Lee had to sell the ABC concept to management. Second, the pilot plant had to be identified. Third, the specific objectives of the pilot beyond just proving the concept had to be determined.Identifying specific objectives for the pilot was considered especially important because the pilot implementation would not be able to satisfy the primary objective of improved cost systems at AMD: to improve management of the company's product mix. Finally, the implementation team had to be identified and trained.

Selling ABC to Management

Lee, in his role as finance director, emerged as the primary champion and corporate project leader of ABC at AMD. Lee believed, "Management commitment and communication of ABC concepts and results were keys to the success of the project." He presented the concept of ABC to Don Brettner (vice president of Far East manufacturing) and the corporate controller, seeking sponsorship for the ABC study. Over the next three to four months, Lee circulated articles on activity-based costing and made several presentations to senior management.

Management's reaction to the seminars and literature reinforced the appropriateness of the decision to run a pilot study before beginning the roll-out. Finance and Manufacturing decided to start a pilot study in August 1991. Lee started to explore potential sites as well as the benefits from using external consulting firms to assist in the initial project.

Selecting a Pilot Site

AMD management chose their test and assembly operations in Penang, Malaysia, as the ABC pilot site. The Penang facility was the largest of AMD's plants and assembled the company's latest and most complex microprocessors. It employed approximately 4,000 people. The reasons for choosing this site included:

- Plant management was receptive to change, having recently implemented JIT successfully.
- The plant's accounting and finance group already had conducted its own mini-ABC study of the purchasing function and was extremely enthusiastic about applying the approach more broadly.
- The yest and assembly production processes were far less complex than those performed in wafer fabrication and assembly manufacturing facilities. Lee and Brettner believed that the pilot implementation would go more smoothly in a simpler environment.

Pilot Objectives

While the primary objective for the pilot study was "proving the concept," other benefits that were expected by the AMD management included:

- *Improved understanding of test and assembly manufacturing costs.* For example, the reported cost per unit of insertion would help the product engineers at the divisions understand the potential economic impact of designing products that required fewer insertions.
- *More accurate cost information about different production strategies at the Penang test and assembly facility.* The ABC system would highlight the difference in costs of the high-volume EPROM and PAL packages produced in JIT cells versus the low-volume military packages produced in non-JIT cells. This improved cost information would provide Operations with the ability to evaluate the cost effectiveness of different manufacturing strategies and decisions. Another example would be to highlight the cost of using specialized testers and handlers. This information would be used to support subcontracting decisions for certain low-volume products.

Team Selection and Training

AMD hired an external consulting firm to assist in the implementation of its pilot project. The consultants launched the project by conducting a two-day training seminar on ABC concepts. A wide multifunctional audience attended the seminar, including manufacturing supervisors, engineering managers, and management information services (MIS) managers as well as financial representatives from other AMD plants in Bangkok and Singapore. The seminar was considered a critical part of the project. It raised plant management's awareness of ABC and created the local management buy-in considered crucial to the project's success. Lee commented on the training program, "The training program generated corporate commitment and visibility for the Penang project. It emphasized the importance of this project to all AMD staff in Penang. The training exposed senior management at Penang to ABC concepts and provided them with the ability to more effectively lead and guide the project."

Local management, along with Lee, helped to select a multifunctional project team of seven AMD employees and two consultants. The project leader was A.S. Leong, who had an operations background and was the section head of the repair and maintenance area in the test facility. The other team members had backgrounds in industrial engineering, product engineering, quality analysis, MIS, and cost accounting. The MIS participant was selected to develop the programs to quantify and collect activity driver data from the manufacturing shop floor systems. Management chose such a large multifunctional team because they believed that the active participation of members from all of the major operations areas would be critical for a successful implementation of the project.

A project steering committee also was created. It consisted of Mercer Curtis, the plant director; Juferi Kasman, the controller; the 10 department managers; and Victor Lee. The steering committee was responsible for resolving any major issues that arose during the project, for example, the number of products to be included in the scope of the analysis.

Implementation of the Pilot Project

Project Work Plan

The project followed a 10-step system implementation approach.

1. *Define scope.* The project team wrestled with the concept of costing some versus all products. It rapidly became clear that costing only a subset of products on any attribute (e.g., production volume) might mask the full impact of the product cost distortions and cross subsidies. Consequently, the project team decided to cost all the facility's products (approximately 120 packages in mark and assembly and 1,200 devices in test).

2. *Carry out activity interviews.* The project team carried out approximately 65 interviews to identify the activities being performed by indirect labor.

3. *Collect labor activity data.* Activity collection forms were circulated to department heads, who used them to assign employee time among the different activities identified in the interviews.

4. *Analyze nonlabor activity.* The project team identified activities related to machine processing and using indirect materials. They attempted to identify machines with similar processing characteristics and indirect materials with similar usage characteristics so that they could be grouped together without introducing serious distortions in reported product costs. Once the machine groupings were identified, machine-related activities such as repair and maintenance, preventive maintenance, and statistical process control were driven to them.

5. *Analyze activity.* Expenses recorded in the general ledger now could be mapped to the identified production-related activities. The list of activities was reduced by aggregating the 80 to 90 activities identified into the 30 to 35 major activities required for accurate product costing purposes. A Pareto analysis was used to identify the less significant activities. These activities were aggregated either with similar activities or with activities having a common objective.

The final activity model of each department was circulated to the department manager, who validated the activity structure. Next, each department's activities were grouped into activity centers defined around the objectives of the department. Exhibits 4-2, 4-3, and 4-4 show the activity centers for each manufacturing area.

6. *Hold activity driver interviews.* Once the list of major activities had been finalized, the project team went through a second phase of interviews to identify the activity drivers that would link activity expenses to products.

7. *Develop activity driver quantities.* Collecting the information about how much of the activity drivers each product used involved extensive programming to extract data from multiple databases.

Exhibit 4-2
ACTIVITIES-BASED COSTING SYSTEM
PENANG TEST MODEL

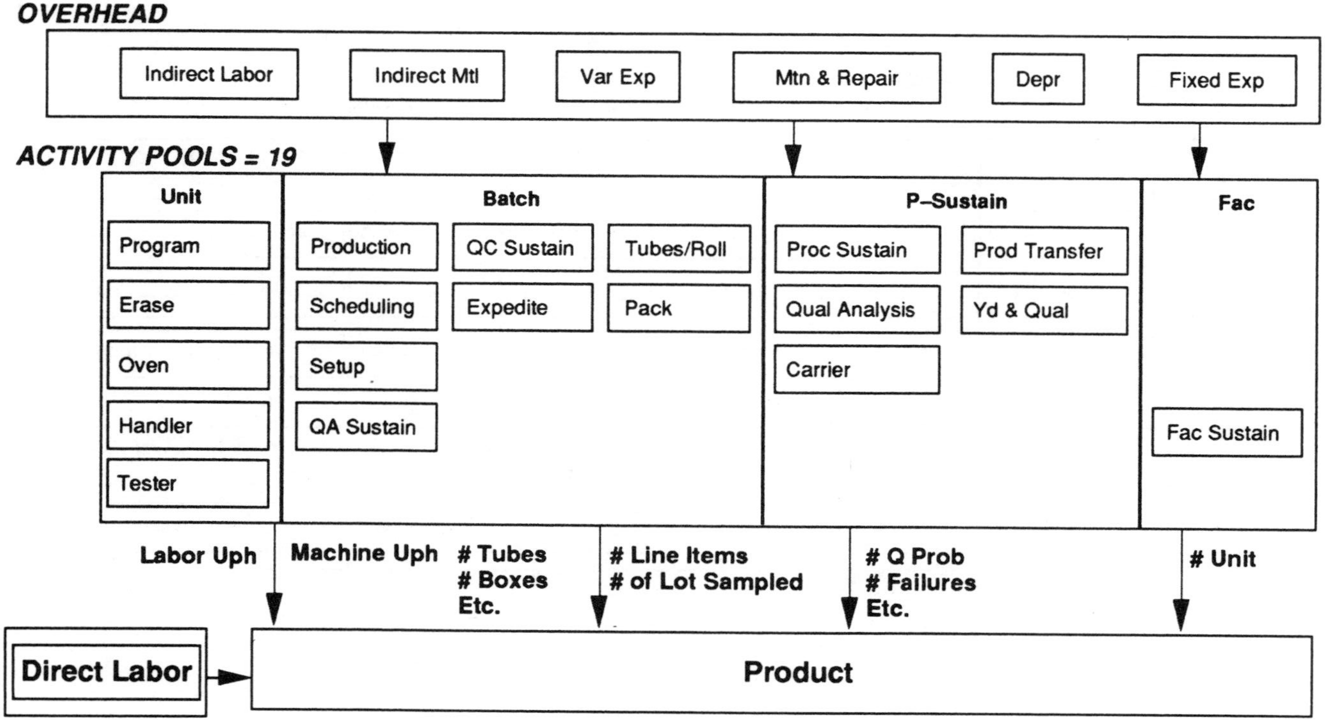

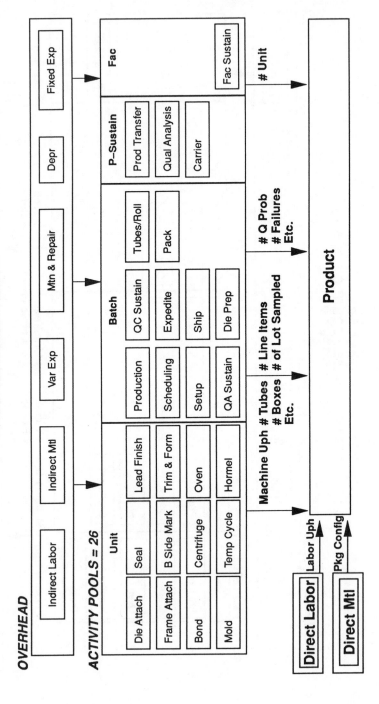

Exhibit 4-3
ACTIVITIES-BASED COSTING SYSTEM
PENANG ASSEMBLY MODEL

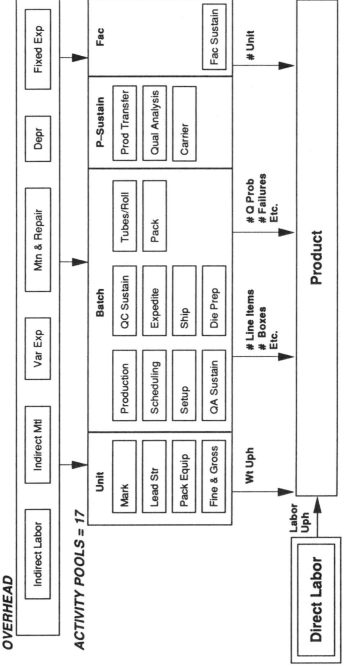

Exhibit 4-4
ACTIVITIES-BASED COSTING SYSTEM
PENANG MARK MODEL

When products' use of drivers was not available from existing information systems, sampling studies were performed to identify typical activity cost driver profiles.

8. *Load and run the model.* The activity expense, activity driver, and product specification data were loaded into the personal computer-based ABC software. The computer model calculated the new product costs.

9. *Verify and analyze data.* After obtaining the new product costs, the project team spent four weeks validating and analyzing the results.

10. *Expect continuous evolution.* The structure of the ABC model at Penang continued to evolve as some of the initial assumptions were refined. The model improvements included additional analysis of the facility-sustaining costs, so that more of them were assigned to products. For instance, utility costs, which originally were treated as facility sustaining, were reassigned to machine centers and then subsequently to the products. Also, certain machine centers were disaggregated further to provide more accurate product costs. For example, the tester machine group was expanded into 12 different groups, one for each type of tester.

Personnel Time and Role of Consultants

While the project team had seven members, most of them were assigned only on a part-time basis. Over the 16 weeks of the project, the equivalent of 2.5 persons were involved full-time. The consultants made two on-site visits. During the first visit, they conducted the initial two-day training seminar and helped with the activity interviews. On the second trip, the consultants helped the team identify the second-stage drivers and launch the data collection process. The U.S.-based consultants continued to play an active role in validating and refining the data once the project was completed, though they did not revisit the plant. The consultants played a relatively limited on-site role because of the extensive travel distance between the home office in San Francisco and Penang. They communicated with the implementation team through E-mail, telefaxes, and weekly conference calls.

Model Design

The structure of the ABC system required that several design decisions be made.

1. *Multiple models.* Given the complex nature of the manufacturing process and the uniqueness of the activities in the different manufacturing processes, the team decided to build three separate ABC models, one each for the assembly, test, and mark areas.

2. *Scope of costs in ABC analysis.* Only the costs of the indirect overhead departments were included in the ABC analysis. The costs of direct labor and materials were imported from the facility's standard cost system.

3. *Machine process activities.* Manufacturing equipment was categorized into groups of machines that performed similar processing activities. The activity costs assigned to these machine groups included repair and maintenance costs, spares costs, utilities costs, and depreciation. Thus these machine activity process costs captured the fully loaded costs of running these groups of machines.

For the test area model, the machine groups included programmers, erasers, ovens, handlers, and testers (see Exhibit 4-2). For the assembly area model, the machines were grouped according to the manufacturing processes, which are die attach, frame attach, bond, mold, seal, B side mark, centrifuge, temperature cycle, lead finish, trim and form, oven, and hermiticity-testing (see Exhibit 4-3). Finally, the mark area model machine groups included mark, lead straighteners, pack, and fine/gross leak machine activity processes (see Exhibit 4-4).

4. *Grouping activities into activity centers.* The team grouped activities into activity centers to provide a more manageable set of activity data for product costing and reporting purposes. Activities with similar cost behavior patterns and/or similar objectives were grouped together.

5. *Value ranking of activities.* The group spent significant time trying to rank activities by the value they added to the finished product. This process proved very controversial. Plant management felt that the on-going efficiency programs would focus employees' attention on the high-cost activities and were concerned that any arbitrary value ranking would misdirect that process. Given these concerns, the team eventually decided not to rank activities by value.

6. *Cost hierarchy.* After activities had been identified and aggregated, the project team categorized them using the manufacturing cost hierarchy (i.e., unit, batch, product, and facility sustaining).

7. *Activity management.* The detailed information on activities

performed and their costs led to a vigorous activity management program. Activity management councils have been set up to use the activity information to improve production processes.

Key Results and Findings

The pilot implementation at Penang successfully achieved its primary corporate objective of "proving the concept." It demonstrated that an economical ABC system could be developed for the semiconductor industry. Locally, the model identified the major drivers of manufacturing cost in the test and assembly facility and revealed the difference in manufacturing costs between non-JIT and JIT production. Finally, the project demonstrated that corporate-wide application of ABC systems could lead to changed decisions in product mix and design by highlighting the distortions arising from the current transfer prices. According to Lee, "ABC provided us with a better understanding of our cost structure and it provided us with the information we required for decision making."

Proof of Concept

The project provided data to prove the intuitive feeling that high-volume standard products were subsidizing low-volume complex devices produced for military applications. Manufacturing had decided to implement JIT cells for the high-volume simple products in assembly and test even though the existing cost system did not validate this decision. ABC demonstrated that the product costs for the standard high-volume products that ran on the JIT cells were significantly lower than traditional costs. It also proved that the low-volume complex military products were significantly more expensive than previously thought. In the words of a local production manager, "ABC provided cost information that acted as a feedback mechanism to validate manufacturing improvement programs. Plant management felt that now they had a cost system that would measure the impact of batch-level activities on product costs and provide a more accurate picture of assembly and test costs for different products."

Local Objectives

The ABC project provided insights into the drivers of assembly and test manufacturing costs in Penang. ABC identified scheduling, setup, and expediting as significant batch-level activities. This insight enabled plant management to identify discrete manufacturing programs that would reduce these activity costs and lead to lower total manufacturing costs. ABC also assisted management in understanding the true costs of running the tester and handler machine groups. Previously, management had concentrated its efforts on reducing direct labor costs. ABC revealed that even though the tester and handler machine groups were fully depreciated, significant repair, maintenance and utility costs were incurred to run these machines. ABC also identified the significant product-sustaining activities—especially engineering—required to assemble and test the products. In summary, ABC provided local management with a much richer tool to understand and manage manufacturing costs.

Corporate Objectives

The Penang project demonstrated that ABC could provide useful information in a semiconductor manufacturing environment. The traditional cost system indicated that the average cost to assemble and test a product was approximately $.48. ABC revealed that the standard deviation of costs around the average product cost was much greater than previously thought. Exhibit 4-5 shows that ABC-reported costs were as high as $3.50 per unit for low-volume complex products, whereas the traditional cost system had indicated that the most expensive product cost only $2.50. This shift in reported product costs helped to demonstrate the value of ABC to the AMD divisions and other manufacturing groups. A manager at a division responsible for the high-volume, simple products felt that "finally the true economics of producing the high-volume simple products was being recognized."

Additional Benefits

In addition to the above objectives, the Penang project provided benefits in regard to the following items: (1) unexpectedly expensive activities, (2) cost hierarchy, (3) key batch and product-sustaining drivers, and (4) product cost distortions.

Unexpectedly Expensive Activities

Two significant scheduling activities were identified: the actual process of scheduling production, and the execution of the production

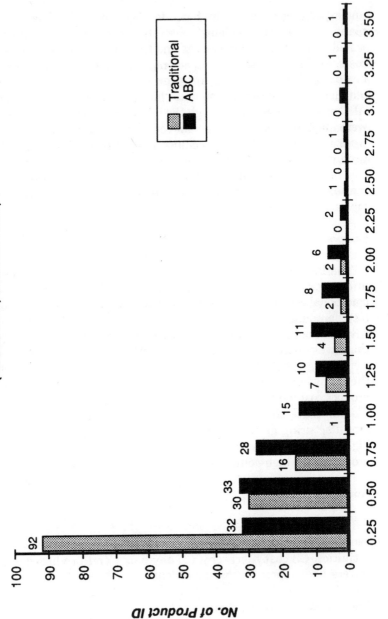

Exhibit 4-5
PRODUCT COST DISTRIBUTIONS
(ASSEMBLY, MARK & TEST)

schedule. The ABC system highlighted the redundant nature of these activities. Also, it identified statistical process control as a major indirect labor activity. As part of AMD's world-class manufacturing program, almost every indirect employee performed SPC in some way or another, so that even though the SPC department actually had only three employees, many more people were involved in SPC. By identifying SPC-related activities wherever they occurred, ABC captured the entire cost of the SPC program. This analysis revealed the testers and handlers machine activities to be the most expensive because of the high cost of repairs, preventive maintenance, and SPC activities performed for them.

Cost Hierarchy

ABC identified significant nonunit-level activities in the back-end manufacturing environment. Of the 19 activities in the test area, only five were unit level, eight were batch level, five were product sustaining, and one was facility sustaining. Similarly, in the assembly area, 12 of the 26 activities were unit level, 10 were batch level, three were product sustaining, and one was facility sustaining (see Exhibits 4-2, 4-3, and 4-4). This categorization of activities helped redirect management's attention to streamlining nonunit-level activities. Previously, the manufacturing improvements had focused on reducing unit-level costs.

Key Batch and Product-Sustaining Drivers

Some of the key nonunit-level cost drivers included:

- Number of line items (for production scheduling and setup activities),
- Number of quality problems that were encountered (for some process-sustaining activities),
- Number of times a product fell below a yield trip point (for yield and quality improvement activities).

The high total of expenses driven by these nonunit-level costs underlined the inaccuracies in the old system, which allocated all expenses to products using labor and machine hours.

Product Cost Distortions

ABC showed that products with low volumes and multiple batches had high manufacturing costs, as did products that used a disproportionate share of product-sustaining activities. In the assembly area, traditional costs ranged from $.009 to $1.21, with a simple average of $.14. The ABC system reported product costs that ranged from $.01 to $15.22, with a simple average cost of $.95. This difference demonstrated that the standard deviation of product costs around the simple average was much higher than previously understood. Under ABC, the standard high-volume products had lower assembly and test costs, whereas the complex military products had much higher assembly and test costs. The complex products had multiple test insertions and went through more complex operations to ensure their functionality. These products also received high batch costs for setup and scheduling because of their low production volumes.

ABC Implementation and Roll-Out Plan

After the Penang pilot project was completed, the co-champions of the project, Lee and Brettner, communicated the findings to various audiences at AMD. Brettner described the Penang results at the corporate director's conference. Lee presented the results to AMD's entire financial management staff at a worldwide controller's conference. The presentations were well received and raised interest levels among divisional managers. The manager for one of the divisions felt, "It was about time that management recognized the need for, and measured, this type of information."

The division manager for a large commodity product line agreed. "Managers need to understand which products are subsidizing other products and to be able to quantify the magnitude of this subsidization."

The CFO of AMD, Marv Burkett, presented some ABC concepts and results to Jerry Sanders, chairman of AMD, and to other senior executive staff. Jerry Sanders and the senior executive staff reacted favorably to the information presented and gave their support to ABC implementation across AMD.

The corporate objective for ABC required implementing ABC throughout the firm. Lee developed a roll-out plan for implementing ABC at the other manufacturing sites. By the end of the third quarter of 1991, AMD had completed the implementation of ABC at its two remaining assembly and test plants in the Far East. Once ABC had been installed at the Asian sites, the systems could be used to set transfer prices for back-end manufacturing. In addition, the ABC-based information was used to prepare the fiscal 1992 budget at AMD.

AMD currently is extending ABC at its wafer fabrication plant in Austin, Texas. Austin was chosen as the first "fab" site for three reasons:

- The core competency of wafer fabrication for AMD is in Austin;
- The Austin fab is a simpler manufacturing environment than some of the other more complex microprocessor fabs; and
- The EPROM wafers (the bulk of the products) processed at Austin also constitute a significant proportion of Penang's products. Developing a model for this plant would give AMD the opportunity to analyze full manufacturing costs for EPROM products by integrating the Penang and Austin results.

AMD plans to complete the implementation of ABC at all its wafer manufacturing facilities by the second quarter of 1992. After all the manufacturing areas are complete, AMD plans to start its product portfolio analysis on a gross margin basis during the third quarter of that year. Between the first and third quarters of 1992, all the assembly and test plants that have implemented ABC will continue to refine their models. The company plans to have implemented a worldwide ABC manufacturing system by the end of 1992 and to have implemented ABC in the sales, general and administrative, and research and development areas by the end of 1993. It plans to have 1993 transfer prices for all manufacturing areas based on ABC information by the end of 1992.

AMD also plans to use ABC not just for transfer pricing but also for activity management, to help streamline inefficient processes. It will analyze divisional and product profitability and, by extending the analysis to the order procurement function, understand order and customer profitability.

Chapter 5

Farrall, Inc.

Executive Summary

Farrall, Inc., a manufacturer of proprietary filter materials with about
$500 million in annual worldwide sales, embarked on an ABC pilot
project in November 1990. The company did a pilot study of ABC
concepts in two facilities that manufactured similar products but that
had substantially different profitabilities. Management wanted the ABC
project to answer several critical questions:

- *More accurate product costs.* How much did transfer prices, based
  on traditionally calculated product costs, distort product
  profitability and lead to bad pricing decisions?
- *Customer profitability.* How were the company's high selling,
  distribution, and administrative expenses influenced by the
  specific demands of individual customers and markets?
- *Resource management/cost reduction opportunities.* In a cost
  competitive environment, how could the company improve
  resource management and reduce costs without sacrificing
  competitive advantage?
- *Investment justification.* What were the costs and benefits of
  capital investments in advanced manufacturing technologies and
  how could they be attributed to specific product lines?

The study also was intended to establish a success model at Farrall
to be built upon for future applications of ABC concepts and results.

The project was sponsored and implemented by members of the
finance function at both corporate and the division. At regular divisional
and international finance meetings, progress reports on the ABC project
were made and results shared. Little awareness of the project, however,
spread outside the finance function to general and operating managers.

The project extended three months beyond the original four-month
schedule, mainly because of limited resources committed to it. The

corporate controller, the ABC project sponsor, felt that "it was better to get to the right numbers than get to inaccurate numbers quickly."

Key insights provided by the project were:

- The most profitable 10% of the customers generated more than 230% of the profits.
- Traditional calculations estimated that 52% of the activities varied with unit volume. The ABC analysis demonstrated that only 23% of activities varied with production volumes; 21% related to each batch or work order.
- Inventory carrying charges made up a significant portion of product costs for low-volume custom products that had been produced in big batches and stored for months.
- Materials-handling information provided the manufacturing manager with new insights into ways of reducing the cost of moving materials in the plant.

Reaction from key management was mixed. Manufacturing Manager Glenn Donahue believed that ABC's greatest value was its tie to quality: "ABC may be a fad within the finance world, but quality is the mainstay to manufacturers due to Japanese competition. Now we can bring ABC to support our quality programs." Bob Spears, ABC advocate and project leader, reacted to the length and effort of the project. "I had no idea it would take such dedication. And I could have used more help."

Tom Flynn, the new business manager, supported ABC with some reservations. "We are not ready to switch our transfer pricing calculations to ABC. Transfer pricing is acceptable today because it's consistent. There is a structured formula for everyone."

Even with the mixed reactions, Farrall currently was selecting new facilities where ABC would be implemented. The corporate controller said that ultimately "I want ABC to generate a standard set of management reports to run our business. ...The question is knowledge. ...With better information, we have better knowledge and can make better decisions."

Company Background

The Company and Business Environment

Farrall, Inc. is a world leader in water clarification technology. The company was incorporated in 1952 after the research of the founder and chairman, Dr. Gregory E. Farrall, had led to a proprietary filter material. Farrall currently has sales in excess of $500 million, to companies in Asia, Europe, the Middle East, Africa, and, of course, the Americas.

Farrall's proprietary porous material and associated housings are used to remove contaminants from water in a broad variety of consumer and industrial applications. Increasing consumer concerns about environmental and health issues has led to high growth for water purifying systems in the home.

Farrall emphasizes customized applications for its products. This differentiation strategy requires it to be close to the advancing and changing needs of leading edge customers. The company has eliminated or de-emphasized a mature product when value-enhancing technology innovation had ceased and the product had reached commodity status.

The company has been highly successful with its technology and strategy. It continues to develop water clarification products and maintains market dominance in its principal markets.

Motivation for the Activity-Based Costing Study

In the late 1980s, Farrall was making substantial investments to acquire expensive equipment required to sustain and grow its businesses. But the company could not measure the cost/benefit of the new equipment or accurately trace capital expenses to the products being produced with the new technology. Corporate Controller Jay Hansen noted, "Our traditional systems showed no correlation between equipment and output." With more and more costly machines on the shop floor, direct labor overhead rates had soared. The existing cost system did not make the benefits of the new equipment visible, nor did it provide signals for management to plan for future investments.

In addition, apparently similar business units that manufactured and sold the same product lines had unexplained differences in profits. The traditional accounting systems did not disclose the cause of the discrepancy. Transfer price calculations between production and sales units and high corporate overhead calculations (which some management believed were not necessarily based on received benefit or use) added to the unexplained differences. Sales & Marketing management were looking at simple and highly aggregated transfer price calculations and asking, "Why can't we learn what's behind the numbers?"

From a market perspective, the original equipment manufacturer (OEM) market was believed to be marginally profitable or even unprofitable. This segment was highly competitive and price conscious and demanded special attention for its customers' needs. When asked to assess the impact of shutting down the OEM market on divisional profitability, Bob Spears, plant controller, responded honestly, "Given our traditional methods of calculating overhead and our aggregate transfer price calculations, I'm not sure I could tell you."

These factors led the company to seek a better system to measure the costs of products, processes, customers, and markets.

How ABC Was Selected

Bob Spears and Carl Winecki (Consumer Products Division controller) had been directed by Corporate Controller Hansen to identify cost system alternatives. They first learned of ABC concepts through seminars and literature from organizations such as the Institute of Management Accountants (formerly known as the National Association of Accountants), Computer Aided Manufacturing-International (CAM-I), and the Department of Defense. The articles and seminars described the value of ABC to early implementors but did not provide sufficient guidance for an in-house project.

Farrall asked for consulting advice from its auditing firm. In a workshop for finance representatives from corporate and selected units around the world, the consultants introduced the fundamentals of ABC, identified what was truly "broken" in the existing cost systems, described how ABC could be applied at Farrall, and, most important, illustrated the potential value of an ABC system to the company. After the workshop, Farrall management decided to investigate ABC concepts by conducting a pilot project in the Consumer Products Division.

The Consumer Products Division

Consumer Products Division's customers included manufacturers and users of home water filtration systems. Farrall chose to pilot ABC concepts in two consumer products (CP) facilities that manufacture the same products. These facilities produced similar products but had quite dissimilar cost structures. One facility, located in Riverside, California, with $30 million in annual sales, served the North America marketplace; the second facility, in Southampton, England, served the United Kingdom and European marketplaces. Both CP plants had embarked on a total quality program, and the ABC project was believed to be a natural complement for this effort.

Consumer products included home filtration systems for use in the kitchen, swimming pools, and hot tubs. Most applications used the advanced technology of the ABSOLUTE and INTEGRAL II filters within a variety of housings. Spears explained, "The manufacturing processes for filters and housings require a mixture of high and low technology, with high capital and people costs."

Approximately 40 different filters were manufactured in a variety of colors, sizes, and specifications, leading to a total of more than 700 individual stockkeeping units (SKUs). More than 25 housing lines designed to house the filters had as many as 10 to 15 versions per line. The market for replacement filters had been growing but was becoming more competitive. Competitors recently had attempted to build filters that fit Farrall's housings. Conversely, Farrall had begun to build filters for competitors' housings.

Farrall's divisions were organized with manufacturing groups that manufactured and transferred products to Sales & Marketing groups for ultimate sale to distributors and OEM customers. The transfer price for products "sold" from Manufacturing to Sales & Marketing was calculated as cost plus a product-specific profit margin, approximately 30% on filters and 10% on housings. Product cost included overhead calculations of up to 600% on direct labor cost and 18% on direct materials cost. Sales & Marketing attempted to maintain a 10% markup on the transfer price. In recent years, Southampton had enjoyed an even higher profit margin, while Riverside had fallen short of the standard 10% profit margin target. Corporate management was uncertain about the causes of these differences.

Preparing the Organization

Farrall's corporate management sponsored and provided financing for the pilot projects. Corporate Controller Jay Hansen selected the two sites and directed them to create project teams to implement ABC within their own organizations, with assistance from outside consultants. Each site was allowed (with certain guidelines) to design its own model. Oversight of the two pilot sites was maintained by corporate and the consulting team. This approach enabled the two designs to be tailored to the different users and marketplaces, while the best features subsequently could be standardized and extended beyond the pilots if proven successful. Hansen wanted the two pilots to establish a success model at Farrall on which to base future use of the ABC concepts and results.

The ABC model was designed to address two primary objectives (see Exhibit 5-1):

- *Product profitability for the manufactured products.* Transfer prices based on ABC product costs would be compared with traditionally calculated transfer prices. Factors leading to differences in product and product-line profitability then would be identified and analyzed.
- *Customer profitability for the Sales & Marketing efforts.* Costs specifically associated with the demands of individual customers and markets would be added to the ABC-based transfer price and compared with the net selling prices, after discounts. This calculation would reveal, for the first time, the profitability of individual customers and market segments.

Exhibit 5-1
ABC PROJECT OBJECTIVES

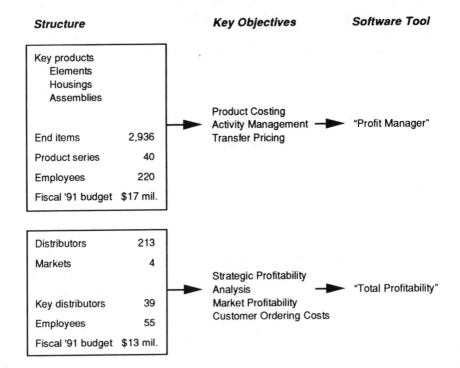

Supplementary objectives for the ABC project were to gain insights into resource management, cost reduction opportunities, and investment justification. Managers were looking for ways to reduce costs without losing competitive advantage. Also, by comparing the high cost of acquiring and using new machines that incorporated advanced manufacturing technology with the lower running cost but much higher maintenance and repair cost of old machines, the ABC calculations would provide information relating to the costs and benefits of capital investments. The comparison between the operating costs of the new and old machines also would suggest strategies for assigning different products to the two types of equipment. Finally, to support the plants' total quality movement projects, ABC was to measure the price of conformance and nonconformance (both internal and external) and identify the extent of nonvalue-added processes.

System Design and Architecture

The ABC implementation began in November 1990, with a two-day meeting at Riverside attended by the corporate controller, Consumer Products Division controller, Riverside business manager, Riverside controller, Riverside manufacturing manager, and the designated Riverside ABC team leader. This initial meeting identified management's business issues and concerns that would form the framework for the ABC system architecture.

The conceptual design session was followed by a two-day implementation training course attended only by project team members. The Riverside project team and their percentage of dedication to the project are shown below.

- Robert Spears, plant controller—25%;
- John McCarthy, Cost Accounting—100%;
- Frank Cohen, Cost Accounting—20%;
- Bruce Coulbourn, Information Systems—20%;
- Christine Sasaki, Corporate Allocations—10%;
- Tim Sander, president of sales company—5%;
- Fred Schmidt, senior vice president of sales—5%.

The approximate full-time equivalent of Riverside team members over the life of the six-month project equalled 1.5 person-years.

Southampton's conceptual design and implementation training followed in December 1990, with similar structure and team makeup.

Due to staff constraints, however, no single person was dedicated full-time to the project.

Both projects followed four key steps to complete the ABC implementation:

1. *Interview and data collection.* Identify activities performed in functional areas and map departmental expenses into the cost of performing activities.

2. *Business process analysis.* Accumulate activities into key business processes, such as procurement, customer administration, and materials handling.

3. *Cost driver analysis.* Assign the activity costs to subassemblies, products, and customers. The team analyzed each business process to identify potential cost drivers. For example, in the procurement business process a key cost driver was the number of line items on a purchase order. Activities varied by the number of unique items on an order.

There was a question initially as to whether the cost driver also should be multiplied by a weighting factor related to the type of raw material, to reflect the raw materials that were more difficult to purchase than the others (due to requirements for specific training and expertise). But further review discovered that this step was unnecessary. Line items per purchase order adequately depicted purchasing difficulties.

4. *Product and customer profitability analysis.* Analyze ABC-calculated product and customer profitability.

Key Design Decisions

The project team made several interesting design decisions based on unique aspects of Farrall's business and objectives.

Direct Labor as an Indirect Expense

The direct labor content at Riverside was approximately 5% of sales revenue. Nevertheless, the plant maintained a significant data collection effort on the shop floor to monitor and report direct labor time, cost, and efficiencies. At the time of the project, Riverside was embarking on a new automated time card system. The discussion of ABC for indirect activities forced management to confront the effectiveness and relevance of the direct labor data collection exercise.

The accuracy of Riverside routing and labor files had been under question for some time. The systems were not relied on and were not kept up-to-date or easily accessible.

Further, the existing cost system assignment of direct labor to products did not distinguish between run time and setup time. Rather than attempt to penetrate the existing direct labor standards to split labor time into separate run and setup time components, especially with the lack of reliance on the current system already, the Riverside design team chose to assign direct labor expenses in the ABC model just like indirect and overhead expenses. Two separate activities were defined for direct labor—producing products and setting up machines. Separate cost drivers then could be selected for each of the two activities: machine hours and number of work orders, respectively.

Southampton chose to continue to charge direct labor in the traditional way. They felt that their routing and labor files were more accurate and assessable than Riverside's. In effect, both run time and setup time were assigned to Southampton's products using a volume driver, and the distinction between unit- and batch-level direct labor activities was suppressed.

Corporate Charges Identified for Type of Activity Only

Riverside received three types of corporate charges based on balance sheet levels of net fixed assets, inventory, and receivables. Another charge was based on corporate services, such as customer service and advertising. These charges were fairly significant and raised key questions:

* Are the amounts accurate on an ABC basis?
* Should corporate charges be allocated to products and, if so, how much and by what method?

Christine Sasaki from corporate, who was familiar with the allocation methods, was assigned to the project to help answer these questions.

The analysis revealed that corporate charges were based mostly on divisional revenue and not usage of corporate resources. Time sheets were kept on only some of the corporate activities. A full-scale study would have been required to provide an accurate assignment of corporate expenses to Riverside. Such a study clearly was beyond the scope of the initial ABC project so the team decided not to question the amount of Riverside corporate charge. It did, however, address whether the corporate expenses could sensibly be assigned to individual products.

The main components of the corporate charge related to R&D of the proprietary material, advertising, customer service, and interest on accounts receivable and inventory. Costs such as interest charges and customer service could be charged to products or customers based on days outstanding (receivables), days in inventory, and number of orders times a weighting factor for average usage of customer service. Costs that were not associated directly with a product or customer, such as corporate-level advertising, were considered facility sustaining, and they were spread to product lines or markets based on production volume or revenue. This procedure produced a fully loaded product cost from which it was relatively easy to exclude the arbitrarily allocated facility-sustaining costs.

Value Ranking of Activities

The design team developed a value analysis scheme for activities to identify process improvement and cost reduction opportunities. The activities were ranked according to their importance for Farrall's objectives and missions, as well as for value they could provide to customers. Lengthy discussions among the team members eventually produced the following definitions:

- Low: No value to either Farrall or the customer. The activity represents errors or mistakes that ideally should not occur. Examples: defects, returns.
- Low-medium: Little to no value to Farrall or customer but currently is necessary to the process. Examples: materials handling, processing quality assurance reports.
- Medium: Supports the objectives and mission of Farrall but does not directly produce a product or generate a sale. Examples: management reporting, general maintenance, and setup.
- Medium-high: Supports production or development of a product or servicing of a customer. Examples: welding shop, packing.
- High: Produces a product or generates a sales order. Examples: assembly and run time.

The team assigned a value ranking to each activity. Spears recalled, "This was a painful process. Everyone had a different definition of what's valuable to them. The concept, however, tied closely to our quality program, and it got people's attention."

Development of Customer Profitability Module

Farrall sold through four main markets, with separate sales representatives in each market:

- HA: Home Appliance Division—kitchen water filters and self-contained water filtration systems,
- LD: Leisure Division—hot tub and pool filters,
- NH: New Housing Division—contract installation in new homes,
- OEM: Original equipment manufacturers—direct business.

A hierarchical structure was built to assign activity costs so that accurate market and customer profitability could be calculated (see Exhibit 5-2). The following hierarchy was developed after interviews with key managers in Sales & Marketing:

- Sales divisions: HA, LD, NH, and OEM;
- Sales representatives: within each division;
- Customers/distributors: reps assigned to a set of customers within divisions (to Farrall a customer is a distributor or end-user);
- Orders: orders for particular products at specific net prices that could be traced directly to individual customers.

Each Sales & Marketing activity was assigned to one level in this hierarchy. For example, customer servicing costs were assigned directly to distributors based on the line items per order. Advertising costs, which had no relationship to an individual customer or sales rep, were assigned at the division level based on actual dollars spent in each market. Costs at higher levels of the hierarchy could be allocated (somewhat arbitrarily) downward, from division to sales rep, from sales rep to customer, and from customer to order, based on unit volumes or sales dollars. Order, customer, and divisional profitability were calculated by subtracting the costs assigned to the customer and order, plus the ABC-calculated product costs, from the sales revenue received from the order or customer.

Data Interpretation

The output from the ABC models provided Farrall's management with new insights into the business. A few of the key activities and cost drivers built into the ABC architecture are listed in Exhibit 5-3. The

Exhibit 5-2
SALES AND MARKETING HIERARCHY

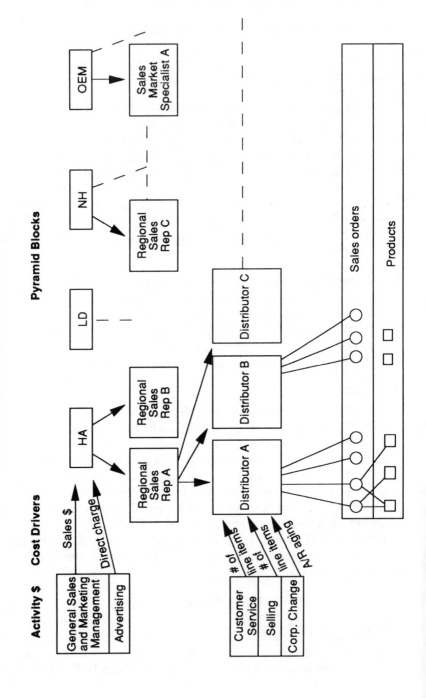

Exhibit 5-3
ACTIVITIES AND COST DRIVERS

Activities/Business Process	Cost Driver
Product development — customer changes	Number of customer ECNs
Procurement	Number of line items per vendor order
Scheduling	Number of production orders
Materials handling	Number of moves (operations)
Inventory management	Average inventory value

analysis focused on: business processes; cost drivers; volume sensitivity; product cost, profitability, and transfer pricing; and customer and distributor profitability.

Business Processes Analysis

Business processes analysis (see Exhibit 5-4) identified and measured the costs of major processes along the company's value chain: from product development through product manufacturing and distribution, culminating in customer service. The business processes analysis enabled management to view its organization across functional organizational boundaries.

For example, the procurement business process encompassed the costs of the activities performed to source, order, and receive raw materials. These activities included the Purchasing Department's sourcing and vendor-relation activities, the Accounts Payable Department's purchase order processing and payment activities, and the Receiving Department's processing activity for incoming shipments. The analysis enabled the organization to see, for the first time, the total cost of its procurement activities.

The business process costs analyzed included: (1) direct production costs, (2) inventory management, (3) materials handling, and (4) quality.

The *direct production costs* category was one of the largest. Costs included direct labor run-time costs, machine depreciation, and energy expenses. The costs in this category were driven to product using machine hours and direct labor hours and yielded results similar to those calculated by the existing cost system.

Inventory management costs included the large corporate charge for days of inventory. Other activities in this business process were the measurement and reporting of inventory values from the cost accounting department, and warehousing and obsolescence charges. Inventory management costs were charged to individual products based on size and on the number of days the products (and their associated raw materials) remained in inventory during the year.

Activities performed in *materials handling,* to move materials in and out of the warehouse and around the shop floor, were separated from inventory management activities because the handling costs were driven by the number of processing steps rather than size or inventory days. By using the number of operations as a cost driver, the products with the

Exhibit 5-4
BUSINESS PROCESSES

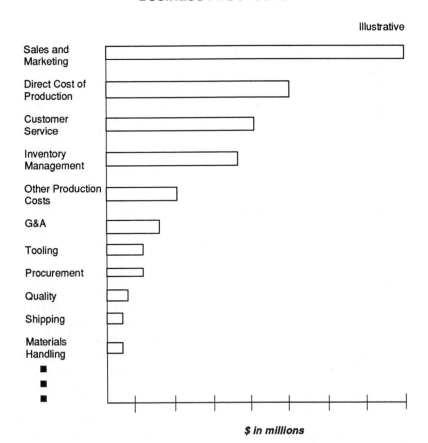

Illustrative

$ in millions

greatest number of production processes or steps consumed the largest amount of materials-handling costs.

The costs of *quality-related activities* (e.g., training, rework, returned goods, inspection) were assigned to a quality business process, a procedure consistent with giving visibility to total quality management (TQM) efforts. The ABC system measured the cost of conformance (training and inspection) separately from the cost of nonconformance (returns, scrap, rework, and redundant activities).

Glen Donahue, manufacturing manager, didn't become enthusiastic about the ABC effort until he saw the tie to the plant's TQM efforts. "Quality is the mainstay for manufacturers," he said. "The ABC model gave our people the right numbers for the first time. It helped us identify the price of nonconformance and tied in 100% with our quality improvement program."

Cost Driver Analysis

The costs assigned by each cost driver, cost driver rates, and the individual cost driver usage by product and customer were calculated and reported (see Exhibit 5-5 for a sample of cost driver rates). These rates can be used as benchmarks to compare costs for similar processes in other units or companies and as targets for continuous improvement.

Exhibit 5-5
COST DRIVERS

Cost per engineering change notice:

■ New product	$37.00
■ Internal modification	96.00
■ Customer change	276.00

Average cost per material handling move $5.60

Cost per work order:

■ Assemblies	11.00
■ Indicators	8.50
■ Filters	87.00

Cost per production order scheduled   42.00

Cost per shipment   16.00

Among the more interesting findings were:

1. *The cost variations in engineering change notices.* The team determined that product development activities were driven by three unique sources: the market, internal ideas, and customer requests. Separate activities were defined to accumulate expenses associated with each of the three sources. The results demonstrated that changes triggered by customer demands were quite costly.

The company recognized that its unique market strength came from providing extensive customer support, but management now understood the need to review the costs and benefits of meeting customer change requests in the future. Furthermore, having identified the cost that is associated with this important service, management intended to focus on process improvement opportunities to reduce the $276 average cost, for example, by improving the engineering process or the way in which changes were communicated to or from the customer.

2. *The cost per materials-handling move.* Materials-handling costs averaged $5.60 per move per product. This activity led to large variations in the unit costs of products, depending on their batch sizes. High-volume products, moved in large batch sizes, used as little as $.79 of materials-handling resources per unit per move. Low-volume and heavier products, such as housings, which moved in smaller batches, used more than $25 of materials-handling resources per unit per move.

Management intended to use these statistics to highlight the products and processes that had the highest materials movement costs. The analysis might affect production scheduling plans to allow for the tradeoff between small batches that increase materials movement costs and large batches that increase inventory carrying costs.

3. *The economics of minimum order size.* By seeing the cost of batch-triggered activities, such as scheduling ($42), shipping ($16), and creating work orders, the company has begun to evaluate whether to increase the minimum order size it would accept.

Hierarchy of Activities

The cost structure for manufacturing expenses (excluding material cost) had only a small percentage of costs driven by unit volume (see the hierarchy of activity expenses shown in Exhibit 5-6). The existing (traditional) system assumed that 52% of operating expenses were variable with unit production volume. The ABC model showed that only 23% of expenses related to unit production volumes. The remaining expenses performed batch or production-order activities (21%), supported the large number of product lines (15%), or were facility related (41%, which of course represented the truly fixed portion).[1]

The hierarchy analysis demonstrated that business expenses were less volume sensitive than the traditional system had led management to believe. This fact changed management's views on the profit leverage during both expanding and contracting business cycles. During

**Exhibit 5-6
HIERARCHY**

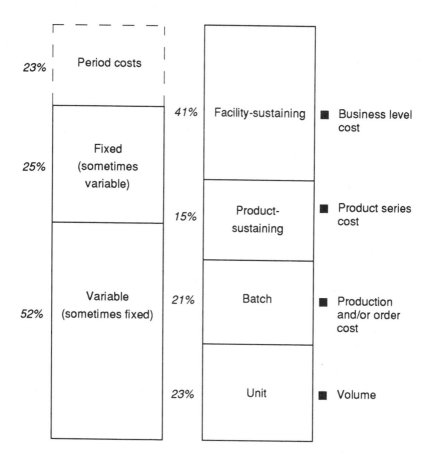

expansion, costs would not rise as greatly as the traditional system had shown. Conversely, during a reduction in volume, costs would not decrease as much as previously believed. To expand on this insight, the company now could see that manufacturing improvement processes aimed at increasing the per unit efficiency of machine time affected only 23% (unit level) of costs, rather than the previously perceived 52%. In contrast, process improvement efforts to reduce the costs of batch and production run activities could affect up to 21% of total expenses. Previously, the benefits from these types of activities were hidden.

Product Profitability and Transfer Pricing

More than 55% of the product value of filters, as shown by traditional methods, decreased more than 20% (see Exhibit 5-7). The housings decrease was not as severe—26% of the housings product value decreased more than 20%. Consistent with the fundamentals of ABC theory, the low-volume, more complex products made up the bulk of the marginal and unprofitable products.

Exhibit 5-7
RIVERSIDE COMPARISON TO TRADITIONAL

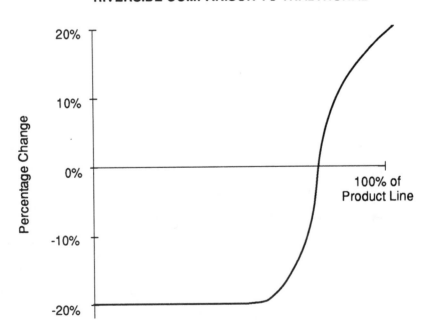

The magnitude of the adjustment surprised even the project's sponsor, Corporate Controller Jay Hansen. He understood that before transfer prices could be reset, based on the new data, a more detailed investigation of the high- and low-volume products from various product lines would be required to gain everyone's confidence.

To illustrate the product cost and profitability analysis performed by the company, a sample of four products is given below:

Product ID	Volume	*Trad.* Cost	*Transfer* Price	*Sales* Price	*ABC* Cost
Filters					
CP22i	2850	$106	$128	$260	$ 78
CP22x	94	$109	$131	$267	$125
Housings					
H40	4	$245	$270	$370	$358
H44	165	$245	$270	$361	$219

The above table shows the volume and the traditional cost based on existing labor and material overhead rates, the transfer price from Manufacturing to Sales & Marketing (cost plus profit), the sales price in the marketplace, and the new ABC cost at the manufacturing site only. The traditional cost can be compared directly with the ABC cost.

The filters selected were very similar except that filter CP22x required a very unique, less popular O-ring. Production scheduling had decided that if several small orders were received for CP22x, it would run a larger batch and store the extra units in inventory pending the next order. This procedure was based on the production manager's intuition that it was cheaper on a per unit basis to spread setup costs over large batches than over small batches.

Housings usually were produced and ordered in much lower volumes than filters and usually were not stocked. Housings frequently were made to customer specifications. Although housings were not Farrall's key differentiating and value-added product, they required a capital and labor-intensive production process.

Influence of Activities on Product Costs

Exhibits 5-8 and 5-9 show the bill of activities for the two filters and two housings that led to the revised product costs.

Exhibit 5-8
PRODUCT COMPARISON — FILTERS

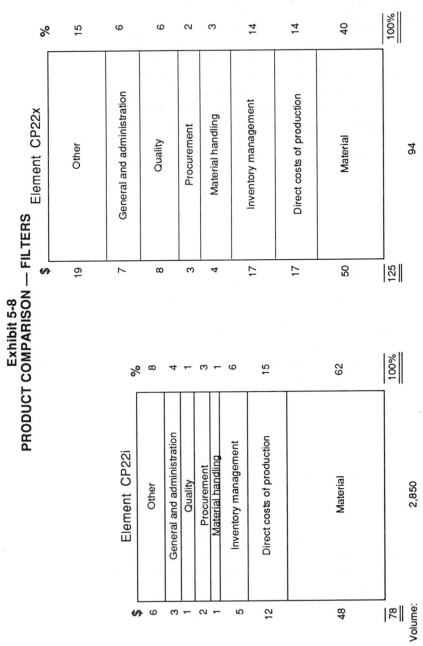

Element CP22x

$		%
19	Other	15
7	General and administration	6
8	Quality	6
3	Procurement	2
4	Material handling	3
17	Inventory management	14
17	Direct costs of production	14
50	Material	40
125		100%

94

Element CP22i

$		%
6	Other	8
3	General and administration	4
1	Quality	1
2	Procurement	3
1	Material handling	1
5	Inventory management	6
12	Direct costs of production	15
48	Material	62
78		100%

Volume: 2,850

Exhibit 5-9
PRODUCT COMPARISON — HOUSINGS

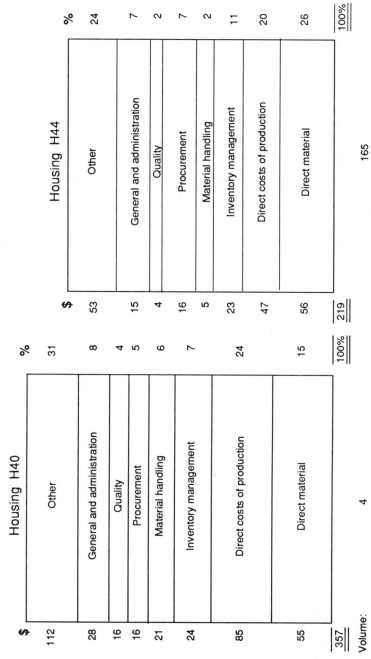

Housing H40

	$	%
Other	112	31
General and administration	28	8
Quality	16	4
Procurement	16	5
Material handling	21	6
Inventory management	24	7
Direct costs of production	85	24
Direct material	55	15
	357	100%

Volume: 4

Housing H44

	$	%
Other	53	24
General and administration	15	7
Quality	4	2
Procurement	16	7
Material handling	5	2
Inventory management	23	11
Direct costs of production	47	20
Direct material	56	26
	219	100%

165

Inventory Management

Inventory management costs consisted largely of the corporate inventory carrying charge. The other costs related to warehousing, cost accounting, and stocking activities. The inventory management costs were charged to the products based on the number of days and value in inventory. Therefore, the filters that were stocked for sale but that were sold infrequently, such as filter CP22x, received a larger part of this cost than did a customized item that was produced to order, such as the H40 housing.

Management now saw the effect of the previous decision to increase batch size on small orders. Batch costs such as materials movement and setup could be low on a per unit basis, but the extra units sat in inventory and accumulated the corporate inventory charge. With this new insight, managers may decide (if determined feasible) to manufacture standard CP22 filters continuously and add special O-rings only as orders for CP22x are received, thereby reducing or eliminating the number of CP22x units held in inventory.

Previously the corporate inventory charge was included in the transfer price calculation but was not distinct at the individual product level. The ABC analysis made this charge visible at that level. Plant managers now could see which products and subassemblies actually were driving the corporate inventory charge and could modify their production and product mix decisions accordingly.

Materials Handling

Materials-handling costs also differed greatly among the filters and housings. The low-volume housing had the highest cost, at $21 per unit. The housings required processing through various machine centers and an assembly area. Housings were also significantly heavier than filters. Using the number of steps involved in the production process, adjusted by the weight of the product or assembly, housings naturally received a greater share of the materials-handling costs.

Management realized that housings were not its differentiating product and that materials handling did not add value to the product. It had started, therefore, to create a program of continuous improvement to reduce the materials-handling costs of housings. If housings could be made cheaper, perhaps a greater share of the market could be gained, which naturally would improve the market for Farrall's filters, both new and replacement.

Procurement

On a per unit basis, the costs of procurement were only slightly different for low- and high-volume filters ($2.39 to $2.66 before rounding effect on the exhibit). The materials purchased for the products were identical except that the CP22x filter required the unique O-ring. Housings, however, had more components and greater freight-in costs due to weight. As expected, housings received a greater share of procurement costs ($16 per unit) than filters. Management now also was reviewing the raw materials procurement process for CP22s to determine if there was an opportunity to use more blanket purchase orders to lower the purchasing cost for this high-volume product.

Quality

Inspection-related costs were charged to products mainly on the number of work orders. Therefore, batch size greatly influenced the calculated per unit cost of quality-related activities. The high-volume filter and housing received quality costs of only $1 and $4 per unit respectively. The low-volume filter and housing, with much smaller batch sizes, were charged $8 and $16 per unit for inspection activities.

In addition, housings required demanding technical specification tests and, therefore, consumed a greater share of quality-related activities. The higher costs for housings again came as a surprise to management. As with materials-handling costs, the analysis of quality costs for housings gave management another opportunity for cost reduction and process improvement efforts.

General & Administrative

G&A activities included financial reporting, general management, human resources development, and other nonproduct or customer-related activities. These costs were considered facility sustaining in nature and were allocated to the products based on volume. General and administrative expenses accounted for under 10% of each product's cost, excluding materials (see Exhibits 5-8 and 5-9).

Influence of Cost Drivers on Product Costs

Product cost differences also were evaluated based on the costs assigned by different cost drivers (see Exhibit 5-10).

Exhibit 5-10
PRODUCT COMPARISON — COST DRIVERS

	Filter		Housing	
	CP22i	CP22x	H40	H44
Inventory value	$4.85	$17.50	$24.00	$24.00
Machine hours	0.00	0.00	27.00	27.00
Inspection	1.30	8.00	17.00	4.00
Shipment	1.50	2.50	17.00	7.00
Material move	0.79	5.09	25.00	5.75

- *Inventory management.* Carrying the low-volume filter in inventory significantly increased the average inventory cost, from the $4.85 for a standard filter to $17.50.
- *Machine hours.* Housings received a $27 machine-hour charge, whereas filters, which were hand assembled, did not receive any machine-based costs. The $27 cost to housings was lower than the $35 cost of conversion charged by the existing system. Management felt that the $27 charge more accurately reflected machine usage costs because the traditional system did not reflect the savings from machines that ran unattended. Management was awaiting the comparison of this rate with the sister plant's rate in Southampton. Ultimately, the more accurate machine-hour charges were expected to be used in capital investment decisions.
- *Inspection.* Cost driver costs varied greatly with respect to inspection. Each inspection cost only $1.30 on high-volume filters, compared to $17 for each inspection on low-volume housings. Using these rates as benchmarks, management expected to develop process improvements to decrease both the number and the costs of inspections performed for housing specifications.
- *Shipment.* The per shipment costs of filters were significantly less than for housings, mainly because replacement filters were shipped in high volumes.

Customer/Distributor Profitability

The customer profitability analysis revealed that the most profitable 30% of the customers contributed approximately 250% of the profits (see

Exhibit 5-11). In fact, the top 10% of customers contributed about 233% of the profits. Many customers were breakeven, and the least profitable 20% incurred losses that accumulated to 150% of total profits.

Two customers from diverse markets were chosen for detailed review (see Exhibit 5-12) to illustrate the causes for these wide disparities in customer profitability. Cunningham Distributors (CD) was the largest distributor in the company's Appliance market. CD had been doing business with Farrall for 14 years, and it received significant quantity discounts.

Accent Spas (AS) was a new distributor in the Leisure division. AS purchased mainly spa and pool filters in low volume and did not qualify for quantity discounts. As a new customer, AS required special attention and training during the year. The ABC analysis clearly revealed the extra activities demanded by new customers such as Accent Spas, for example, in corporate receivables, selling activities, and management and advertising costs.

Exhibit 5-11
CUSTOMER PROFITABILITY

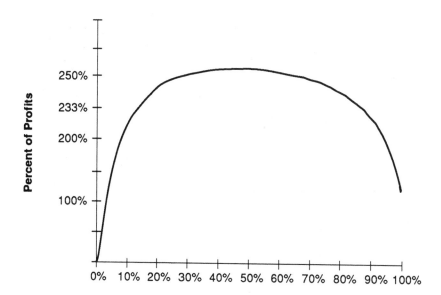

Percent of Customer Base

Corporate Receivables

AS consumed a much greater portion of the corporate receivable charge ($3.89 per unit purchased vs. $0.19 for CD). This charge was allocated to customers based on dollar days of receivables outstanding. Farrall's credit policy automatically gave extended credit terms for qualifying new customers. AS's receivables were outstanding longer and therefore received a higher working capital charge.

Selling Activities

AS also used a greater per unit share of Farrall's sales representatives' assistance. Sales reps visited customers to establish relationships,

Exhibit 5-12
CUSTOMER COMPARISON

Market	Appliance		Leisure	
Customer	CD		AS	
Volume	40,510 Units		3,007 units	
	Dollars	Per unit (avg)	Dollars	Per unit (avg)
Sales	$2,830,031	$69.86	$134,275	$44.65
Cost of goods sold				
Material	$493,844	$12.19	$22,771	$7.57
Facility	417,505	10.31	14,187	4.72
Product	143,085	3.53	4,915	1.63
Batch	224,404	5.54	6,729	2.24
Unit	218,438	5.39	10,643	3.54
	$1,497,276	$36.39	$59,245	$19.70
Gross Profit	1,332,755	32.90	75,030	24.95
Advertising	$55,982	$1.38	$6,089	$2.02
Corp. receivable chrg.	7,777	0.19	11,709	3.89
Customer service	21,134	0.52	2,030	0.68
Distribution mgmt.	1,396	0.03	11,080	3.68
Selling activities	376,364	9.29	34,033	11.32
Marketing acitviites	40,352	1.00	11,556	3.85
Other	155,654	3.84	1,561	0.52
	$658,659	$16.26	$78,058	$25.96
Net Profit	$674,096	$16.64	$(3,028)	$(1.01)

train their personnel, and identify new business opportunities. Expense reports were used to assign the expenses of these activities to customers. A new customer such as AS attracted a disportionately high portion of these costs.

Fred Schmidt, senior vice president of sales, understood the results but did not agree with the implications:

> I don't agree with using expense reports as a basis for charging customers for this service. The service is available to customers. New customers and small-volume customers just tend to use it more. However, I don't think that we should penalize them just because they need more hand-holding than other customers.

Managers generally agreed, however, that the ABC model helped them to understand better the economics of their new customer activities and how much it costs to change a distributor.

Distributor Management and Advertising Costs

Activity costs assigned at the division level were allocated, often equally or based on volume, to the individual distributors within the division. Thus, division management costs could be fairly similar for each division but could be higher for a distributor in a division with only a few other distributors versus one in a division with many distributors. Clearly, on a per unit sold basis, AS was charged with greater distributor management costs than CD.

Advertising costs also were measured at the division level and spread to individual distributors based on sales volume. More dollars were incurred in the after-market division on a per unit basis than in the more mature market of industrial customers.

Management Acceptance of the ABC Study

Senior management had many different perspectives on the ABC study. The new worldwide vice president of operations saw a presentation in England and wanted ABC applied to all manufacturing sites. Sales & Marketing management had yet to respond, either positively or negatively, to the project.

Several planned presentations and workshops, both in the United States and England, helped to spread information about the ABC pilots throughout the Farrall organization. The subject was presented at the annual international controller's meeting in April 1991. Workshops were held for selected management to discuss results and key design decisions. Reaction was mixed among various segments of the organization.

Sales & Marketing

The project had been driven from the finance side of the organization, beginning with the corporate controller. The Sales & Marketing division, especially in the United States, showed little interest and offered little support throughout most of the project. No one from Sales & Marketing attended the Riverside conceptual design session. As the output from the study was shared at various stages, Sales & Marketing management began to see ways the data could affect or even benefit them. But gaining understanding and acceptance was a slow process.

At one interim meeting, dummy customer cost drivers were used to display the types of information that Sales & Marketing could receive. This presentation sparked enough interest to make Sales & Marketing management decide to help the team find realistic customer cost drivers.

Sales & Marketing management was most enthusiastic about the greater detail now provided in product cost calculations. They felt that the ABC bill-of-activities and cost-driver information provided greatly improved insights into the sources of product cost calculations and was much superior to the highly aggregated transfer price figures they had received from the existing cost system. One sales manager stated, "I can explain these figures to my customers now. Before, I couldn't support the reported costs of my products."

In contrast, the Southampton site had maintained a stronger link with its Sales & Marketing group throughout the project. From the beginning, representatives of Sales & Marketing took an active role in the process. John Benton, Sales & Marketing controller in Southampton, expected to use the ABC data to influence customer management and discount policies. "It can be used right away to support our day-to-day discount decisions," he said.

New Riverside Business Manager

In discussion of ABC as a management tool, Tom Flynn reflected, "We must try to design products that will not require so much support. We have different discount structures that bear no resemblance to support. We must understand where and why we are profitable; gut feel may not be correct." However, Flynn felt differently about using ABC for transfer pricing:

> We are not ready to switch off current transfer pricing calculations into ABC. Transfer price is acceptable today because it's consistent. There is a structured formula for everyone. Part of the problem is that Sales & Marketing want better information to pressure Manufacturing into reducing costs. They don't see ABC as helping them understand how customer decisions drive manufacturing as well as selling and marketing costs.

Flynn conceded that as of July 1991, no decisions on pricing, customer mix, or manufacturing process technology had yet been made. He wished to see the next generation of the model before acting but recognized the long-run potential impact from ABC information:

> The company faces a lot of strategic choices over the next three years. We need to be able to assess alternative scenarios: closing plants, combining plants, focusing plants, changing distribution channels. Management needs better information to do the what-if analysis. ABC, with its better segmentation of cost data, will likely be helpful for this analysis.

Riverside Manufacturing Manager

The Riverside manufacturing manager, Glen Donahue, said, "I saw a tape on ABC concepts and was sold right away. Now I know where the costs are. They are not hidden (in the variances) any more." Donahue felt strongly that the tie to quality was ABC's greatest asset:

> Everything we do with the quality program requires communication. ABC supports communication. It helps us identify the cost of nonconformance and where there are redundancies. Quality is the mainstay to manufacturers due to the Japanese competition. We can use ABC to support our quality programs.

Corporate Controller and ABC sponsor Hansen did not share Donahue's enthusiasm for ABC's link to TQM. He explained why:

> I do not believe that ABC should be sold as a system to measure the cost of quality. It's a side benefit. There are so many nonfinancial measures of the cost of quality that ABC cannot address. You can only get a partial sense of it.

Currently, Donahue's cost reduction and improvement programs already included the use of ABC data. He said:

> I'm using the data in a variety of ways. To begin with, we are creating a new distribution center to attack the high costs of materials movement. When I saw the dollars spent in maintaining the routings, I found out that the bulk of the industrial engineer's time is just key punching. For less money, someone else is key punching and my industrial engineer is now focused on more important areas where we need help.

Donahue also indicated that he felt the information provided a better basis for discussing the departmental budgets for the upcoming year. He was reassigning people based on their abilities to perform key tasks that had been revealed in the activity analysis.

When asked of his involvement with the implementation process, Donahue responded:

> In retrospect, I wish that my people had been more involved in the process. Our exposure was limited. I wasn't sure what ABC was about. Next time, I'd dedicate at least one of my people to the project.

Bob Spears, Project Leader

Bob Spears spoke about lessons learned about the implementation process. Looking back he could identify the key ingredients to success:

- Make sure management is committed.
- Make sure department heads know that their people will be interviewed and will need to spend some time with the implementation team.
- Get substantial data processing support.
- Dedicate the project leader 100% to the project, no less.
- Don't hard code the model; create it in a flexible database.
- Make an action plan to get things done.
- Hire consultants to wrestle with the concepts and create or uphold executive buy-in.
- Communicate constantly. We didn't have enough meetings; we met monthly—it should have been weekly.

Spears felt that the information helped to create awareness of what drove the need for people's activities. He described the situation.

We had to overcome the fear that ABC was to be used to criticize people's performance. We're trying to take the emotion out of performance and measurement.

We can now talk about a nonvalue-added activity, not an individual's performance. We're more focused on process improvements rather than measuring an individual's actions.

Key Corporate Sponsor Jay Hansen

Jay Hansen spoke about the length of the project:

The project teams on both sides of the Atlantic watched their initial April 1991 deadline fly by. The teams were struggling to get data with the limited resources they had. Quite often, just getting key people's attention was difficult. We initially targeted our deadline for the April 1991 international controller's meeting. But as both projects were taking longer, I thought it best to take our time to get to the right numbers than try to pull something together in a rush. But we did go ahead and present what we had to date on the ABC project at the international controller's meeting. It sparked a lot of interest. People became interested in seeing more of what was finally done.

I think it's important to get to the right numbers quickly, but I think it's equally important to keep people aware of what's going on during the process.

Dick Wilcox, VP of Worldwide Operations

Dick Wilcox was the new vice president of worldwide operations. He stated, "ABC will be vital for helping us understand our business better. However, we must standardize our methods before extending the method throughout the company. For example, we can't have two sites treating direct labor differently."[2]

The Future of ABC at Farrall

Based on the pilot results, corporate management had decided to continue implementing the ABC concepts at their manufacturing and sales facilities worldwide. Two new plants and sales organizations, with more diverse product lines than the Riverside and Southampton plants, had been identified for the next ABC implementation. The chosen plants did not include plants that produce products purchased by federal agencies, because these divisions first needed to confront how to navigate through government cost regulations. The plants were similar to Riverside because they had unexplained low profitability. ABC was starting to be viewed as part of the turnaround strategy for underperforming divisions.

The Riverside and Southampton teams were updating their models so as to use the fiscal year 1991 actuals and the fiscal year 1992 budgeted data. In early January 1992, the Southampton and Riverside project teams were scheduled to meet at corporate headquarters to evaluate and discuss their findings. Certain product and customer costs and cost driver comparisons would be made there. The different ABC architecture decisions, such as the direct labor decision, also would be reviewed then.

Where does the ABC sponsor Hansen see the future of ABC?

Eventually I'd like to select the appropriate ABC information and then move to a standard set of management reports to run our business. The question is knowledge. ABC provides more information to our manufacturing and marketing managers than they ever had before. With better information, we have better knowledge and can make better decisions.

Epilogue

On January 16, 1992, the Riverside and Southampton ABC teams met in New York City to compare the structure and information from the models developed at the two locations. Present were: ABC team leaders, corporate representation (Jay Hansen and Carl Winecki), and controllers from two divisions where the next ABC implementation would occur.

The objectives of the meeting were to:

- Identify and evaluate different design decisions made by the two teams;
- Assess ABC's ability to address its original objectives of investment justification, profitability, and transfer pricing;
- Determine the next steps.

Design Decisions

Although each model used slightly different cost drivers and business processes, three distinct differences in model design were identified and discussed: the treatment of direct labor, freight costs, and corporate charge.

Direct Labor

Direct labor had been treated differently by the two teams. As described, Southampton had chosen to apply direct labor to products in the same manner as with their traditional system. This treatment required them to load the direct labor routing files into the ABC model to calculate direct labor per product. Riverside treated direct labor similarly to indirect labor. Activities (run time and setup) and cost drivers (direct labor and number of setups) were identified.

The teams had yet to compare the differences caused by the two methods of calculating individual product costs. People anticipated, however, that the Riverside model direct labor costs would be less volume sensitive, because part of these costs were applied to products based on the number of setups rather than on the basis of a pure volume driver (direct labor hours).

The participants decided that the traditional direct assignment of labor costs would be more familiar to most people. Riverside agreed to run its model again using recently updated labor and routing files. Southampton, however, recalling the extra effort required for data processing to load the labor and routing files into the ABC model, agreed to assess the amount of effort it took to load the direct labor files. A final decision as to how to treat direct labor on an on-going basis would be made after these two tasks had been completed.

Freight Costs

Southampton records freight as part of materials costs, while Riverside treats freight as a component of overhead. Riverside assigned freight costs to products using cost drivers. While total product costs for the same product will be the same under the two methods, Southampton will have higher materials costs and Riverside will have higher procurement costs. The different classification arises from differences in the way freight costs are recorded and processed at the two plants. No decision was made as to which method would be preferred.

Corporate Charge

Riverside analyzed the components of the corporate charge (accounts receivable, inventory, and fixed assets) and drove them to products and customers using an appropriate cost driver (e.g., number of days outstanding for accounts receivable). Southampton drove much of its corporate charge based on sales (or turnover). Participants expressed a preference for Riverside's approach, which appeared to be more accurate.

ABC's Ability to Address Original Objectives

The original objectives were investment justification, profitability, and transfer pricing.

Investment Justification

The teams recommended not using ABC for investment justification decisions. Andy Smith, Southampton project leader, felt that their current MAPICS package provided adequate information to support investment decisions:

> With MAPICS and our financial information systems we can look at investment decisions at a top level, such as the discounted net present value from purchasing one machine. But we can't look at the impact that investment has on the whole product base. Maybe that's where an ABC what-if analysis adds value.

Carl Winecki disagreed:

> MAPICS only handles savings from reductions in direct labor costs but not indirect costs. What about the costs of repair and maintenance or setup of machines? How will these indirect costs be included in an investment decision using MAPICS? We have to learn to map our activities to materials handling and other activities. Just as the Japanese create their target costing—we need a clear method of understanding every component of cost, especially our indirect costs.

The Riverside team also did not feel as comfortable with using only MAPICS for investment decisions but admitted that they had less experience with MAPICS than Southampton had.

Profitability

The teams concluded that the accuracy of ABC product costs depends on the validity of the cost driver. Riverside had sharper divergence between its ABC and traditional costs than Southampton. Further investigation determined that almost 70% of Southampton cost drivers were volume based, while only 40% of Riverside's were unit-level drivers. Agreeing that 70% appeared high, the teams decided to evaluate Southampton cost drivers in more detail at a subsequent meeting. The teams concluded, however, that product comparisons could be performed more easily if design differences relating to corporate charge, freight costs, and direct labor were eliminated.

Transfer Pricing

The team recommended, "If we accept that a refined ABC gives more accurate cost, then we could use ABC for an annual update of transfer prices." This hedged recommendation, however, revealed the disagreement about whether ABC actually calculated more accurate costs. Southampton, with its many volume drivers, did not see vast differences in its product costs. Participants felt that before ABC could be used for transfer pricing calculations, ABC product costs needed to be scrutinized for accuracy. Jay Hansen was concerned about this cautious recommendation. He said, "Transfer pricing is essential to our management process. If we don't use ABC for transfer pricing, do we want to go forward with ABC at all?" The meeting ended with mixed and unresolved opinions on this subject.

The Next Steps

It was quickly agreed that a critical next step was to compare the model structures in greater detail and recommend an "ideal ABC model" for future sites. This task would be accomplished by creating activity, business process, and cost driver dictionaries for each site. With a complete description of these components, the two teams could determine the right combination of activities, business processes, and cost drivers. This recommended "ideal ABC model" would be presented to management within four weeks. The "ideal model" would enable other divisions to implement ABC with a more standardized approach, and management would find it easier to compare results across sites.

At the end of the meeting, participants reflected on the future for ABC at Farrall. John Benton, Southampton Sales & Marketing controller, commented on customer profitability. "We don't have an alternative system at the moment. We calculate divisional and distributor profitability right now, but we allocate expenses based on turnover [sales]. ABC is a much better alternative." Benton also commented on the option of using ABC only for customer profitability. "A problem arises if we continue to use traditional transfer prices. A customer could be unprofitable not because of his buying behavior but because of the products he purchased. We would not know for sure [about customer profitability] unless we use ABC for product costing also."

John McCarthy, Riverside project leader, firmly believed ABC gave the managers at Riverside better information even without changing transfer prices. He stated, "ABC is an excellent tool for managers. You can see how activities impact the profitability of our lines. I would like to reduce the number of drivers in the next pass to make it easier, but as a management decision tool, ABC is excellent."

The group discussed how often the data needed to be updated. After considering many options, most concurred with the views expressed by Bob Spears. "It depends on the decisions we need to make. Probably to understand customer buying patterns, quarterly customer profitability reports would be good. However, for transfer pricing and product costing purposes annually should be adequate."

The day concluded with the expectation that the two teams would design the standardized ABC structure that would become the basis for new implementations. Riverside and Southampton would run the models again under the new structure. A full comparison of the models then would be performed, although everyone wanted the other sites to begin concurrent implementation of a customer profitability ABC.

When asked if there was a current opportunity to begin sharing results beyond the finance group, Marc Woodward, Southampton CFO, was cautious. He stated, "You have to be very careful in showing any data you're not completely comfortable with. If it's not precise enough, people can take the results and make them support a particular decision or anything else they want. I think we have to be very accurate before we show these data around."

Notes

[1]The team felt that the 41% of expenses initially assigned to the facility-sustaining category portion was likely too high. The category probably included some product- or process-sustaining activities that should be reassigned in the next iteration of the model.

[2]Recall that Southampton and Riverside had chosen different ways to assign direct labor costs to products. Southampton was using the traditional way with routings and standards, while Riverside had assigned direct labor expenses as if they were overhead, using volume and batch-level drivers to assign the costs to products.

Chapter 6

Williams Brothers Metals

Executive Summary

Williams Brothers Metals (WBM), a family-owned metal fabrication and distribution company, had just completed one of its most financially successful years. However, times had changed for this business, which traditionally had generated healthy profit margins. Margins were growing tighter with weakening demand, and costs were increasing. In reponse, the company embarked on an ABC project to gather cost information that would be used to target business improvement opportunities, to reduce cost, and to rank profitability by product lines. The company also wanted a better understanding of its profitability, by customers, orders, and territories. According to Steve Owens, executive sponsor of the ABC project, "We know intuitively what is a good order or a bad one. We need something more than intuition, we need a system."

ABC was piloted within a region that contained three processing facilities and all corporate support functions. The ABC team, led by the finance organization, concentrated on providing product profitability and cost of activities information.

The ABC architecture became very complex, and the project effort was extended months beyond the original deadline due to factors such as:

- Transfers and transshipment between locations and their effect on location profitability;
- The need to allocate corporate support functions to the processing locations (which had never been done before);
- Refinement of data in order to build credibility for the results.

When the results ultimately were presented to owners/managers, the data were perceived as flawed by some due to the use of inaccurate cost drivers. Some questioned the validity of the data when they saw products for which they were responsible contributing negatively to the business. Others felt their expectations were not met and that the project was completed much later than expected. Overall, however, the executive management team felt that ABC was worth further investment of effort.

As Jim Curry, VP finance and ABC project director, stated, "Profitability by product is less meaningful to our business. It should only be a by-product of a study like this. It should not be our main objective. Activity analysis is our true benefit." As such, Curry refers to future studies as ABM, "activity-based management."

Company Background

Williams Brothers Metals was founded in 1935 in Long Beach, California, by Albert Williams. Today it remains a privately owned company run by active owner/managers who are the family members of its founder. Over the years, WBM has expanded to seven locations in the Midwest and western portions of the United States, the geographical area the firm services. WBM distributes a full range of specialty metal products to a wide variety of industries. Its customers are quite diverse, ranging from small companies to Fortune 500 companies. The majority of sales include value-added processing services, such as leveling, sawing, shearing, and polishing.

To enable the firm to provide timely services to its broad range of customers requires an inventory of approximately 20,000 different stock-keeping units (SKUs). "We are like a bank; we carry inventory and finance receivables," states owner/manager Ronald Williams.

The existing transaction accounting system at WBM captures the costs of organizational units. It is not used to measure or control either processing or location costs. The system's reports focus on product gross margins, departmental costs, and company-wide profitability. Location profitability never existed (see Exhibit 6-1). Transfer prices had been established based on material cost and a fixed charge for freight and processing depending on the number of cuts.

According to Steve Owens:

> I wanted to implement a cost accounting system, and I thought ABC made sense. Rather than calculating costs of various activities on an ad hoc basis, we wanted a system to organize our costs of activities. We wanted to know relative product profitability, whether certain types or sizes of orders were more or less profitable, and whether we could charge a sale with a reasonable cost of producing it.

Jim Curry, VP finance, described the situation.

Gross margins was our key financial measure. We looked at volume, price, and product gross margins. But quite often, orders were received for small dollar amounts with many different items on them. Without a system to measure the costs associated with filling these orders, they looked profitable. Our old volume measures encouraged managers to push more sales with less regard to profit contribution.

Over the years, the business environment was changing for WBM, with competitive pressures causing the firm's historically healthy gross margins to shrink. With operating costs increasing, management knew operations had to become more efficient. As owner/manager Lenny

Exhibit 6-1
THE TRADITIONAL VIEW OF COSTS

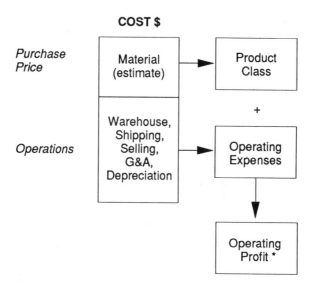

*Before capital costs, rent, returns, and allowances

Gibson stated, "If we don't understand our costs, we could wake up one morning and find ourselves bleeding."

According to Curry, "We were faced with tighter margins, higher competition, and increasing costs. We had to take a significant amount of cost out of our overhead." In response, Curry read articles and attended seminars to find ways to measure and control costs better. In July 1989, at the suggestion of Steve Owens, he attended a Harvard Business School executive seminar that exposed him to ABC theory. During the months that followed, Curry had a series of meetings with his management to broaden their awareness of ABC. "The theory had gone far (in the manufacturing industry), but we struggled to see its applicability to our distribution business."

In July 1990, Curry invited consultants experienced with ABC implementations to discuss possible pilot opportunities at WBM. "We had struggled, unsuccessfully, to build our own model, but we didn't have the staff or the resources. Meanwhile, there was software already built and experience already gained in the marketplace. We needed outside help to get started," states Curry. WBM embarked on an ABC project with the guidance of a consulting firm in November 1990. Management expected the project to be completed in February 1991.

Preparing the Organization

There were three executive VPs, all owner/managers. Steve Owens was responsible for operations, distribution, finance, and certain product lines. Lenny Gibson was responsible for the external sales group, branch operations, and certain product lines. Ronald Williams was responsible for the internal sales group and certain product lines.

The Southwest (SW) Region was selected as the pilot site for ABC. The region includes two Long Beach plants within five miles of each other—one on Cherry Avenue (CA) and another on 19th Street (19th). A third plant was located in Arizona (AZ). Each facility maintains its own inventory and performs related processing for specified product lines. The sales force primarily serves customers within its geographic territory and takes orders across the product lines offered by WBM.

Most corporate support functions are performed centrally for all regions, including the SW Region. These functions include product management, finance, management information systems (MIS), inside and outside sales, and human resources. Product management is responsible for setting prices, managing inventory, and purchasing material. Corporate support offices are located in the SW Region.

Getting Started

A project leader, Mary O'Connor, was relieved of her daily responsibilities within the finance department and dedicated to the ABC project on a full-time basis. "I had never even heard of ABC until Jim Curry told me I would be working on this project. I read some articles to prepare myself, but I had no idea what it was really all about until it was almost over."

The project began with a two-day conceptual design session taught by the outside consultants and attended by WBM's project team. No other members of management, aside from Curry, attended this session. The design session identified many issues facing WBM's business. These issues included:

- *The complexity of interbranch transactions.* What is the cost of transfers and transshipment? What is the cost of delivery to a customer when multiple branches are involved?
- *Customer satisfaction.* How can we measure the cost of on-time, accurate deliveries? What is the cost of our specialized packaging? What is the cost of entering and processing orders?
- *Cost reduction opportunities.* Where and how can we reduce costs and still remain competitive?
- *Product profitability.* Which are our more profitable product lines? How can we determine the profitability of an order?

These issues were developed by the project team. However, management recognized that ABC would not provide all the answers to these issues. Rather, they viewed ABC as an information base to help them begin identifying solutions to the problems surrounding cost reduction, strategic market refocusing, and sales order profitability.

The implementation project required approximately two people devoted full-time, 30% of Curry's time, and MIS personnel on an "as-needed" basis. Consultants were used to support and participate in the model design (from one to many), which in the end was significantly different from the initial design.

The key objectives of the ABC system as determined by the project team were:

- Determine product profitability within the SW Region.
- Perform a "proof of concept" that ABC will provide information relevant to WBM's distribution business.

System Design

The project team followed the major steps of implementing ABC (preparation and training, activity analysis, cost driver analysis, and analysis of results). However, due to the uniqueness of their distribution business, key design decisions required careful consideration to ensure that the ABC model reflected the economics of the distribution business. These key design decisions included common costs, profit centers, transfers of cost, business processes, product classes, cost drivers, and financial data.

Common Costs

As described earlier, the SW Region comprises three physical facilities and a corporate headquarters function. The first decision the team faced was how many sites to use to capture cost in order to compute product profitability by site. (A "site" cost structure included direct costs associated with processing and delivering products to customers, plus an assignment of common or headquarter costs that reflected activities performed for each site.)

After much discussion, the team decided on five sites (see Exhibit 6-2). One site was designated the "common site" and contained the common costs for shared services. Three sites were created representing each of the SW processing facilities and warehouses (CA, 19th, and AZ). A fifth

Exhibit 6-2
TEAM-IDENTIFIED SEPARATE SITES

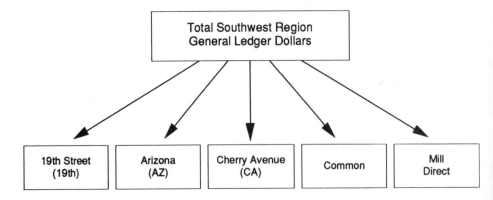

site, "mill direct," was created to capture the costs of servicing customer orders that do not draw inventory or use processing capabilities of company locations but are shipped directly from the mills to a customer.

The next task was to assign costs to each of the five sites using data from the general ledger of the SW Region. Many costs, for example, plant manager salary, were assigned directly to the three warehouse sites—CA, 19th, and AZ. Corporate costs for support activities were assigned directly to the common site.

Support costs charged directly to the common site had to be assigned to the four other sites (see Exhibit 6-3). Common site costs were distributed to the other sites by identifying the activities performed at the common site and their appropriate cost drivers. For example, the costs of the selling activity at the common site were assigned to the other sites based on the number of sales orders processed for each site.

Ultimately, each site contained total activity costs consisting of direct costs of its own activities plus assigned costs from the common site on an activity basis.

Profit Centers

In order to report profitability by site, certain costs and revenues had to be recast to reflect the multitude of intersite transactions. In the existing financial systems, sales are credited to one of two different

Exhibit 6-3
COMMON COSTS

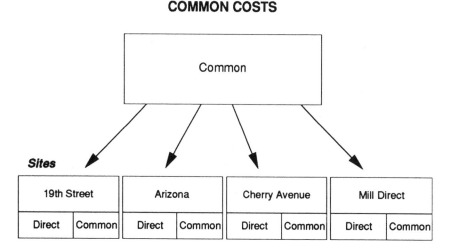

branches, depending on the customer who is associated with a specific branch. However, often the last warehouse is only an intermediary handling or staging point before delivery to the customer.

Most of the processing costs were incurred at the warehouse that stocked and processed inventory prior to sale. Consequently, profit centers were established for ABC reporting purposes and were referred to as the "stocking site." Revenues for orders and costs related to fulfilling the order had to be recast by the project team and be transferred to these stocking sites or profit centers.

Transfers of Cost

There are two types of cost transfers—transfers and transshipments. Transfers are physical movements of material without a customer order. Material is received by one warehouse, unloaded, processed, reloaded, and then moved to another warehouse for additional processing or to be stored in inventory. The final warehouse becomes the stocking point to the customer when a sale is made and the goods are pulled from that warehouse's inventory. For transfers, the costs to unload, process, and load at each warehouse prior to the customer sale had to be transferred to the stocking site (see Exhibit 6-4).

Transshipments are intermediate handling points, or staging points, prior to delivery to a customer. For transshipments, the costs of unloading and loading at each warehouse had to be transferred back to the stocking site where the sales revenue was credited (see Exhibit 6-5).

Transferring the cost of transfers and transshipment to the stocking site makes it possible to report profit center profitability as well as order profitability, due to the information gained about the overall cost of material movement and the number of times material is moved before it reaches the customer (see Exhibit 6-6).

Business Processes

To gain an improved understanding of its business processes and to facilitate management reporting, WBM organized activities into manageable and logical groupings that provided a functional rather than organizational perspective. Five groupings were identified as follows:

- *Customer management:* activities related to selling, marketing, and maintaining customers. It also included an imputed carrying cost of accounts receivable charged to each site.

Exhibit 6-4
COST OF TRANSFER

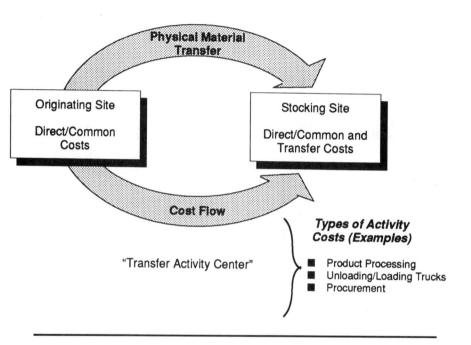

"Transfer Activity Center"

Types of Activity Costs (Examples)

- Product Processing
- Unloading/Loading Trucks
- Procurement

Exhibit 6-5
TRANSSHIPMENT ACTIVITY CENTER

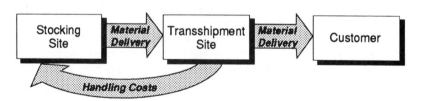

"Transshipment Activity Center"

Types of Activity Costs

- Unloading
- Loading

Exhibit 6-6
ABC VIEW

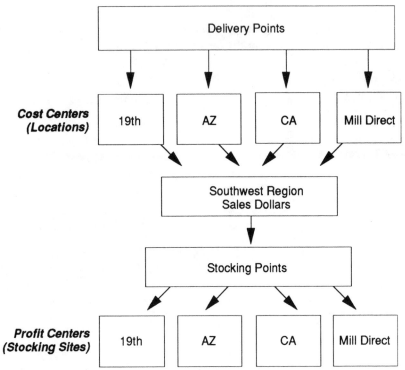

- *Product processing*: activities related to processing material including leveling, shearing, and polishing.
- *Distribution management*: activities related to loading, packing, and outbound material handling.
- *Inventory management*: activities related to unloading trucks, scheduling, procurement, transfers, and transshipment. Inventory carrying charges were imputed and charged to the products.
- *Support*: activities related to personnel management, finance, MIS, and general administration.

Product Classes

"Product" in WBM's business is a specified grade, shape, thickness, length, and width of metal, which could represent more than 20,000 distinct SKUs. When asked, the product managers requested cost information about major categories of products (i.e., product classes) for pricing purposes. There were currently 23 product classes. They felt that assigning costs any lower to include a multitude of lengths and widths would be less relevant for pricing. Most pricing and product decision making are determined at the product-class level.

Cost Drivers

Costs had to be assigned to the 23 product classes in a manner that reflected their consumption of activities. The ABC team's selection criteria for the cost drivers included the following: Is the driver indicative of how we operate the business? Is the information accessible? Is the driver acceptable to the organization?

Some of the more notable cost drivers were:

- *Delivery cost driver:* stops, weight, and distance. Delivery costs varied by the number of stops, the weight of the material, and the distance traveled. On a per unit basis, this driver allocated a greater proportion of the delivery costs to orders that went to the farthest destination zones. This driver was intended to assign costs without penalizing large-volume orders.
- *Loading cost driver:* number of items, weight, and handling difficulty. Loading varied by number of items in each order, weight, and handling difficulty. In this respect, orders with more line items received a greater share of the loading costs.
- *Sales & Marketing cost driver:* number of inquiries, number of orders, and size of orders. The activity analysis brought to light the varying levels of difficulty in filling an order. Therefore, individual line items per order were used to reflect the assumption that larger orders required greater effort.

As the team selected cost drivers, it was assumed that much of the operating data were not captured in the current systems and that special efforts to capture the data would be needed in the future. However, to the surprise of the project team, cost driver data and other information, such as transfers and transshipments, were accessible. "For example," Curry noted, "we had no idea that the original site was maintained on a transshipment record. The MIS group provided valuable assistance in extracting data from the existing systems. We were able to utilize existing data in new and relevant ways."

Project leader Mary O'Connor recalls, "When we started, we didn't know what was available in the systems. Designing cost drivers was a big deal. You really need to have good systems in place before you start an ABC project."

Financial Data

The general ledger was the primary source of the cost information with certain imputed costs (e.g., cost of capital) added to represent the total cost of operations. Specific considerations included the following:

- Financial costs of the prior year were used. Operating data for cost drivers primarily used the same period.
- A capital cost was imputed for inventory and accounts receivable investments at 9% per year.
- All sales were net of sales returns and allowances.
- Executive salaries and related costs were excluded.
- All company-owned properties were restated to a rental basis.

The resulting architecture (see Exhibit 6-7) drove costs to activities and then to product classes within each profit center site. The final model for WBM had approximately 250 activities, 35 activity centers, and 20 activity cost drivers.

Implementation Process

Throughout the months of implementation, Curry attempted to prepare the organization for the ABC results. ABC concepts were presented periodically in various general management meetings. Supervisors and managers were asked to comment and review the data on their departments. An open door policy was established in the finance area so anyone curious about the project could learn more.

The project was driven mostly by Curry's financial group. "However, Operations people helped us," recalls Curry. "They performed special analyses to collect cost driver data. For example, the packaging cost driver was developed by them based on a special study to determine the relative complexity in packaging different products."

The project completion date extended from February 1991 to August 1991 because of the complexity of the model design, Curry's desire to have credible information for management prior to presenting preliminary results, and summer vacation schedules. "The original

Exhibit 6-7
ABC VIEW OF COST

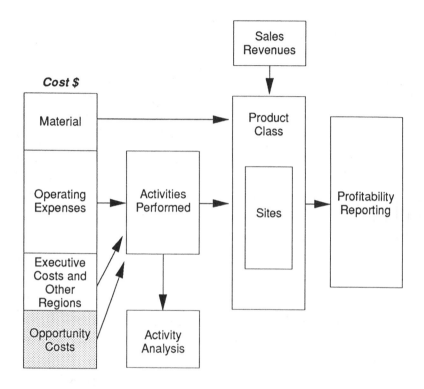

design [of one site] was too simplistic. But designing five sites also raised many questions. We went down a very complex path," recalls Curry.

Findings and Results

Results were presented about four key areas: (1) product class and location profitability, (2) activity and business process analysis, (3) value analysis, and (4) hierarchy.

Product Class and Location Profitability

The project team developed profitability reports for each product class, in total and by location (see Exhibit 6-8). Curry commented:

Exhibit 6-8
ABC PRODUCT PROFITABILITY REPORTS

STOCKING SITE PROFITABILITY – ILLUSTRATIVE DATA
ALL PRODUCTS
FOR THE 12 MONTHS ENDED DECEMBER 31, 19XX

	CA $	% Sales	19th $	% Sales	AZ $	% Sales	Mill Direct $	% Sales	Total $	% Sales
Product Volume	62,000		78,000		53,000		25,000			
Gross Sales	$515,000	100%	$650,000	100%	$440,000	100%	$210,000	100%	$1,815,000	100%
Material Cost	453,200	88%	455,000	70%	334,400	76%	178,500	85%	1,421,100	79%
Gross Margin	$61,800	12%	$195,000	30%	$105,600	24%	$31,500	15%	$393,900	21%
Processing Costs	5,150	1%	19,500	2%	8,800	2%	0	0	33,450	2%
Product Margin	$56,650	11%	$175,500	27%	$96,800	22%	$31,500	15%	$360,450	19%
Business Process:										
Inventory Management	$15,400	3%	$39,000	6%	$17,600	4%	$4,200	2%	$76,250	4%
Distribution Management	15,500	3%	58,500	9%	30,800	7%	4,000	2%	108,950	6%
Customer Management	10,300	2%	38,000	6%	22,000	5%	6,500	3%	77,600	4%
Support Services	5,150	1%	14,000	2%	8,800	2%	2,100	1%	29,050	2%
Operating Expenses	$46,350	9%	$149,500	23%	$79,200	19%	$16,800	8%	$291,850	15%
Operating Margin	$10,300	2%	$26,000	4%	$17,600	3%	$14,700	7%	$68,600	3%
Contribution	($15,450)	-3%	$0	0%	($4,400)	-2%	$8,400	4%	($11,450)	-1%

Exhibit 6-9
PRODUCT PROFITABILITY RANKED BY SALES $ (ALL SITES)

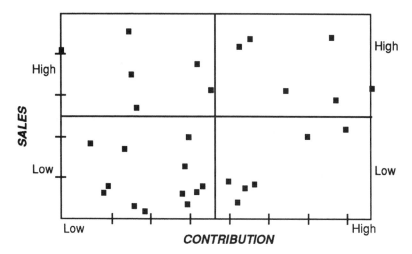

Our most profitable site was mill direct business since shipping directly to customers incurs very little material handling costs, other than freight. The least profitable location was CA. The ABC results have raised the issue of closing CA. We had considered it before but never had the data to evaluate it. ABC has put a lot of issues on the agenda.

In addition, the contribution of each product class on an ABC basis was compared to its sales (see Exhibit 6-9). Surprisingly, most product classes fell into the low sales and low contribution quadrant. This information could be used to assess future decisions relating to inventory levels, number, and processing capability of stocking sites and product mix.

Activity and Business Process Analysis

"The review of activities within business processes provided insight into the potential to improve the organization," states Curry. For example, within the customer administration business process, the credit and collection process was the highest dollar activity (see Exhibit 6-10). It reflected the time and effort expended by executives, salesmen, product managers, and finance to collect outstanding balances.

Exhibit 6-10

ILLUSTRATIVE DATA
CUSTOMER ADMINISTRATION

ACTIVITIES	$	%
Credit and Collection	$300,000	31.9%
Process Order Entry	250,000	26.6%
Customer Service	200,000	21.3%
Support to Sales Force	100,000	10.6%
Support to Branches	50,000	5.3%
Testing *	25,000	2.7%
Other	15,000	1.6%
Total	$940,000	100.0%

* Quality control personnel visit customer sites to assess discrepant material claims.

In the Sales & Marketing business process, certain activity costs were found to be lower than management expected (see Exhibit 6-11). "Prospecting is less than 5% of our sales and marketing efforts. Maybe we should be willing to invest more time," commented Ronald Williams.

In comparing business process costs by location, varying degrees of cost effectiveness were highlighted. Exhibit 6-12 illustrates distribution management specific activity costs by location. On a per weight basis, the 19th site was far more costly than the other sites. "This site has a lot of

Exhibit 6-11

ILLUSTRATIVE DATA
SALES/MARKETING

ACTIVITIES	$	%
Preparing Quotes for Customer	$261,750	34.9%
Visit/Travel to Customer	309,700	41.3%
Advertising Expense	48,800	6.5%
Prospecting	33,600	4.5%
Pricing Orders	42,900	5.7%
Other	53,250	7.1%
Total Activity Center	$750,000	100.0%

Exhibit 6-12
COMPARISON OF ACTIVITY COSTS

Business Process	19th	By Site ($000) AZ	CA	Other	Total
Distribution Management:					
Truck Loading	$475	$210	$140	–	$825
Equipment Maintenance	390	140	290	–	820
Packaging	500	165	410	–	1,075
Common Carriers – Branches	50	42	175	$35	302
Common Carriers – Trade	30	50	10	150	240
California Fleet	1,600	225	525	30	2,380
Arizona Fleet	90	790	35	2	917
Material Handling	300	225	50	–	575
Transfers	175	7	5	30	217
Total	$3,610	$1,854	$1,640	$247	$7,351
Volume (in lbs.)	80,000	55,000	65,000	28,000	228,000

small orders. That's probably why it's more costly to operate than the other facilities, which process larger orders," explained Curry.

Value Analysis

For purposes of cost reduction and to gain a better understanding of the value of activities, WBM assigned a value code at the activity level. The coding scheme used was as follows:

- 9—High value: adding value to the product and/or customer,
- 7—Medium to high value,
- 5—Medium value, necessary evil,
- 3—Activity that is not necessary or one that could be improved,
- 1—Nonvalue-added (i.e., errors): activities that should not ever occur.

Exhibit 6-13 depicts the results of using this ranking to assign value codes to activities. As expected, the greatest share of the activities (more than three-fourths) were coded as of medium to high value to the company. However, 16% were viewed as activities that could be improved or eliminated.

Exhibit 6-13

**BREAKOUT OF ACTIVITY COSTS FOR ALL SITES
BY VALUE CODE**

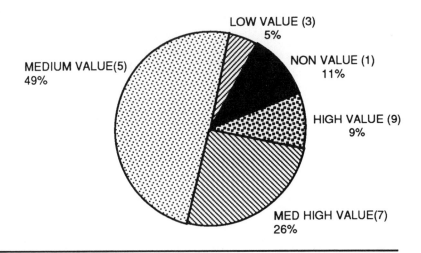

Hierarchy

The activity hierarchy for WBM was tailored to fit a distribution business. The unit-level activities at WBM related to individual customer orders. Batch level then was defined as shipments or movements of products to fulfill customer orders. Product-sustaining costs were such things as machine maintenance and product management. Facility-sustaining costs related to general plant costs and support service activities that were not product specific.

The results are shown in Exhibit 6-14. Facility costs, at 22%, emphasize the high cost of doing business out of three or more locations. Batch costs, at 21%, reflect the cost of shipping and moving material among multiple warehouses. Order (unit-level) activities consumed 41% of total costs, demonstrating the volume sensitivity of their distribution business.

"People were amazed at the results. We would have expected more fixed [facility] costs, rather than unit," Curry said. "Virtually all costs can be controlled and managed to the level of order volume—much more than we had thought."

Exhibit 6-14
BREAKOUT OF ACTIVITY COSTS FOR ALL SITES
BY HIERARCHY CLASSIFICATION

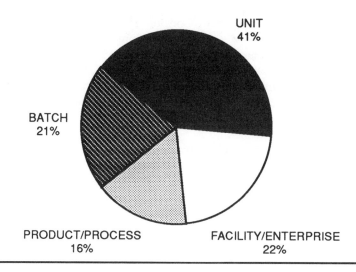

UNIT
41%

BATCH
21%

PRODUCT/PROCESS
16%

FACILITY/ENTERPRISE
22%

Management Acceptance

WBM management believes that an ABC system will be invaluable to help manage their business in the '90s. However, for various reasons they are still struggling to fully accept the ABC data and the insights it provides. Ronald Williams, whose two largest products appeared unprofitable, believes the information is "fundamentally flawed. ..."

> I agree that we need to understand what products cost us. But [the ABC] product profitability was built on assumptions which are completely wrong. For example, number of orders was used to drive Sales & Marketing costs to products. That's crazy. One order can take five minutes, another five days. Those differences should be built into the model.

When asked about other uses of ABC beyond product profitability, Williams responded, "The activity analysis gave us information we can act on. For example, I had no idea how much double handling was going on. And maybe we should spend more money on prospecting new business."

Steve Owens expected a decision model to help decide what orders should or should not be taken. Product managers and management at WBM intuitively understood their margins and their cost. Owens observed:

> However, we were seeking a better way to understand the cost of filling various types of orders and looking at costs from different perspectives. This we still have not accomplished. I don't believe I got what I wanted. We need customer profitability and order profitability to run our business. We need to know when to take an order and when not to. There was not sufficient communication throughout the process. I wanted to be involved, to shape it, but instead, I didn't even get what I wanted.

Lenny Gibson saw the link to transfer pricing at the August 1991 presentation:

> Transfer pricing is a major issue to us. I didn't see the link between ABC and transfer pricing until the final presentation. Our intent is to view each branch as a profit center. We need to know the true cost of moving material to branches.

When asked for his view of the process, Gibson responded:

> We need more teaching. I was too remote from the process. I only recall one meeting in August. We need to drive this concept forward, and Curry can't do it alone. It has to come from executive management. Too much time has elapsed already.

Jim Curry, vice president finance, concludes that ABC "affected the way people think." Although Curry admits he went down a very long and complex path and should have shared more of the results along the way, he is convinced that:

> People need to be empowered to control costs in their own areas. ABC helps that to happen. Supervisors can now see how their department's activities affect costs. They can see that just doing the activity more efficiently isn't always the answer. By controlling the cost driver, they can also keep watch on the number of times they do the activity. People are so much more aware of costs.

Referring to the complex architecture of five sites, Curry continued.

"No one ever criticized the theoretical design. The project just took so much longer than we expected. Every minor design change took hours or days of data manipulation." Looking back, it's easy to recognize the communication gaps:

> I should have focused on the activity and business process analysis earlier, while the cost drivers were being collected. That would have given people a sense of the results. But we were all too focused on product profitability. I thought that if I didn't show complete results, it would lose credibility.
>
> People become stakeholders in projects like this. They naturally react when they see that the products they are responsible for are actually losing money. They read the last page in the mystery novel first and disregard the rest. In the end, one wrong cost driver, sales orders, threw every bit of credibility out the window.

Could it have been avoided? Curry says:

> Probably. We should have come to some numbers quicker, even if they didn't reflect the economics of our transfers and transshipment. In the end, the business processes were a real hit. I could have showed that to them three months into the project.

Future of ABC at WBM

Does ABC have future at WBM? Steve Owens states:

> Absolutely. We are just beginning to understand how we can use it. But more people need to be involved in the next phase. I want a system that will enable us to know our cost and to use this information to cost different types of orders. We should be able to maintain a cost system that allows us to view cost from different perspectives and, where necessary, to peel the onion so as to analyze the impact of various costs on our business.

Curry plans to update the current model with 1991 data; however, his approach will not be merely loading new financial numbers. He is planning to use this chance to get more people involved. Curry anticipates that process improvement teams would use the ABC information to:

- Assess the validity of the original design decisions regarding activity definition, hierarchy, value codes, and drivers within their business process. The teams will be responsible for improving the original model.

- Assess the cost effectiveness of each activity by evaluating dollars spent on an activity relative to the value activity adds to a product. This assessment will help focus on where money is being wasted and where cost reductions can be achieved.
- Identify improvement methods for less cost-effective activities.
- Develop "standards" (i.e., measures) for tracking performance on a periodic basis.

"What good are all these efficiency programs, if we can't measure ourselves toward something?" asks Curry. "Ultimately, I envision information that will reflect costs of taking an order and linking it to customer profitability. That would make everyone happy."

Chapter 7

ARCO Alaska, Inc.

Executive Summary

The Finance, Planning, and Control Department (FP&C) of ARCO Alaska, Inc. (AAI) is responsible for reporting, analyzing, and monitoring financial activities within AAI. In a commodity environment where prices are market driven and the costs of operations and support increase each year, FP&C is constantly trying to find ways to measure, analyze, and manage costs better.

After a few limited attempts to analyze costs on an activity basis, a broader scale activity-based analysis (ABA) study was undertaken in the summer of 1991, with the help of an outside consultant. FP&C believed that the information from the pilot study could be used to demonstrate how operational demands affect controllership activities and costs.

The Controller's Group within FP&C, sponsored by Dan Casey, the controller, piloted the ABA study. The Controller's Group consisted of 175 people responsible for activities such as budgeting, financial reporting, accounting, and contract and joint interest auditing. The cost of these activities would be charged to operating oil fields based on the field's use of each service or activity.

Summer interns were hired to perform the project. Due to the interns' limited availability and the department's desire to use the ABA data in the up-coming 1992 budget process, the project was given a seven-week deadline. The management group committed to the quick-paced project but later admitted some disadvantages from accelerating the project to this degree. Steering committee member Randy Eldridge admitted, "Timing was too fast. We got some immediate benefits but with a few penalties, such as difficulties in obtaining management acceptance and buy-in during the process."

The manager of policy and internal control, June McHaney, concurred. "The process was rushed due to our own schedule. There was very little time for managers to fully review the assumptions made by the ABA team. The more manager involvement up front, the better."

The pressures to complete the project on time kept the ABA team from encouraging management participation. As a result, many managers became skeptics rather than supporters.

Toward the end of the project, the downturn of the economy required ARCO to institute a headcount reduction program throughout the company, and managers were suddenly faced with reducing the number of employees. The ABA data were used to help turn what would have been subjective decisions into objective decisions.

Eldridge said, "The data enabled us to look at activities first and then people."

FP&C Vice President Joe McCoy stated:

> When other departments made the same reduction decisions they just reduced headcount by 10% across the board. They did not have the quality database that the Controller's Group had. Cutting headcount without a detailed study can have adverse long-term effects. And how will these departments react to another reduction program? That could really hurt them if they aren't prepared with data like ABA.

Company Background

Atlantic Richfield Company (ARCO) is one of the largest crude oil and natural gas producers in the world. ARCO Alaska, Inc., a wholly owned subsidiary of ARCO, produces the crude oil for ARCO's West Coast refining operations. AAI's 430,000 barrels a day of Alaska's North Slope crude oil account for approximately 5% of total U.S. daily production of crude.

AAI's 2,700 employees are involved in the discovery, development, administration, and operation of fields located throughout Alaska. The high costs of finding, developing, and operating such large fields create financial barriers that are difficult for a single company to overcome.

To alleviate these financial burdens, major fields have multiple owners, who share development and operating costs in proportion to their equity stake. In most cases, one of the co-owners is selected to operate the field and is compensated by the other co-owners for the cost of running it. Co-ownership and operating agreements are highly complex. All co-owners invest heavily in staff and resources to audit and manage the terms of the agreements.

In addition to several smaller fields in South Alaska, AAI co-owns and operates three major oil-producing fields on the North Slope of Alaska.

They are Prudhoe Bay—Eastern Operating Area, Kuparuk, and Lisburne.

Prudhoe Bay, in operation since 1977, is the largest producing oil field in North America, with more than 1,000 production and injection wells. AAI operates one-half of this immense field. The field near the Kuparuk River, with approximately 700 production and injection wells, is the second largest producing field in North America. AAI is the sole operator of Kuparuk. The field at Lisburne is a smaller field, with approximately 70 wells that produce about 40,000 barrels of oil per day.

AAI also conducts major exploration projects and land development in Alaska and its surrounding waters. Exploration projects, like oil field production, have multiple co-owners and an operator to share the costs and risks. The exploration projects have made significant discoveries at Point McIntyre on the North Slope and in Cook Inlet, located in south coastal Alaska.

Major departments within AAI include:

- Finance, Planning, and Control;
- Two business units (Prudhoe/Lisburne and Kuparuk/Cook Inlet) that include engineering, operations, drilling, and health, safety, and environmental departments;
- Exploration;
- External Affairs;
- Human Resources.

The Need for Activity-Based Analysis

All oil companies came under severe competitive pressures during the 1980s, when not only did the price for oil fail to reach a previously predicted value of $50 per barrel but actually declined to below $20. Oil was traded as a commodity, and success required a company to be a low-cost producer. AAI recognized the need to understand its costs better.

Additional cost pressure occurred in 1985 when AAI separated from its parent, ARCO, to become a separate company. Prior to 1985, AAI obtained much of its support services, such as computer systems, planning and budgeting activities, and general ledger accounting support, directly from the ARCO Oil & Gas Company in Dallas, Texas. When AAI became a separate profit center, it could no longer use the general accounting support services of ARCO. Separate field accounting became necessary. When AAI was created as a subsidiary, the controllers function was established. In a short period of time the FP&C

Department (and other support areas) doubled in size to handle the increased volume of transactions. Thus both external and internal forces influenced the FP&C group to find better ways to understand, measure, and manage costs.

Finance, Planning, and Control Department

AAI's Finance, Planning, and Control Department prepares company-wide financial reports and supports all business units' finance, planning, and control needs. Joe McCoy, the vice president of FP&C, described its function. "We are a service organization. We provide financial information for the fields, our parent (ARCO), and ourselves (AAI) to run the businesses."

Subdepartments within FP&C are:

- Controller's Group,
- Materials and Purchasing,
- Planning and Evaluation,
- Administrative and Information Services.

Preparing for Activity-Based Analysis

The Controller's Group consisted of 175 people (160 of whom were located in Anchorage, Alaska, and the remainder at the field locations). It was responsible for financial reporting, general accounting, internal auditing, and budgeting at AAI. The organizational structure of the Controller's Group and its key functional areas are highlighted in Exhibit 7-1. In performing its mission, the group consolidates and analyzes all forecasts and budgets; coordinates internal controls and policies; manages accounts payable and materials; audits all co-ownership agreements; handles all revenue, production, and tax accounting; writes reports for shareholders; and provides financial support to field operations.

The existing cost system at AAI accumulated labor costs and expenses (e.g., supplies, travel, contractor costs, fringe benefits) by department but did not give visibility to what was being performed or for whom. The Controller's Group began to look for new ways to measure and control its costs. Much of the initial effort was led by Thad Bydlon, manager of the Kuparuk, Cook Inlet/ Exploration and Land Business Group. He explained, "We were looking for ways to add value to our reporting and analysis mechanisms."

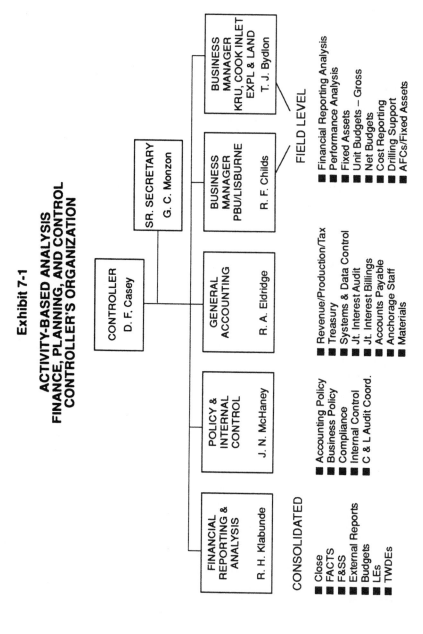

Exhibit 7-1

ACTIVITY-BASED ANALYSIS
FINANCE, PLANNING, AND CONTROL
CONTROLLER'S ORGANIZATION

CONTROLLER
D. F. Casey

SR. SECRETARY
G. C. Monzon

FINANCIAL REPORTING & ANALYSIS
R. H. Klabunde

POLICY & INTERNAL CONTROL
J. N. McHaney

GENERAL ACCOUNTING
R. A. Eldridge

BUSINESS MANAGER PBU/LISBURNE
R. F. Childs

BUSINESS MANAGER KRU, COOK INLET EXPL & LAND
T. J. Bydlon

CONSOLIDATED

■ Close
■ FACTS
■ F&SS
■ External Reports
■ Budgets
■ LEs
■ TWDEs

■ Accounting Policy
■ Business Policy
■ Compliance
■ Internal Control
■ C & L Audit Coord.

■ Revenue/Production/Tax
■ Treasury
■ Systems & Data Control
■ Jt. Interest Audit
■ Jt. Interest Billings
■ Accounts Payable
■ Anchorage Staff
■ Materials

FIELD LEVEL

■ Financial Reporting Analysis
■ Performance Analysis
■ Fixed Assets
■ Unit Budgets – Gross
■ Net Budgets
■ Cost Reporting
■ Drilling Support
■ AFCs/Fixed Assets

An initial activity-based analysis (ABA) was performed in 1988. Randy Eldridge, manager of general accounting, recalled the departmental breakdown of activities.

> We did a functional analysis then and assessed whether an activity was critical, necessary, or fiduciary. But we had defined activities at too low a level. The effort served to illustrate that it was worthwhile to understand what we do, why we do it, and whom we do it for. We knew we needed to understand our business better.

In the summer of 1989, with the assistance of a summer intern, a small ABA study was performed using a field operation as the test site. Bob Allaire, then internal business consultant within Thad Bydlon's business group, recalled:

> Our goal was to provide a more valuable way to look at costs for our field managers. The results were dramatically different from what the field management had been seeing. The results sparked our interest because we knew that activities are the driving force of our costs.
>
> Before proceeding further with analyzing field operations, we decided to demonstrate the concept of ABA more fully in our group within the controller's department. Meanwhile, we had begun to circulate ABC articles to help disseminate the concept.

The Kuparuk business group consisted of 24 people. Members of the group determined whether activities were decision-making, cost recovery, or fiduciary. The results were presented to Joe McCoy, vice president of FP&C, and it was proposed that the study be extended to include the entire controller's department. Other managers quickly gathered similar data with limited resources and tools, but a full-scale analysis was not done. These small-scale internal ABA studies had been greeted with mixed results. Bydlon recalled:

> The assignment of costs to activities was enlightening. We could quickly see the potential benefits of activity management. But it was so limiting. We did not value rank activities or try to understand why they were happening, or for whom. We knew we needed to increase the scope of the study the next time.

In January 1991, Dan Casey became controller and in charge of the controller's department. He understood the potential value of the ABA studies and suggested that another, broader-scale study be undertaken. Bob Allaire felt that the next study should be assisted by people experienced and credible in ABA. After some research, he selected a consulting firm to assist AAI in a proof of concept study.

The consulting firm was invited to Anchorage in June 1991 to discuss its methodology and approach. The consultants, after a general ABC introduction, proposed a "cost object" approach whereby the costs of activities would be assigned to the cost objects' demand for or consumption of each activity. Bob Allaire explained:

> We defined the operating fields to be the cost objects for the department's activities. Previously we had just analyzed activities without linking activities to what benefitted from or created a demand for the activities. This was the first time I had looked at activity analysis in this way. The theory really gelled in my mind at that time. We got Dan's and Joe's approval to go forward immediately.

Dan Casey stated four broad objectives for the study:

- Develop an activity-based analysis (ABA) of the staff functions of the controller's department;
- Document and understand the cost behavior of the controller's department;
- Evaluate activity-based analysis for the controller's department and its application to other staff and operating units in ARCO Alaska, Inc.;
- Present findings and recommendations to the controller and FP&C management.

AAI assigned two summer interns to work on the pilot analysis. Bob Allaire and Gary Light (supervisor of headquarters accounting) acted as co-project leaders and assisted on a part-time basis. A steering committee—Randy Eldridge and Dick Klabunde—guided the project, to wrestle with issues as they arose and to approve all design decisions. The steering committee established a demanding seven-week deadline to complete the project because of the limited availability of the interns and the desire to use ABA data in the 1992 budgeting process that would begin in August. The project plan envisioned five main tasks:

1. Overview presentation to the management of the controller's department about ABA and the project's objectives and scope.

2. Architectural design of the model.
3. Activity definition and costing.
4. Cost driver identification and collection.
5. Model computation and analysis of results.

Model Design and Architecture

Time Period and Nature of Resources

The ABA team chose to collect one year of data in order to capture the underlying cost-activity relationship over a sufficiently long time period. Actual expenses for the first six months of 1991 and the latest estimate for the remaining six months were included in the study. Total expenses captured were approximately $16 million.

To begin the process of assigning costs to activities, the team defined four categories for review: (1) labor related, (2) travel, (3) training, and (4) contractor. More than 95% of the expenses were labor related and were driven to activities based on surveys (as discussed in a later section). The travel category was mostly for employee training and North Slope operational audit travel. The training category covered primarily course fees or incremental expenses to attend conferences or seminars. Contractor costs were for various special projects, such as the ABA study.

Collecting Costs by Relationship Level

Before surveys could be performed, costs had to be segregated into "reporting relationships" to represent supervisors and their staff. This level was necessary for collecting activity data. All supervisors later were asked to identify the activities performed by their staff. There were 25 such reporting relationships: the managers of the five functional groups, the supervisors of 19 subgroups, and the controller's administrative staff (see Exhibit 7-2). For ABA purposes, these reporting relationships were referred to as "resource groups." The ABA team decomposed existing cost reports from the five high-level groups into the 25 resource groups. Direct assignments or a salary code distribution were used to obtain costs within each resource group.

Determining Cost Objects

In most manufacturing ABA applications the cost objects are the products produced. For AAI the most obvious cost object or product is a

Exhibit 7-2

RESOURCE GROUPS

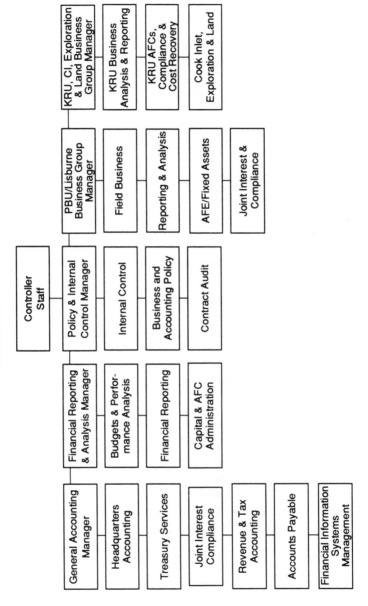

Controller Staff

Policy & Internal Control Manager
- Internal Control
- Business and Accounting Policy
- Contract Audit

Financial Reporting & Analysis Manager
- Budgets & Performance Analysis
- Financial Reporting
- Capital & AFC Administration

General Accounting Manager
- Headquarters Accounting
- Treasury Services
- Joint Interest Compliance
- Revenue & Tax Accounting
- Accounts Payable
- Financial Information Systems Management

PBU/Lisburne Business Group Manager
- Field Business
- Reporting & Analysis
- AFE/Fixed Assets
- Joint Interest & Compliance

KRU, CI, Exploration & Land Business Group Manager
- KRU Business Analysis & Reporting
- KRU AFCs, Compliance & Cost Recovery
- Cook Inlet, Exploration & Land

barrel of oil. The Controller's Group activities, however, produced budgets, financial reports, audits, and analyses for the fields themselves, the co-owners, or their corporate offices. The ABA team decided that these services were the outputs produced by the Controller's Group, not barrels of oil, and the "objects" for these services are the fields or groups requesting or benefiting from the service.

The team determined that fields most likely consume resources differently depending on whether AAI owns and operates them or just operates them. The following classes of cost objects were identified:

- Fields (separated as an owner and operator),
- Exploration projects,
- ARCO Alaska, Inc. management,
- ARCO corporate management.

The complete list of the 14 cost objects is shown in Exhibit 7-3.

Defining and Obtaining Activities

Each of the 25 resource groups was asked to complete a form outlining activities performed by its staff. These forms were developed after interviews with the five key functional managers to determine the activities performed by each subgroup. Supervisors were encouraged to add activities as necessary. They also were asked to assess the percentage of time each activity was performed for the 14 cost objects. These assessments or "management estimates" became the basis for driving activity costs to the fields or AAI management. In some cases, resource groups mainly supported specific fields. Most resource groups, however, provided services to several cost objects to some degree.

Exhibit 7-3

COST OBJECTS

Prudhoe Bay Owner	Cook Inlet Owner
Prudhoe Bay Operator	Cook Inlet Operator
Lisburne Owner	Exploration & Land Owner
Lisburne Operator	Exploration & Land Operator
Point McIntyre Owner	AAI Management
Point McIntyre Operator	ARCO Management
Kuparuk Owner	
Kuparuk Operator	

Quite often similar activities were identified in various resource groups servicing different cost objects. For example, budget activities are performed by many groups such as the Prudhoe Bay/Lisburne Field resource group and the Cook Inlet/Exploration and Land resource group. Management was aware of these similar activities, but it was not aware of the amount of time spent and the cost in aggregate by each individual field.

Problem in Defining Activities

Due to the time constraints of the project, supervisors and managers were given limited time to complete, review, and discuss the activity forms with the ABA team or in the management group. In many cases essentially similar activities were defined differently by different people. In total, 308 activities were identified, a much higher number than expected. The ABA team attempted to "standardize" some of the activity terminology, but in many instances differences remained.[1] A subsequent review estimated that the actual number of different activities was probably closer to 225 to 250.

The ABA team concurrently was creating an activity dictionary (a listing and definition of each activity) based on the completed forms. As more and more inconsistencies were noted, managers and supervisors asked the ABA steering committee for time to complete and agree upon the activity dictionary and then complete each activity form again. The ABA team estimated that such a review would delay the project by at least two weeks, possibly more. Given the potential delay, the steering committee decided against performing a special review of the activity dictionary. In addition to the resource and time constraints already imposed on the project, the decision was based on the following considerations:

- Some of the activity differences could be corrected relatively quickly,
- A future step in the activity analysis would group activities into major business processes; this step would help to standardize activities.

Defining Activity Attributes

The ABA team wanted to classify each activity's contribution to the department's mission. It defined value and reason codes for each activity.

Value codes were defined as high, medium, and low. The criterion for evaluation was the activity's ability to support the individual resource group's mission. For example, performing accounts payable processing in the accounts payable resource group directly supported the mission of that group (which was to perform the accounts payable function) and, therefore, was coded as high value. Additional examples include: (1) low—checking data errors, (2) medium—training, and (3) high—invoice attesting.

Reason codes identified "why" the activity was performed: (1) regulatory—required by a regulatory agency or GAAP (generally accepted accounting principles), (2) contractual—required by legal contract, (3) management request—requested by AAI or ARCO, (4) business unit request—requested by a business unit, (5) none of the above. For example, preparing corporate reports was coded as management request, as it is performed at the request of the parent company.

Managers and supervisors were asked to define value and reason codes for each of their group's activities. The replies were inconsistent. Some people viewed an activity such as budgeting as low value, whereas others viewed it as high value. Clearly, a standard definition of value did not exist. But because each value assessment concerneed the resource group's own mission, the team did not override the individual managers' assessments.

Determining Business Processes

The project team grouped the 308 activities into more aggregate business processes—that is, collections of activities performed to accomplish a major service or function. For example, all the activities related to managing authorizations for commitment (AFC) were grouped into a business process called "AFC management." To capture the total costs of training, the costs (labor, travel, and other expenses) of all activities related to training were grouped into a business process called "training." The team identified and created definitions for 20 business processes (see Exhibit 7-4).

Identifying Cost Drivers (and Activity Drivers)

The final step in the design process identified the cost drivers used to assign activity costs to the cost objects. Cost drivers reflect the underlying use of activities by each cost object. When managers were asked what caused activities to occur, their initial answers related to the price of oil. "If the price of oil changes, our activities may change dramatically," stated project co-leader Bob Allaire.

After much discussion, the consulting team explained that Allaire and others were referring to the fundamental economic events that trigger activities or change the activity level, such as changes in the price of oil, policies, or contracts. Such events are often difficult to quantify and therefore cannot be used to link costs to products (or in this case to the operating fields).

Examples of activity cost drivers are numbers of invoices, checks processed, and budget line items, that is, the quantity of work performed by each activity but not necessarily the fundamental determinant of the actual quantity of the activity cost driver.

The ABA team discovered that quantifiable cost drivers did not exist for many of the activities performed by the 175 people in the Controller's Group. Doug Everhart, supervisor of Prudhoe Bay cost reporting, stated, "Our office environment is more difficult to quantify, tasks are less

Exhibit 7-4

BUSINESS PROCESSES

Accounts Payable
Administrative & Treasury Services
Administrative Management
AFC Management
Allocations
Budget – Capital & Expense
External/Internal Audit
External Reporting
Fixed Assets Management
Internal Control & Business Policy
Internal Reporting
Joint Interest/Cost Recovery
LE/TWDE
Operational Audits
Operational Reporting
Other Operational Support
Planning & Evaluation
Revenue Accounting
Special Corporate Request
Special Projects
Systems Development & Support
Training

Exhibit 7-5
SAMPLE OF COST DRIVERS

Cost Driver	Activity
Number of Invoices	Accounts Payable Management
Number of AMP Transactions	Material Control
Headcount	Administrative Management
Number of Time Sheets (3b–16)	Technical Labor Reporting
Net Assets	Fixed Asset Control
Number of Contractor Audits	Audit Reporting

repetitive, and fewer data are collected, than on the typical shop floor of a manufacturer." While all activities had clear beneficiaries, it was difficult to measure or to count the benefits in an objective manner without detailed time sheets.

The consultants pressed the team to search for quantifiable cost drivers, especially ones that subsequently could provide useful performance metrics. Several quantifiable measures were identified to serve as objective cost drivers (see examples in Exhibit 7-5). When objective drivers were not available, the "managers' estimates" collected during the interviews to fill in the activity forms were used to measure the usage of activities by the different operating fields. An example of the final ABA architecture, from resources to cost objects, is shown in Exhibit 7-6.

The Seven-Week Project: Problems Encountered

The ABA team worked at a quick pace. It devoted little time to educating managers and sharing information along the way, anticipating that the results would be disseminated at the end of the project.

Therefore, education and buy-in by the ultimate users (managers and supervisors) were postponed. Time pressures forced the ABA team to focus on completing the project rather than on allowing management to understand the process and contribute to it. As a result, some of the managers became pessimistic during the project while they were waiting for results.

Project co-leader Gary Light conceded, "You can't evaluate a project that moves so quickly. At times we just had to make some calls, without asking for other people's opinion. But in the end, we got the information quicker, probably cheaper, and we learned a lot about our business in a short period of time."

Steering committee member Dick Klabunde remembered the problems that the project members encountered due to the lack of standardized activity definitions. He said, "Next time we have to prepare an activity dictionary first, no matter how much it slows down the process."

Exhibit 7-6
RESULTING ABA STRUCTURE

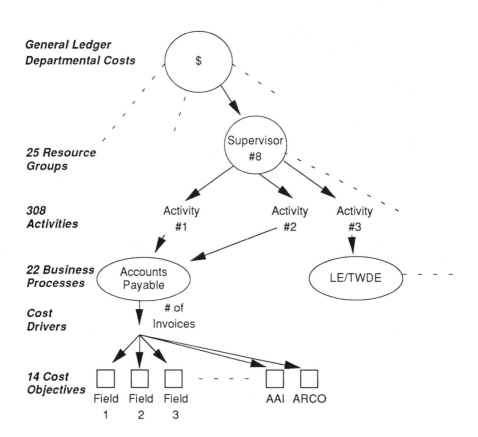

Shift in Sponsorship During Project

During the start of the project in June 1991, Dan Casey was transferred to ARCO Corporate in Los Angeles. Casey originally had approved the project with concurrence from his management team. Casey's position was not filled until the new controller, Mark Blincoe, arrived three months later. The steering committee members, Klabunde and Eldridge, acted as direct sponsors to the project.

Meanwhile, pessimism continued to grow. As a result, the ABA team found it difficult, if not impossible, to gain the attention and acceptance of all the managers and supervisors. In response, the consultants encouraged a mid-project presentation to Joe McCoy, vice president of FP&C. All managers were invited to attend. Seeing some actual data from ABA, managers began to understand its value, and the project forged on. In subsequent discussions, however, managers felt the change in sponsorship did not affect how they viewed the project's success or failure. They believed that the management team were the sponsors.

Eldridge described the situation. "Our skepticism was from the time pressures, not from any sponsorship issue. We were all sponsors to the project, some of us more so than others. Most likely, only the external consultants felt negative pressures from the loss of the initial sponsor."

Change in Objectives Toward the End of the Project

In the last three weeks of the project, managers called the consultants into a meeting and asked them, "Can the ABA data be used to identify staff reductions in a headcount reduction exercise?" During the summer of 1991, the oil and natural gas markets headed downwards. After the Gulf War, crude oil prices dropped by $4 to $6 below prices prevailing in the summer of 1990. Natural gas oversupplies also were lowering prices. The U.S. recession was squeezing margins at the pumps. The net result was significantly poorer financial performance and a need to reduce spending throughout the firm.

A reduction-in-force (RIF) was placed on AAI in late summer 1991, targeting a headcount reduction. The managers and supervisors in the FP&C Department, in general, and the Controller's Group, in particular, had to decide quickly how to make the mandated personnel cut.

All the managers and supervisors in the group now had activity data for each person in their department. Activities could be evaluated based on value to the organization, by reason for occurrence, and by dollar amount.

The consultants cautioned against making staff reduction decisions straight off the ABA data. For example, if AAI cut out a process that used the equivalent of 5.2 people, they might eliminate portions of jobs of 10 different individuals performing the function. An actual reduction in headcount could not be achieved until the remaining responsibilities of the 10 positions were reduced or restructured. The consultants further explained that the ABA data measure how activities consume resources for a given time period but do not measure the cash savings that would occur if certain activities were eliminated. As the new controller, Mark Blincoe, stated months later, "Getting rid of an activity that takes one half hour of someone's day just means that the person can either go home earlier or do something else for the half hour. Savings will not be incurred until identifiable people have been let go."

The consultants explained how the ABA data could be used to identify redundant activities, less valuable activities, and high cost activities on which to focus headcount reduction efforts. The ABA project team redirected its attention toward presenting information useful for evaluating manpower and expense usage by activities and providing insights into target areas for resource reduction and redeployment.

Full-Time ABA Project Team Member Hired

The ABA project members were summer interns and external consultants. Both FP&C management and the consultants were concerned about the lack of in-house capability to sustain ABA projects. The AAI project leaders, Bob Allaire and Gary Light, were involved from a design perspective but not from a detailed data collection, entry, and analysis perspective.

Sid Elliott, a recently hired MBA graduate, was assigned to the ABA effort during the last few weeks of the project. He became involved in the presentation and analysis of the project information. Concurrently, through one-on-one discussions with the summer interns and consultants, he gained a detailed knowledge of the model structure. He would serve as AAI's ABA resource and provide the continuity for any future ABA applications.

ABA Results

Results from the ABA pilot study were presented to Joe McCoy and all managers on August 12, 1991 (less than eight weeks from the start of the project). The presentation covered the areas below.

- Value and reason code analysis,
- Business process analysis,
- Cost object analysis,
- Cost driver analysis,
- Integrated analysis,
- ABA team's recommendations.

Value and Reason Code Analysis

The value code analysis indicated that managers believed that only 4% of their activities were low value and did not support the mission of their group (see Exhibit 7-7). This percentage was much lower than expected. Co-project leader Gary Light explained this finding:

> No wonder it was so low when the value ranking was relative to the group's mission. Each group writes its own mission statement. On the next ABA study I'd like to see the value ranking be done, not on the individual group's mission, but on the Controller's Group mission as a whole. The next assessment should be made on whether the activity directly supports the generation or protection of company assets or cash flow—and that's all. Using this criterion, the percentage of low-value activities would be a lot higher and more meaningful to us.

Exhibit 7-7

VALUE ESTIMATE

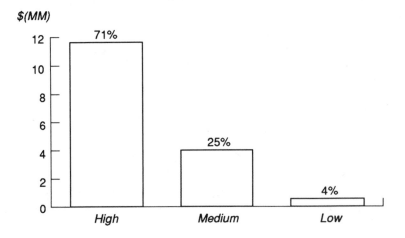

Exhibit 7-8
REASON CODE

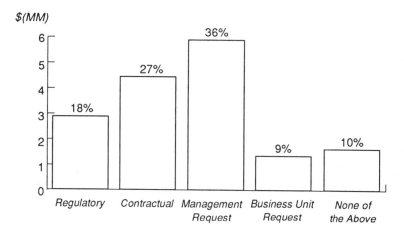

Other managers agreed with Light's new criterion for value ranking. The value coding in its current state was less useful to the managers as basically all activities were considered "high," which they knew was not always the case. Even the limited identification of low- and medium-value activities, however, turned out to be useful for implementing the RIF program (as subsequently discussed).

The reason code results (see Exhibit 7-8) showed that the greatest share of activities (36%) arose from requests from AAI or ARCO management. Only 18% and 27% were regulatory or contractual, respectively. A further analysis of the value and reason codes (see Exhibit 7-9) showed that most low-value activities were not done for regulatory or contractual reasons. The team thought, "In theory, we should only be doing low-value activities that we are legally or contractually bound to perform. Therefore, we would want the low-value activities to be made up of almost all contractual and regulatory activities."

Business Process Analysis

Joe McCoy's mid-project presentation had highlighted the results of the business process analysis (see Exhibit 7-10). It was the first cross-functional analysis ever made. As had been expected, accounts payable consumed the greatest amount of resources. Surprisingly, however, the third-largest consumer of resources was administrative management. This process represented the hiring and firing, staff meetings, and performance evaluation efforts. Reaction to the business processes were mixed. Some managers questioned a few of the roll ups and provided the team with good suggestions for future ABA analysis.

Doug Everhart saw value in the analysis from the start. He said, "When I first saw the results of the business processes in that mid-project meeting with Joe McCoy, I began to see the value in how ABA data can be sliced and diced, and how you can see the big picture, too."

Exhibit 7-9

VALUE BY REASON CODE

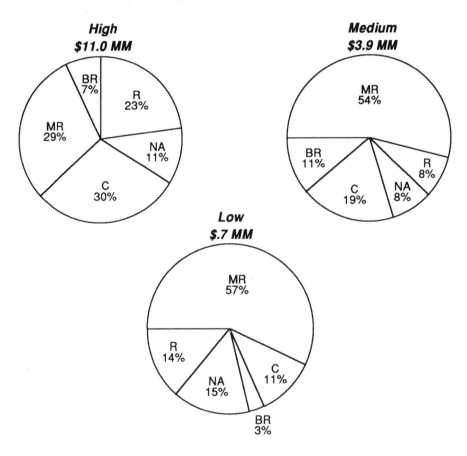

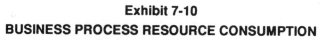

Exhibit 7-10
BUSINESS PROCESS RESOURCE CONSUMPTION

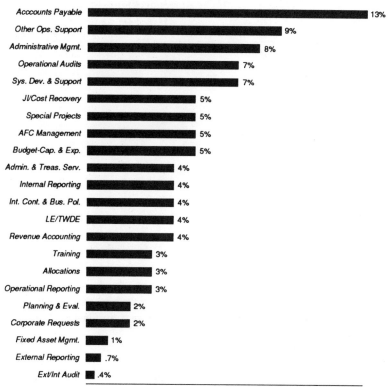

Acccounts Payable	13%
Other Ops. Support	9%
Administrative Mgmt.	8%
Operational Audits	7%
Sys. Dev. & Support	7%
JI/Cost Recovery	5%
Special Projects	5%
AFC Management	5%
Budget-Cap. & Exp.	5%
Admin. & Treas. Serv.	4%
Internal Reporting	4%
Int. Cont. & Bus. Pol.	4%
LE/TWDE	4%
Revenue Accounting	4%
Training	3%
Allocations	3%
Operational Reporting	3%
Planning & Eval.	2%
Corporate Requests	2%
Fixed Asset Mgmt.	1%
External Reporting	.7%
Ext/Int Audit	.4%

Accounts Payable

Exhibit 7-11 presents the activities performed within the accounts payable process. Only 40%—invoice processing (24%) and coding and keying (16%)—represent actual accounts payable processing. The remaining activities relate to review and control functions, inquiries, errors, and nonrelated functions. Randy Eldridge commented on these insights.

We had been struggling for a long time on improvement opportunities in the accounts payable area. Now I can see what we are really doing and what it is costing us. Some people argue that process-oriented activities

Exhibit 7-11
ACCOUNTS PAYABLE BUSINESS PROCESS ANALYSIS

Activity Name	Cost Percentage
Process Management	35%
Invoice Processing	24
Coding and Keying	16
Control Functions/Attesting	9
Vendor Inquiry	7
AMPS Maintenance/Errors	4
Mailroom	4
Accounts Payable – Others	1
Total	100%

such as accounts payable could be outsourced or perhaps moved down to the lower 48 states, where labor isn't as expensive as in Alaska. Now I'm armed with data to make the decision.

McHaney concurred on the value of the accounts payable analysis for decision making. "The accounts payable data revealed how expensive we were. I see how we can use this information to reduce the cost of processing an invoice."

Budgeting Process

The budgeting process requires many estimates and re-estimates. The LE is the "latest estimate." The TWDE is the "third work day estimate." Almost all groups perform some activities related to the LE/TWDE process.

Most managers considered these activities as of low value and done for internal use rather than at the request of the fields or ARCO. Management decided to focus on the LE/TWDE process for headcount reduction, and eliminated some of the required schedules, thereby reducing the demand for the activities.

Exhibit 7-12
GROUP PERSON YEARS BY BUSINESS PROCESS

Group	AFC Mgmt.	Alloc.	Internal Reporting	JI/Cost Rec.	LE/ TWDE	Ops. Audits	Other	Actual Person Years
PBU	4.4	3.2	0.5	2.4	2.7	0.2	21.7	35.0
KRU	3.9	3.5	1.8	1.4	1.1	0.1	15.1	27.0
FR&A	0.4	0.0	2.8	0.0	0.7	0.0	5.1	9.0
GA	0.8	0.9	0.7	5.5	0.7	4.3	71.1	84.0
BP&IC	0.0	0.0	0.0	0.0	0.0	5.7	8.3	14.0
Controller	0.0	0.0	0.0	0.0	0.0	0.0	5.0	5.0
Equivalent Person Years	9.5	7.6	5.8	9.3	5.3	10.2	126.4	174.0

(These numbers are disguised.)

Business Process/Person-Year Analysis

Bob Allaire suggested calculating the person-years required for each business process (see Exhibit 7-12).

Unlike a manufacturer, we don't have materials and machine costs. In our environment, we have primarily people costs. Therefore, looking at the number of people it takes to perform an activity gives us a better indicator of what can be done. Looking at activity dollars doesn't give the full picture because dollars per hour are not always the same.

Mark Blincoe supported the person-year analysis. He said, "This is where our discussions begin. The person-year presentation tells us, very simply, how many people it takes to get something done."

Cost Object Analysis

The cost object analysis is depicted in Exhibit 7-13. As expected, the large Prudhoe Bay field (PBU) consumed the greatest share of activities (32%). Surprisingly, however, AAI itself required the second largest

Exhibit 7-13
COST OBJECT RESULTS

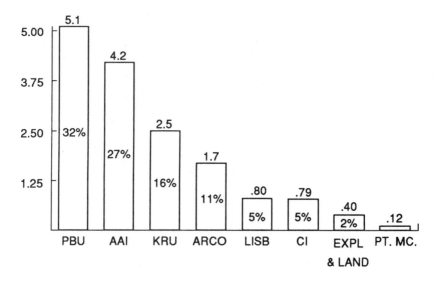

share of activities (27%). The team also calculated the headcount in each cost object's functional group with the ABA-calculated equivalent-persons per cost object. For example, the Prudhoe Bay business unit consists of 35 people, but the ABA analysis revealed that the Prudhoe Bay field required 52 equivalent people to support it (see Exhibit 7-14).

This calculation showed that although a functional group may be designated to support a specific field, the group supports other objects as well and also receives support from other functional groups.

Exhibit 7-15 shows how Policy and Internal Control's resources are used by four cost objects: the Prudhoe Bay field, AAI, the Kuparuk field, and ARCO. McHaney commented on this presentation: "I found the cost object analysis interesting. I never knew precisely how much time our group spent for one field versus another. This information will be really helpful in evaluating where to direct resources in the future."

Cost Driver Analysis

Many of the cost drivers used to assign activity dollars to cost objects were the "management estimates" obtained during the activity analysis.

Exhibit 7-14
PBU BUSINESS GROUP VS. PBU COST OBJECT

Prudhoe Bay Business Group		35.0	Headcount
Resources consumed outside Prudhoe Bay cost object:			
■ ARCO	3.3		
■ AAI	3.5		
■ Lisburne	5.2		
■ Point McIntyre	0.5	(12.5)	
Remaining Prudhoe Business Group Equivalent Headcount		22.5	
Additional Resources Demanded by Prudhoe Cost Object:			
■ General Accounting	24.0		
■ P&IC	4.0		
■ Other	1.5	29.5	
Prudhoe Bay Cost Object		52.0	Equivalent People

Exhibit 7-16 shows the unit costs calculated for several of the quantifiable cost drivers used in the analysis.

The average cost of administration per person was considered quite high and varied among the departments. These data highlighted the high costs of decentralizing personnel responsibility to individual subdepartments. A few departments were combined into one during the RIF program based on this insight.

Recommendations

The team concluded with recommendations for ABA's future:

- Use the ABA results and process in the development, analysis, and description of the 1992 Controller Group's budget;
- Develop a plan for phased expansion of ABA to the entire FP&C department;
- Make available summary results of the study to other AAI and ARCO organizations.

Exhibit 7-15
POLICY AND INTERNAL CONTROL GROUP

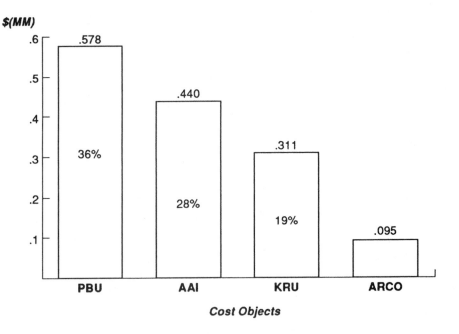

Cost Objects

Management Acceptance and Use of ABA

Despite the initial problems relating to managers' buy-in due to the quick pace of the project, the ABA data were used in the RIF process. The controller's organization eliminated 21 persons, ranging from clerks to supervisors. It gained efficiency by reducing or eliminating activities and combining subdepartments.

AAI managers commented on the role of ABA in the RIF process. Randy Eldridge said:

> We first looked at activities, than at people. We started with activities to eliminate. The ABA data showed us where there were a lot of redundancies, especially in the review process.

ABA co-project leader Gary Light described the effect on him.

I was able to move to another department with other responsibilities. My old job was supervisor of headquarters accounting. A key part of my group's responsibility was to calculate and report the capitalization of residual overhead. The ABA data showed that we were adding no value to our group by performing this task. The capitalization of residual overhead may or may not be a fiduciary requirement per generally accepted accounting principles. So, we've asked for a ruling on discontinuing it and meanwhile we have de-emphasized it.

Meanwhile, Light moved out of his previous job and into another department, after headquarters accounting was consolidated.

June McHaney, manager of policy and internal control, commented:

I always felt that some of our time spent in the policy support area was not as leveraging as the other areas within my group. I made a decision to reduce the amount of certain business policy activities, via headcount reduction of two people, choosing first the activity to reduce, then the individual. As a result, the overall time spent in the policy area is much more effective. I also combined two subdepartments within my group. I already suspected that consolidating subgroups within my department was a good idea, but ABA confirmed it. This eliminated one supervisor.

Exhibit 7-16
RATE PER OBJECTIVE DRIVER

Average Cost of Processing an Invoice	$ 10.00
Average Cost of Training per Person	3,069.00
Average Cost per Contractor Audit	10,173.00
Average Cost per AMPS Transaction	0.45
Average Cost of Administration per Person	6,958.00
Average Cost of Processing 3B-16:	
PBU, Lisburne, Pt. Mc.	32.00
Kuparuk	32.00
Cook Inlet, Exploration and Land	16.00

(These numbers are disguised.)

Dick Klabunde, manager of financial reporting and analysis, said:

> Our estimating process was always built from the bottom up. This caused
> a lot of effort. By using a top-down approach, at a higher level, we reduced
> headcount by two to three people overall, including one person in my own
> group due to the ABA efforts.
>
> I looked at all the low-value activities to determine which of them could
> be cut. I was requested to cut two people in my group. But the ABA data
> gave me evidence that eliminating two people would have hurt the com-
> pany. So, I was given permission to eliminate only one person. About 70%
> of the person's activities were actually eliminated and the other 30% were
> shifted to others. Without ABA I probably would have been more uncom-
> fortable. It would have been only my view and very subjective. I would not
> have been able to prove the two-person issue.

Joe McCoy commented:

> RIF gave the organization a chance to change. Other departments didn't
> have the benefits of ABA data and they didn't have the same focus. They
> just reduced headcount across the board. Although other organizations
> may have been successful in this RIF process, second cuts may be difficult
> without the benefits provided by ABA.

Dick Klabunde added to Joe's comment:

> Just cutting headcount across the board can't work in the long term—espe-
> cially if another RIF comes along.

Mark Blincoe, controller, stated:

> It was a real breakthrough. Now people understand that what they do
> costs the company money. ABA is an event-oriented analysis of a support
> group. Without ABA, it's difficult to get your hands around how many peo-
> ple you need to get something done. ABA data helped us understand the
> impact of each event.

Doug Everhart, supervisor of Prudhoe Bay cost reporting, concurred:

> It is an on-the-shelf listing of what my people are doing. Every month we
> used to prepare variance analyses to explain why costs went up or down.
> We went through all sorts of special analyses to explain differences. ABA,

in theory, provides that special analysis. We should be more proactive now in explaining why costs differ from one period to the next.

Gary Light extended these thoughts:

ABA confirmed what we thought. Activities are the driving force of our costs. Now we can see how our activities contribute to the bottom line.

June McHaney added:

Price is not controllable in our environment. We can control only our exploration activities and our costs. ABA detects inefficient activities, helps us streamline activities that are not competitive, and shows us low-value activities we can eliminate entirely.

Joe McCoy identified another use for ABA:

It can help us in outsourcing decisions. Some of our competitors are using other companies to do their processing activities, such as general ledgers and accounts payable transaction processing. The ABA data can help us make the right "make versus buy" decision for these financial activities. And, it can also prove to our co-owners the charges for our processing activities.

Sid Elliott, project team member, felt ABA provided a basis for further analysis.

ABA does not provide clear-cut answers. Rather it provides a basis to begin asking questions. It becomes a 'road map' versus a 'destination.'

Cost Object Analysis

Managers recognized that the impact of the cost object analysis was minimal because of the limited scope of the project. Gary Light believed:

The pilot project was based on the expenses of only 175 people in one department. In order to view the total resources used by the fields, a full-scale analysis must be done. For example, systems department costs are not included here, and they probably vary greatly among the fields.

To do a more complete analysis of cost objects, you would need the executive management committee on board. We are not really going to change the demands from the fields just to become more efficient inside. To change the demand from outside users requires executive support and a bigger ABA study. Until that happens, the cost object analysis will not include fully loaded costs to make meaningful decisions.

Randy Eldridge concurred:

Cost objects are not fully developed yet. We really couldn't use it. However, if extended on a broader scale to include all expenses in FP&C, it would become more meaningful for co-owner discussions and negotiations.

Bob Allaire added:

Clearly, cost objects become more meaningful the higher you are in the organization. The controller's department is just a small piece of all the costs demanded by the fields. But with a complete activity analysis for the Alaska company in place, field management could use the cost object data to better understand how operational demands affect controllership activities and costs. Ultimately, management could use the information to assure that only the highest-value activities are emphasized and low-value activities are reviewed for elimination. The result would be the potential for activity and cost reduction across the company.

Future of ABA at AAI

Randy Eldridge commented on the acceptance of ABA. "The management team has continued to support the ABA process."

Recently hired full-time ABA team member, Sid Elliott, has moved out of his full-time role in ABA and into the joint venture audit function. At the time of our subsequent discussion he was updating the ABA data:

I'm reviewing the data and value rankings with all the managers. There was a push to do ABA on our 1992 budget, but I think RIF has put that on hold and no mandate exists yet for me to go forward. So, I'm just cleaning up and reviewing everything with the managers. An activity dictionary is basically complete, and I'm concentrating on finding better cost drivers than the management estimates that were used the first time.

Managers like June McHaney feel ownership now. When asked how she obtained ownership in such a difficult, quick-paced project, McHaney answered:

The RIF forced me to look at the data and make decisions on it. I can see that ABA gives us a good grasp of where people spend their time. Productivity can be monitored at this level. I can also see other ways to use the data. For example, we are spending too much time in certain phases of a contract audit. The data will substantiate our feelings that if we can change behavior, we can affect costs. If we're ready to sell a field, we should spend less time on working with this field.

We would also like to eventually discuss with corporate the burden their internal control demands place on us. Our costs are driven fundamentally by the number and types of audits this organization is required to do. But any changes must be done slowly. The education process must be good. The system is meaningless if the data are bad and not enough time is given to educate users.

Mark Blincoe believes that ABA has a long way to go before its message is spread throughout the company. He said, "It is only known in Joe McCoy's financial group. Very little has gone outside."

Months after the ABA study had been completed, the team made a presentation to Jim Weeks, Joe McCoy's peer and senior vice president of the Prudhoe Bay/Lisburne Operations Business Unit. This presentation led to discussions about the next ABA project, which could occur within Weeks's organization by focusing on the engineers located in Anchorage first and then extending into actual field operations. A formal plan for the study had yet to be established. Original ABA advocate Bob Allaire summarized the future opportunities at AAI:

> There remains at AAI, in my mind, an opportunity to become more efficient and cost effective. Activity-based analysis provides a mechanism to measure progress and make decisions about these two goals. It provides management with information to reallocate resources to high-value activities, target efficiency improvement opportunities, eliminate low-value activities, test the demand for activities being performed, evaluate the cost of activities to the benefit, provide the opportunity to redesign expectations, and, thereby, add value to the entire enterprise.

Note

[1] For example, one group defined reporting as "reporting," while another group defined it as two activities: "internal reporting" and "external reporting." It subsequently was determined that the breakdown of internal and external reporting costs would be meaningful to track.

## Chapter 8

Monarch Mirror Door Company

Executive Summary

Monarch Mirror Door, a privately held company, implemented ABC to support its strategic decision making. The business had grown rapidly over the company's 30-year history, with significant expansion into new product lines and markets. But declining profitability accompanied by growing competition had forced Monarch's management to rethink its market strategy.

Monarch's customers ranged from huge national home improvement firms and mass merchandisers to local new construction contractors. Products varied from standard mirror doors to specialty and custom-made wall decor.

With the intense proliferation of products and markets, management faced several key questions:

- What are our true product margins?
- What is the cost of doing business in each of our different markets?
- What products should we be delivering to which markets?

Chief Financial Officer Mike Laney recognized that his existing cost systems lacked relevant information to address these questions. He championed an ABC project at Monarch, though it took nearly three years to get management approval. He said, "Top management at first felt it was too new. There were no success stories in the market. ABC was too 'leading edge' for a small company like ours to try it."

Once approved, ABC was implemented during a five-month project in the two main manufacturing facilities. The project's goal was to measure product and customer profitability. Laney claimed:

We learned a lot about our business. The study made us review and question each and every market we were servicing. For example, the new construction industry is a very costly market to serve. We now recognize that maybe we should be aligned with a distributor who can sell and install these products for us. In addition, our international market is extremely costly. We've basically stopped trying to grow sales in this market.

An unexpected benefit from the project came when a major customer awarded one manufacturing facility certification as a supplier based on ABC-derived quality information. Project team member Alan Meek noted, "The customer became convinced about the validity of our TQM process based on the data we collected and presented to them."

Company Profile and Business Environment

Company History

Monarch Mirror Door Company (Monarch), a privately held company, was established in 1962 in Glendale, California. Initially, Monarch had little competition as a manufacturer of wardrobe mirrored doors. Monarch's founder, Oscar Kain, was the first person to design and patent a wardrobe door that operated from a bottom track attached to the floor. Other companies at the time were using a top channel attached to the door jamb. Kain's design made the doors lighter and easier to operate.

The product was marketed mainly to the rapidly expanding and lucrative Southern California new construction industry. By 1978, annual sales had grown to $12 million, and Monarch's operations had expanded significantly and outgrown the Glendale facility. The business was moved to larger facilities in nearby Chatsworth, California. Monarch now was successfully selling nation-wide to building materials outlets and the new construction industry through a distribution network of four fabrication warehouses. In 1986 Monarch continued its expansion efforts and acquired Wondura Products in Tupelo, Mississippi.

The Wondura acquisition added a new line of decorative wall mirrors to the firm's portfolio of products. When purchased, Wondura had annual revenues of approximately $12 million. After the acquisition, all four of Monarch's warehouses (located in Texas, Illinois, New Jersey, and Florida) were closed down, and mirror door production lines were added to the Tupelo facility. Management believed the Tupelo facility could service its Midwest and Eastern customers adequately.

With its extended line of products, Monarch began to sell in new markets beyond the building materials and new construction industry, including mass merchandisers, original equipment manufacturers, and international. Monarch's base of approximately 800 customers quickly grew to more than 1,500 after the acquisition. Mike Laney, financial director, recalled, "In some cases, we expanded into markets we had no experience in." Despite this lack of experience, the expansion was successful and the firm's customer base grew rapidly.

Today, Monarch Mirror Door Company employs more than 850 people, who design, manufacture, and market a wide range of wardrobe mirror doors, mirrored wall decor, and specialty windows in the Chatsworth and Tupelo facilities. Combined 1990 sales were approximately $70 million.

Market Strategies

Monarch sells 700 standard products and more than 10,000 custom products. As Mike Laney stated, "We design everything for everyone." Custom products are manufactured primarily in Chatsworth, where they amount to approximately 20% of the facility's annual sales. These products are plate mirror and nonstandard-size wardrobe doors sold primarily to the new construction industry. The Tupelo facility's production of custom products amounts to less than 1% of its sales.

National Sales Vice President George Borowski commented on the company's marketing strategy. "Our manufacturing costs are low but are offset by our selling and distribution costs. Our competitors are more regionally focused and don't have the high selling, general, and administrative costs that we do. We try to be innovative and are always looking for ways to enhance our image."

Monarch services three target markets, which are organized into strategic business units (SBUs):

- Building materials outlets (e.g., Home Depot, Builders Square, Hechingers);
- Mass merchandising industry (e.g., Target, Walmart);
- New construction industry, primarily in Southern California.

Monarch is the market leader for mirror products in the building materials outlet industry and the only mirror manufacturer who services all three SBUs. This fact can be attributed to Monarch's size, the geographical location of its manufacturing facilities, and the number of years it has been operating. As one of the largest mirror products manufacturers (and one of the few that manufactures its own mirrors), Monarch has more resources available than its competitors. Monarch grew at a time when few competitors existed. Expanding into additional markets with similar products was relatively easy because only minor modifications to existing products were needed.

Monarch also serves some small markets, including original equipment manufacturers (OEMs) and the international market. The Chatsworth facility services all five of Monarch's markets while Tupelo concentrates on the building materials outlets and the mass merchandising industry.

Major Product Lines

Monarch has five product lines (percent of sales is shown after each):

- Mirrored doors—45%,
- Wall mirrors—30%,
- Pullman mirrors—15%,
- Shower doors—2%,
- Specialty windows—8%.

1. *Mirrored doors.* Monarch manufactures three main types of mirrored doors. The frames for the doors are fabricated from aluminum, steel, or wood. The aluminum-framed door is the original and oldest mirror door design at Monarch. The wood-framed wardrobe door is the premier product in this line. Both of these types of mirrored doors are purchased primarily by the new construction industry, which frequently will order custom sizes. The aluminum and wood mirrored doors account for about 20% of all custom products that are ordered in Chatsworth.

Steel-framed doors have the highest sales volume but also a lower margin. The steel-framed doors are purchased primarily by building materials outlets in standard sizes and palletized quantities. These doors also are sold to the new construction industry, usually to be installed in less expensive types of housing (apartment buildings or townhouses). Monarch produces a steel-framed door with a vinyl panel specifically for this market. This vinyl panel door is interchangeable with the regular steel-framed mirrored door. Thus, it is easy for contractors to offer it as an upgrade to new home buyers.

Consumers consider the mirrored door product line more of a decorative item for their home. Competition is based on unique features such as color and design. Thus, this product line generates high profit margins.

2. *Wall mirrors.* Wall mirrors differ by the type of frame with which they are made: brass, plastic, and wood. Some mirrors are produced without frames. The plastic and wood frames are offered in several color choices. All four types are available in a number of standard sizes and are sold in boxed quantities. Wall mirrors are purchased both by mass merchandisers and home centers. The wall mirror line is commodity-like: high volume, low margin, and highly price sensitive.

3. *Pullman mirrors.* Pullman mirrors are sold exclusively to the new construction industry. Pullmans are plate mirrors cut to any size up to 72" x 130", to be installed in new houses, usually in bathrooms. This item accounts for more than 80% of "custom" product sales. Pullman mirrors normally are sold to contractors along with wardrobe doors.

A contractor can order any size mirror in three different thicknesses (4mm, 5mm, or 6mm) in increments of 1/4" up to the maximum size. Contractors can order the mirrors cut to size with the edges polished and ready for installation. They also can purchase "custom pullmans," which are cut oversized at Monarch and then cut and polished to fit at the job. The custom pullmans are three to four times the price of regular pullmans due entirely to the job-site labor costs.

4. *Shower doors.* Monarch buys both components and finished products from a shower door manufacturer and assembles the components in-house. This line is sold primarily to the new construction industry as a complement to sales of the wardrobe doors and mirrors. Although there are standard sizes, a majority of the work is for one-time special sizes that have to be measured and cut to the builder's specifications.

5. *Specialty windows.* Monarch produces a small line of leaded glass decorative windows made in one of two shapes (octagonal or oval) and approximately 10 different patterns. Monarch had purchased this line from a window manufacturer in 1988 as a complement to existing product lines. Although the decorative window is typically a higher margin product than the other lines, sales have been flat.

Sales of mirrored doors in the first six months of 1991 had dropped noticeably, to $16.6 million compared to $21.5 million for the same period in 1990, a 23% decrease. The same comparison for wall mirrors showed sales remaining unchanged at $11.7 million. This product mix shift raised management's concern that competitors were "cherry picking" the high-margin products.

Monarch's Cost System

Monarch used a traditional cost system. Both direct labor rates and direct material usages were calculated from engineering studies. Standard costs for them were updated annually. Overhead was allocated to products based on a percentage of direct labor. These figures were used for inventory valuation and product costing purposes, but actual manufacturing costs were not compared with standard costs. Thus no variance reporting occurred.

Mike Laney explained, "Our old system (of developing a product cost annually) was OK for a steady state market with few products and a limited number of customers. But with all the changes and new markets we were entering, it became totally inadequate."

The Need for ABC

While Monarch was expanding its product and market base, a number of new competitors had emerged. At present, Monarch competed against smaller companies that focused on wall decor products or mirror door products (but not both) for a few key customers. These "focused competitors" with regional distribution channels had been effective in competitive pricing against Monarch.

During the late 1980s, major competitors were:

- Contractor's Wardrobe Company, located in the Los Angeles area. It manufactured a similar line of wardrobe doors and marketed to building materials outlets and the new construction industry in Southern California.
- Hoyne Products, located in the Southeast. It produced an extensive line of wall mirrors and mirror doors targeted for mass merchandisers and building materials outlets.

Recently Monarch's national customers, especially the mass merchandisers, had been demanding more services such as bar coding, electronic data interchange (EDI), special packaging, shortened order cycles, larger discounts, and more lenient payment terms. The firm's information systems could not give management information about the impact of meeting these demands on the company's internal resources.

Monarch also had been affected by the nation-wide recession in the housing industry. Starting in 1990, as new construction in Southern California slowed, sales to this SBU had decreased considerably.

These issues forced Monarch's senior management to look closely at their business and to ask critical questions about the products they were manufacturing and the markets they were servicing. If management could identify which products, customers, and markets were the most profitable, they could decide which products and markets to emphasize, which to abandon, and which to focus improvement opportunities on. Management faced four key issues:

1. *Product costs.* More accurate product costs were needed to aid in pricing and other product-related decisions, especially for custom products. Why were low-margin products losing market share? How were inaccuracies in the current margins affecting current pricing policies?

At the product line level, more accurate costing information was needed for strategic decisions. It was essential to find the best opportunities for pruning or streamlining product lines. A number of product lines had been added in recent years (including a majority of the wall decor) and required considerable amounts of engineering, sales, and marketing resources. What effect did this strategy of continually introducing new products have on current costs, as well as on pricing and product mix decisions?

2. *Market profitability.* Senior management was concerned with the number and type of markets now being served. They needed to understand the cost of doing business with customers within each SBU in order to make decisions about growing or abandoning markets in the future.

Managers at the Chatsworth facility were particularly concerned about the downward trend of the Southern California new construction industry. Sales in this area historically had been strong, but harsh economic conditions and increased competition over the past few years were eroding revenues while costs remained relatively constant.

Both divisions (Chatsworth and Tupelo) now also were questioning their costs of servicing the mass merchandising industry. Mass merchandising customers were very large, usually nation-wide chain stores with tremendous buying power. They accounted for a majority of Monarch's wall decor sales (high volume, low margin). The huge chains were demanding more services from their suppliers, free of charge. Management believed that the costs of doing business with customers in this market segment might be exceeding revenues, but they had no accurate information to support this intuition.

3. *Manufacturing costs.* Monarch manufactured identical products in its two facilities. Management wanted to compare the manufacturing processes and costs in the two plants. In addition, each facility produced unique products. The Chatsworth facility originally was designed to manufacture mirrored wardrobe doors while the Tupelo facility had been designed to produce wall mirrors. Understanding costs for the unique products was also important.

After the Tupelo facility had been purchased, resources were dedicated to operational "fixes" there so that it could produce the mirrored door production lines. Laney recalled:

> Tupelo needed attention. Among all the fixes, we also established a TQM program there. Business stayed as usual at Chatsworth. Then before we knew it, Chatsworth became overburdened. It became apparent that we needed to understand costs at both facilities.

4. *Cost of quality.* Operations management at the Tupelo facility was initiating several programs to improve efficiency in the manufacturing process. A total quality management process throughout the Tupelo organization was already in effect. Additional programs being implemented included: (1) JIT, through an on-line software system connected with the production control and purchasing systems; and (2) design for manufacturability (DFM), to address the rising engineering costs as product life cycles became increasingly shorter.

Management wanted to measure the impact of all three improvement initiatives (TQM, JIT, and DFM) and to be able to tie them to cost reductions. This process would require reliable and current information on product costs as well as standardized performance measures.

Senior management had investigated different programs to address these issues and at times had conflicting opinions as to the best strategy. Mike Laney first learned of ABC through business publication articles and books from academic authorities. He said, "I recognized, early on, the benefits such an implementation could have on Monarch. But I knew that it was too 'leading edge' for the company. The process had to be taken on very carefully."

Preparing the Organization

Mike Laney initiated Monarch's interest in ABC. He stated, "At the time, ABC was so new. It had no track record; very few companies had actually implemented an ABC program. I knew that the success of bringing ABC into Monarch would rely on an education process for both my staff members and senior managers."

Starting in March 1988, Laney began to circulate articles on ABC and related subjects continually. He sent key people to ABC seminars, held breakfast and lunch learning sessions, and incorporated discussions on ABC, where possible, at management and departmental meetings.

People in Laney's financial group accepted the potential benefits from an ABC system fairly quickly. They already were well aware of the distortions in the existing system of calculating product costs. The ABC methodology would give them the tools to obtain more accurate cost information to support the company's decision-making processes. As Laney expressed it, "We knew how much we were spending in aggregate, and we knew our products and customers, but we did not know our activities. Therefore we could not understand or manage resource consumption.

The financial group determined that the biggest benefit of an ABC implementation would be to understand how activities cause resources to be demanded. This knowledge would help the organization manage spending by understanding which activities were demanding the most resources. For instance, both engineering and marketing costs had grown steadily as new products were designed and introduced to the market, but no one really understood how and which products were creating the demand for these costs.

Senior management saw the potential benefits of implementing the ABC methodology but still had some reservations. In 1989, with the three improvement projects (TQM, JIT, and DFM) yielding good benefits, Laney invited three consulting firms in to help educate top management about ABC and to sell them on the idea. The initiative was turned down because management still considered ABC a new and untested methodology with few actual implementors and success stories. Laney recalled, "It was too state-of-the-art and too expensive. For a small company like Monarch, the risks were too great."

Laney continued his education process, however. Approximately one year later, in July 1990, when more had been written about ABC and several large, well-known companies actually had gone through an implementation with satisfactory results, a second proposal by Laney to implement ABC in Monarch was accepted. He said, "I kept presenting ABC awareness sessions to my group and senior management. I kept watching ABC develop in the marketplace. Eventually, they took one big leap and let me try my ideas."

Role of Consultants

Laney felt that he would need the assistance of ABC-trained and experienced consultants to make this project successful. "I couldn't take a chance with someone like me who was still learning," he stated. He began an interview process with several Big Six accounting firms. His criteria for selection were the number of prior ABC engagements in which the consulting team had participated and the emphasis they placed on training and "transferring knowledge" to their clients.

Preparation to Implement the Project

Laney decided to implement ABC at both manufacturing sites (Chatsworth and Tupelo) rather than just do a pilot study at one. Senior management at both sites wanted the ABC information to help them run their business. This decision forced the team to decide whether they should develop models for the two sites simultaneously or sequentially. In addition, issues such as the time periods to be used and whether the same time periods were needed at both sites had to be resolved. The project team deliberated extensively to make decisions on:

- The scope and objectives of the Chatsworth and Tupelo implementations,
- Selection of team members and role definition,
- The start times for each site's implementation,
- The time periods to be studied,
- Training for Monarch management and other project members.

Identification of Scope and Objectives

Senior management at Chatsworth knew that any changes or new procedures, no matter how beneficial, would not be well received at the facility, given the recent layoffs and newly established procedures. Therefore, they decided to focus the ABC project at Chatsworth at a more strategic level—to provide management with high-level profitability and activity analysis needed to make strategic product and market/customer decisions. Tupelo was not faced with the new procedures or layoffs and, as a result, was able to collect activity data at a more detailed level.

To summarize the objectives:

- Chatsworth—strategic implementation: (1) gain more accurate product costs and (2) gain more accurate customer costs at the SBU level.

- Tupelo—strategic and operational implementation: (1) gain more accurate product costs and (2) identify key performance metrics to measure total quality management, JIT, and design for manufacturability initiatives.
- Chatsworth and Tupelo: (1) compare costs and activities for similar products manufactured at both locations, (2) increase knowledge of ABC throughout Monarch and prove the applicability of ABC to the mirror products manufacturing industry, and (3) move beyond the initial implementation and incorporate ABC data into the current information system.

A subsequent study determined profitability by SBU at the Tupelo facility.

Creation of ABC Teams

Two teams were created and dedicated to the projects, with oversight from Mike Laney and the consulting team. Team members were selected based on functional talent and availability. The Chatsworth implementation included the following, dedicated full-time to the project:

- One person from Finance familiar with the existing costing system and the product and bill of material files,
- One person from Information Systems with experience working with the Operations department.

The Tupelo implementation team consisted of:

- One person from Information Systems who previously had worked in Production Planning,
- One Finance person familiar with the general ledger and current costing system,
- One Operations person with an engineering background who was familiar with the product and bill of materials files.

Corporate provided:

- The corporate treasurer, who acted as the team leader in Chatsworth. He assisted in resolving any issues or problems

throughout the implementation and helped to make key decisions as they developed.
- Two outside consultants to provide education, conceptual insights, and detailed implementation knowledge throughout the two implementation projects.
- Mike Laney, who was the overall project leader, monitoring the project and providing advice on the overall architecture and conceptual design.

Timing of the Two Projects

The project team decided to start the Chatsworth project two months ahead of Tupelo because:

- Corporate support functions were located in Chatsworth. These activities were to be included in the ABC project and, as such, would make Chatsworth a lengthier project;
- Chatsworth facility had a large number of custom products (over 5,000 custom products were manufactured there during the time frame of the study) which would add to the complexity of the implementation;
- The staggered start times would allow the Tupelo team to learn from Chatsworth's team members during the two months prior to the start of their own implementation.
- Staggered start times could also benefit the use of outside consultants since the two teams would not reach any critical point requiring heavy assistance simultaneously.

Time Period of Data for Review

The ABC project team decided to collect and review only six months of data for both the Tupelo and Chatsworth plants (rather than the more typical one year of data). The ABC teams felt that six months was a good reflection of what had happened over the course of one year and that the data would be quicker to collect if only a six-month period were used. Also, they felt that no additional insights would be gained from a study of one year of data. But deciding on the right six months time frame required special discussion.

Tupelo management believed that in order to properly reflect the seasonality of their business the study must use data from the second and third quarters of the fiscal year. Chatsworth management knew that their business was not as sensitive to these seasonal changes and were confident that using data from the first and second quarter of the fiscal year would properly reflect their business. For ease in obtaining the data, the Chatsworth ABC team chose to use first and second quarter data. Managers and the project team eventually determined that the differences in the time frame of the data for each location would not distort any comparison between the two sites.

Building ABC Awareness and Education

The project at Monarch began with Laney and the outside consultants leading a one-day training and awareness session in July 1990 at the Chatsworth facility. All senior executives, managers, and other key people were present. The concepts and need for ABC in today's manufacturing environment were key discussion points. The session included an open discussion in which all managers discussed their business issues and concerns. For example:

- Where did each see the business going and what would it look like in several years?
- How would each like to see the business grow?
- What information was needed to perform their jobs better and to meet individual and departmental goals?
- What information available through an ABC implementation appears most useful?

Individual issues were noted for inclusion in the initial design of the ABC architecture. Incorporating these issues and concerns as part of the architecture helped to ensure that ABC would become a useful tool for all functional groups of the organization. A similar session was held for the Tupelo facility approximately two months later.

Project Duration

The implementation at the Chatsworth facility lasted approximately 22 weeks. The estimated full-time equivalent (FTE) was approximately 1.75 persons during the 22 weeks. The Tupelo implementation was completed in 14 weeks with an FTE of 2.0. The Chatsworth implementation was longer because the model included custom products (more than 4,000), thus making driver collection and data validation more time consuming.

Implementation: System Design and Architecture

Project plans were created for both sites based on the decisions made in the preliminary phase. The development process used nine steps:

1. *Scope of the project.* The Chatsworth implementation focused on all general ledger expenses including those related to corporate offices. Due to the presence of the corporate-related functions Chatsworth required two models: (1) product cost model and (2) customer-related expenses model at the SBU level. The Tupelo implementation incorporated all general ledger expenses into one product cost model.

2. *Activity interviews.* The team interviewed key managers and supervisors to determine the activities performed within each department. The interviews also included managers from Production Control, Purchasing, Maintenance, and Marketing. In the departments with a large number of employees, such as Sales Support and Operations, supervisors also were interviewed to be certain that all key activities had been identified. The activity interviews focused mainly on product-related activities, though the Chatsworth interviews also identified customer-related activities at the SBU level. Based on the interviews, an activity dictionary was created, with precise definitions. Exhibit 8-1 shows sample activities identified through interviews. The dictionary was updated and used as a reference throughout the project. It helped prevent misconceptions concerning the activities.

3. *Employee activity percentages.* The team next sent an activity form to each department manager. This form contained the name of the manager, the employee names, and the activities that the manager had identified during the interview. The department manager either filled out the percentage of each employee's time devoted to the activities or else gave the form to the employee to complete. As the Chatsworth team began to collect activity data two factors emerged that affected the collection of activity information.

- The effect of layoffs. Due to economic and competitive conditions, the Chatsworth facility had experienced a layoff of both factory and office personnel during the study. To obtain a full array of activities performed, the ABC team members sometimes had to include in their activity analysis employees who were no longer with the company to ensure that all activities, including ones no longer assigned formally to anyone, would be included in the analysis.

- *Special manufacturing studies.* An extensive study of Chatsworth's manufacturing line and packaging and shipping procedures recently had been conducted by another outside consulting firm. The study produced changes in production scheduling and the initiation of several new procedures and reporting requirements throughout the factory. While operations management people assisted the ABC project by providing information and data, they did not want the ABC results to cause any additional changes. Operations management believed any further changes or new procedures would not be received well by their factory personnel.

4. Direct labor analysis. The direct labor rates from the traditional system were used in the ABC analysis, but direct labor employees

Exhibit 8-1
MONARCH MIRROR DOOR COMPANY
ACTIVITY DICTIONARY–SAMPLE ACTIVITIES

Activity	*Description*
Moving Material	Handle both work-in-process and finished goods. Move WIP between operating stations (machine centers). Move finished goods to storage.
Inventory Control-Raw Material	Perform raw material cycle counts on a weekly schedule. Maintain all receipts and issues of raw material in MAPICS system on a daily basis.
New Product Development	Develop and analyze potential new products or services. This includes the design, a materials list, the manufacturing process, and safety and quality testing.
Order Processing	Input new orders to on-line order system. Check all newly printed orders – verify pricing, products, quantities, and customer information.

were not classified as "direct labor" for 100% of their time. The variance between actual direct labor wages paid and total direct labor absorbed through the bill of materials was computed and assigned to nondirect labor activities identified by department managers.

5. *Machine center activity analysis.* The team listed all machine and equipment-related expenses. It identified six machine groups for each facility, based on the type of raw materials they processed. The expenses assigned to the six machine centers were equipment depreciation, power, replacement parts, and maintenance contracts. To reflect the cost of operating these machine groups, maintenance activities and downtime activities also were included. Assigning equipment depreciation directly to the machine centers was difficult for the teams at both sites. All equipment depreciation appeared in one account, and little back-up data were available on most of the older equipment to properly assign the depreciation expense to individual machines. At both sites, the teams turned to the Maintenance and Engineering personnel most familiar with the equipment. Ultimately depreciation was charged to each machine center based on the estimated replacement value of the equipment in that center.

6. *Activity amounts and analysis.* Once all the activity forms were returned and the direct labor and machine center analysis were completed, the relating general ledger expenses were mapped to the activities and machine centers using the identified percentages. This procedure resulted in all general ledger dollars being assigned to activities or machine centers. At this stage, the team had identified more than 75 different activities, a number considered too cumbersome to manage or interpret. The activities were reviewed again by the ABC teams. Many similar activities subsequently were grouped together. In the end, each site had approximately 30 activities.

As the next step, the 30 activities were classified within the hierarchy of activities, that is, unit, batch, product-sustaining, or facility-sustaining (see Exhibit 8-2 for the Tupelo results). The Chatsworth model had no activities classified as "batch" because no data were kept at this level. Some batch-level activities were known to occur so this omission was noted and deferred for future ABC analysis. The Chatsworth customer model substituted "customer-sustaining" for "product-sustaining" for each SBU (see Exhibit 8-3 for Chatsworth results).

7. *Identification of cost drivers.* Following the activity analysis, ideal cost drivers were identified for all activities. An "ideal" cost driver represented the cause of each activity. Unfortunately, because data were limited, the ideal cost driver often did not exist so a next-

Exhibit 8-2
MONARCH MIRROR DOOR COMPANY
TUPELO DIVISION
COST HIERARCHY SUMMARY

	Percent of Total Costs
Fixed Facility Costs	20.8%
New Product Support Costs	0.4
Product-sustaining Costs	21.2
Batch-sustaining Costs	2.4
Unit Level Costs	55.2
	100.0%

best "surrogate" driver was identified. For example, the ideal cost driver for materials movement normally would be obtained from a product routing file. A routing file was not used at Monarch, so the team created a surrogate driver that measured the number of machine centers in which a product was processed. The logic for the surrogate driver was that a product using several machine centers would be moved more often than one processed in only a single center.

Both project teams found that identifying and collecting activity cost driver information was the most time-consuming part. Much of the relevant information existed off-line and required a considerable amount of programming or manual efforts. Production control information was kept manually so that the teams had to enter these data themselves on spreadsheets before it could be accessed by the model.

Exhibit 8-3

MONARCH MIRROR DOOR COMPANY
CHATSWORTH DIVISION
COST HIERARCHY SUMMARY

Percent of Total Costs

Fixed Facility Costs	12.4%
New Product Support Costs	0.5
Intercompany Support Costs	0.7
SBU5 Support Costs	0.1
SBU4 Support Costs	0.3
SBU3 Support Costs	6.9
SBU2 Support Costs	1.8
SBU1 Support Costs	6.3
Product-sustaining Costs	9.2
Unit Level Costs	61.8
	100.0%

8. *Loading data and running costing.* Once the activity cost drivers were collected, they were downloaded into the ABC software program so that product and customer costing could be calculated.

9. *Data verification and analysis.* The final phase of the project verified the data and analyzed the resulting product and customer costs. The entire team was active in this phase, especially Mike Laney and the consultants. Including changes, it took approximately four weeks.

During the review, it became apparent that the models should be changed. Certain cost drivers needed to be replaced as better ways were identified to drive activities to products or customers. In the Chatsworth product model, one procurement activity had been driven to all products using the number of raw material parts per product. The team found this activity was done only for a few parts. The driver was changed so that only the products using those raw material parts would be assigned the procurement activity costs. Many of the enhancements were fairly simple and could be completed quickly. Other more difficult changes were noted for future enhancements because senior management was anxious to see preliminary results.

Findings and Results

Mike Laney, referring to the profitability results by SBU and product line, stated, "The greatest benefit of the two pilot implementations was that ABC provided us with a better understanding of our business. We now had the strategic information required to make decisions."

The results of the initial ABC implementations at Chatsworth and Tupelo proved many of management's intuitive insights, though there were a few surprises.

Surprising Results

Mass merchandising SBU had very low or no profit potential. Exhibit 8-4 shows the ABC-calculated net profit for each SBU. The mass merchandising market has a negative margin. Customer-related costs are low in this SBU because of large purchase volumes, but purchases are concentrated in wall decor, and this product line (see Exhibit 8-5) has a negative margin. A separate and subsequent study of Tupelo's SBU profitability yielded the same conclusions.

While in principle Monarch might improve the profitability of this SBU by encouraging customers to buy a different mix of products, mass merchandisers mainly are interested in purchasing inexpensive, prepackaged items that their consumers can pick up easily from a display shelf and carry home. Monarch's other product lines do not meet this criterion. A more appropriate plan of action in this case would be to analyze the manufacturing related activities for this product line and look for opportunities to reduce or eliminate costs.

Machine center costs were higher than anticipated. The study highlighted maintenance and repair, unscheduled downtime, and replacement parts costs by machine center. Management felt that the costs reported in these categories were surprisingly high. The project teams investigated further. Their review revealed that most of the maintenance and repair activity was unscheduled. The old age of much of the equipment caused many machine failures, leading to a great deal

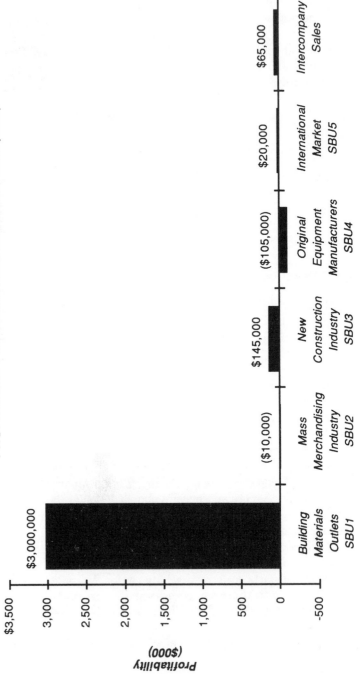

Exhibit 8-4
MONARCH MIRROR DOOR COMPANY
CHATSWORTH DIVISION
PROFITABILITY BY STRATEGIC BUSINESS UNIT (SBU)

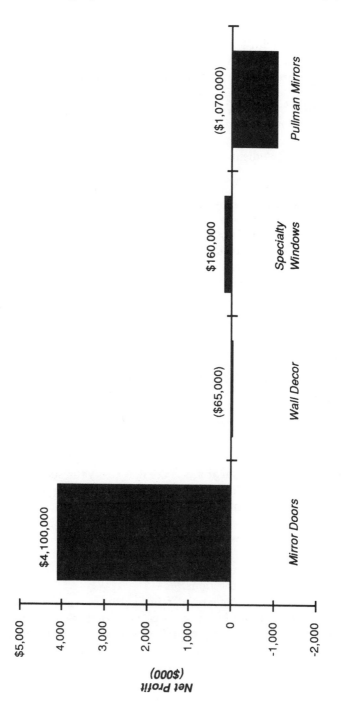

Exhibit 8-5
MONARCH MIRROR DOOR COMPANY
CHATSWORTH DIVISION
NET PROFIT BY PRODUCT LINE*

* *Excluding Facility Expenses*

of unscheduled downtime. This information helped management to understand all the costs involved with running older equipment. Although replacing equipment would have reduced much of the maintenance, repair, and downtime costs within machine centers, this course of action was not at present an economically feasible alternative.

ABC's role in TQM assisted Tupelo in achieving certified supplier award for a major customer. Prior to the ABC study, Tupelo was trying to become a certified supplier for Sears, one of its major customers in the mass merchandising market. Alan Meek recalled:

> When I saw the activity data relating to quality come out of the ABC project, I decided to present it to Sears. They could now see in black and white the quality program we had implemented. ABC helped to quantify our world-class manufacturing processes and the results from our TQM program. Sears awarded us with vendor certification, an unexpected benefit from our ABC efforts.

The quality cost information shared with Sears related to activities such as inspection, downtime, rework, and returned goods. In addition, management plans to measure and monitor the costs of quality.

New construction industry SBU was the most costly. Exhibit 8-6 shows the activities performed for each of the five SBUs. Out of 15 customer support activities identified, the new construction industry (SBU 3) consumes 14, six of which are done only for this SBU. As a consequence, SBU 3 incurs $1.3 million in support costs, more than any other SBU. Unique activities for the new construction industry relate to installation and delivery functions. This SBU also requests most of the custom sizes. This is typical given the nature of the new construction business. But management was surprised to see how costly the special sizes and extra activities were. Considerable resources were being consumed to obtain a relatively small profit.

Expected Results

Additional insights from the ABC analysis conformed more to management's expectations.

Product and customer proliferation causes higher overall costs and is eroding total profitability. Many costs existed solely to support the large number of products manufactured and customers served. The hierarchical activity cost analysis showed that 24% of total expenses were incurred for product- or customer-sustaining activities. These expenses were most significant at the Chatsworth facility, where more custom products were being made and all five SBUs were being serviced. *Comparisons of identical products manufactured at the Chatsworth and Tupelo plants did not uncover major discrepancies in ABC costs.* Both plants were found to be operating with fairly similar cost structures. Exhibits 8-5 and 8-7 show profitability by product line for both locations. Mirrored doors and specialty windows are manufactured in both locations. Just prior to the ABC implementation, management had moved production of one entire product line from Chatsworth to Tupelo. In Tupelo's ABC model, this line turned out to be one of the most

Exhibit 8-6
MONARCH MIRROR DOOR COMPANY
CHATSWORTH DIVISION
ACTIVITY INTENSITY ANALYSIS BY SBU – SG&A COSTS ONLY

Activities	SBU1	SBU2	SBU3	SBU4	SBU5
Advertising and promotion	✔	✔	✔		
Selling	✔	✔	✔	✔	✔
Install mirrors			✔		
Install doors			✔		
Commissions	✔	✔	✔		
Executive support	✔	✔	✔	✔	
Damaged merchandise	✔				
Customer service	✔	✔	✔		
Install measure			✔		
Install shower door			✔		
Order processing		✔	✔		✔
Take sales order			✔		
Process billing	✔		✔		
Schedule delivery			✔		
Miscellaneous support	✔	✔	✔	✔	✔
Total number of activities	8	7	14	3	3

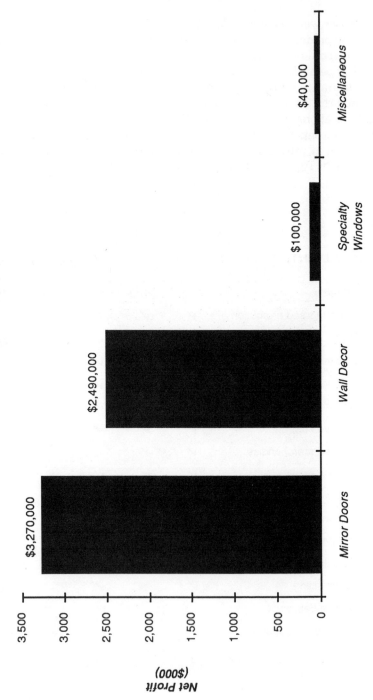

Exhibit 8-7
MONARCH MIRROR DOOR COMPANY
TUPELO DIVISION
NET PROFIT BY PRODUCT LINE*

*Excluding Facility Expenses

profitable. (Data were not available on Chatsworth because the decision was made prior to developing the ABC model). Management felt the data helped to validate the decision, since Tupelo's customers were the major purchasers of this line. Management expected that future product decisions could be informed with ABC data, not just intuition.

OEM and international markets were marginal. OEM and international markets already were being questioned when the ABC study began. The ABC information on market profitability (see Exhibit 8-4) reinforced this feeling. Laney described the likely outcome from this finding, saying, " Since the ABC implementation, we have developed and initiated an exit strategy for the OEM market and have held off any attempt to grow our international market. The ABC data put certain decisions on the table. We now had data to support our decisions."

Management Acceptance

Monarch's management met in a group session to discuss reactions to the ABC project. CEO Bob Merkow saw a linkage between ABC and pricing decisions. He stated, "We need to use ABC as a pricing model, especially when determining discounts. In a world that's changing (referring mostly to overhead and distribution costs), we need to be as accurate as possible with our product costs.

Sales VP George Borowski believes that the ABC information will force the company to focus on which markets are most profitable and which type of businesses should be emphasized:

We manufacture and distribute nationally. Our competitors, however, operate mostly regionally. The ABC information showed that our distribution costs vary greatly between markets and products. Should we be regional distributors or should we continue to manufacture nationally but sell to regional distributors and stop trying to service our customers from a national base?

The Southern California new construction market had been our original product focus but is now revealed to be quite unprofitable. I can understand that because we have an infrastructure in place dedicated to that market, no matter how slow it is. But we should rethink our strategy in this market. Again, I look to the way we are distributing to and servicing this market.

Manufacturing manager Ken Rounds believed that the ABC information could support his strategic product decisions.

I can use the data for certain make versus buy decisions. We are considering producing a new line of medicine cabinets. I would like to see ABC inform that decision up front so that we can anticipate our costs before we commit to in-house manufacturing.

Tupelo Vice President of Operations Don Eckenrode saw the value of ABC at the operational level:

I see a role for ABC to measure and monitor all of our programs of improvement. It can help to set priorities for these programs. When Sears awarded us supplier certification because of the ABC data we showed them, that's when I knew ABC had an important role in our world-class manufacturing efforts.

Conclusion and Next Steps

Currently, the project team at Monarch is updating the models at both locations with 1991 fiscal year data. The team plans to continue updating the ABC models quarterly. Mike Laney wants eventually to use the quarterly data in monthly ABC financial reports on customer and product profitability. He feels, "I don't believe it will ever replace my traditional system for inventory valuation. But it will become the tool for management decisions."

Senior management plans to continue using ABC for strategic purposes by reallocating resources among products and markets based on their calculated profitabilities. Tupelo management wants to use ABC as an operational tool for plant performance measurement to support the initiatives in TQM, JIT, and DFM programs.

Epilogue

After the conclusion of the study, Monarch was sold to Stanley Works of New Britain, Connecticut, in October 1991. Stanley has used the data to aid in the strategic repositioning of the company and its product lines. The ABC information proved very valuable in this circumstance.

Chapter 9

Steward & Company

Executive Summary

Steward & Company, Inc. is a broker/dealer that provides trading execution services to large institutional investors. Fred Benning, Steward's president and CEO, sponsored the activity-based costing study so that support expenses could be assigned more accurately to the firm's products and to the account executives (the account managers/liaisons to the institutional accounts). Benning wanted to understand better the cost and profitability structure of Steward. "It is important for us to be able to generate information quickly regarding the profitability of our lines of business and accounts so that we can respond rapidly to the changing conditions in the marketplace," he explained. Benning's enthusiastic support and commitment to the project greatly facilitated the acceptance of the ABC results.

Steward's key objectives for the activity-based costing study were to develop an accurate model of product and account executive profitability. Steward had nine key products. The study focused on overhead expenses (their nondirect costs), which included branch, G&A, and transaction and data processing costs.

The short duration of the study, conducted over a 12-week period, did not allow all the data to be collected and validated to the extent that the Accounting and Finance Department desired. Steward's management still reacted favorably to the concepts and already had made several decisions to de-emphasize certain product lines and to reorganize the business based on the preliminary results.

Company Profile and Background

Steward is a broker/dealer whose principal business is the execution of transactions in equity securities for institutional investors. Steward is one of the leading national firms engaged in the distribution and trading of blocks of equity securities. It conducts such activities primarily in the "third market," a term used to describe transactions of listed equity securities made away from national securities exchanges. In the past, the company's revenues have been derived predominantly from trading blocks of listed and over-the-counter equity securities with or on behalf of institutional investors. Steward had 450 employees and total revenues of $200 million in 1990.

Steward's core customers are institutional investors such as investment advisers, banks, mutual funds, insurance companies, and pension and profit sharing plans. Institutional investors usually purchase and sell securities in block transactions. These customers value trading execution that is timely and executed at competitive prices, based on negotiated commissions.

Steward's CEO, Fred Benning, described the company's philosophy:

> Our company competes via the speed of change—the ability to respond quickly to the needs of our customers. Steward's strength is relationships and my job is to be the director of quality. Quality comes from our being a focused niche player. We want to be a partner with our clients, not simply a vendor.

Among Steward's competitors are large investment banking firms such as Morgan Stanley, Goldman Sachs, Bear Stearns, and First Boston, which have larger capital resources and extensive research services to offer to customers. Brokerage houses such as Merrill Lynch offer execution services in return for "soft dollar" payments for research and other services, a practice that had climbed to 40% of commission dollars, up from only 5% only several years ago. Mutual funds also funneled some of their trading business to brokerage houses as a reward for promoting sales of their funds.

Up to 1986, Steward performed primarily block trading of listed and OTC (over-the-counter) stocks. Subsequently, it added new businesses that increased the complexity of its operating environment. By 1991, Steward was trading futures, options, international securities (foreign denominated stocks), and ADRs (American depositary receipts). The firm had added a corporate finance and taxable fixed income capability. It also had developed a technology group that offered sophisticated analytical software and automated trading for a "fourth market," in which institutional buyers and sellers could trade assets directly with each other.

Benning described the demands that the new businesses made on the cost and profit measurement system of the company, saying:

> My philosophy includes avoiding businesses we can't make money in.
> Therefore, we must know our costs accurately to enable us to make wise
> decisions regarding outsourcing or to point out areas where we can be more
> productive and do things smarter and better. We also need to be able to
> generate information quickly regarding the profitability of our lines of
> business so that we can respond rapidly to the changing conditions in the
> marketplace.

Larry Black, director and head of Steward's core equity business, concurred:

> The size of the pie is dwindling due to external forces, and we have to make
> sure we spend our money on the right businesses. We need new informa-
> tion to tell us: What does a product really cost us? What does an account
> executive cost us? What does an account cost us? What activities really
> bring in revenue? Where should our effort be expended?

Black's assistant, Bill Connors, echoed these comments:

> We had grown rapidly over the last few years and become a much more
> complex organization. New business lines were continually being added
> and our telecommunications and data processing costs were escalating
> rapidly even though the number of AEs had increased by only ten percent
> to fifteen percent.

The Need for ABC

Benning had been searching for a better way to allocate costs of support resources. He wanted the rapidly growing support department expenses assigned to the products or account executives (AEs) that used the support services. He had read an article in INC. magazine in 1988 that suggested the gains from more accurate assignment of support department expenses. Benning asked the Accounting and Data Processing departments to develop a chargeback system. He explained:

> When I looked at all the activities we were performing and all the efforts
> we were expending, it was clear to me that the support areas were not
> being guided by the marketplace. All activities received the same priority.
> The squeaky wheel got attention. Priorities had to be administered all the

time which was not the ideal way to manage a rapidly changing organization. The management team had difficulty allocating resources since we didn't really know what the resources were actually doing.

I believed each department could be a profit center and charge other departments for its services. However, it seemed there was little passion for the idea and, in the midst of other projects, not much happened. Our support areas kept growing to support a broader range of businesses. But I didn't want to be in the accounting or data processing businesses since we can't make money in those businesses. I knew, as a small company, that we had high EDP requirements and that it was expensive to maintain the investment in this rapidly changing technology. I decided to outsource our hardware computing to a vendor that could give us continual access to state-of-the-art hardware and specialized software. The outsourcing accomplished some of the visibility for support costs that I had hoped could have been done internally by more accurate assignment of internal support department expenses.

Ron Knight, director and head of the technology group, recalled the situation:

There was a general feeling by the management team that we really didn't know our product profitability and that the G&A allocations weren't right. Most allocations were on headcount. To keep allocated overhead charges to our departments down, individual department heads had started to use more temporary employees and consultants. But these actions created even more work for the accounting department.

Mary Scott, chief financial officer, explained the existing profitability reporting system:

The profitability report had grown more complex over time as we continued to add additional lines of business. The report, called the 'gold book,' used a traditional approach for allocations. The costs that could be identified as direct were charged directly to the products. However, many G&A costs could not be directly identified with a particular user or product and were allocated on the basis of headcount or number of tickets. Number of tickets was used to allocate much of the operational functions and the MIS expenses. Increasingly, senior management challenged the appropriateness of using the information.

In 1990, Benning and Andrew Bane, chief administrative officer, listened to an audio-tape about activity-based costing and felt that the procedure offered promise for Steward. Bane recalled:

> I felt that ABC might help us allocate our costs more accurately without everyone having to keep timecards. The complexity of our business had changed and the P&L owners were complaining about costs for services they didn't believe they used. My objective for ABC was to identify the cost of administrative functions based on use rather than on arbitrary measures like headcount and tickets.

Preparing the Organization

Scott and Peter Van Harten, vice president, Accounting and Finance, started to solicit proposals from consulting firms for assistance in an ABC study. They attended one firm's seminar on ABC in February 1991 and, based on the approach described, selected the firm to lead the ABC project. The consultants delivered a one-day kick-off meeting, in the spring of 1991, to introduce the project to key Steward personnel and to develop an understanding of Steward's key business reasons for conducting the project.

Due to internal resource constraints, Steward was unable to dedicate someone full-time to the project. Consequently, much of the work was performed by the consultants. They communicated extensively with Scott, Bane, and Van Harten, who served as the steering committee for the project and met weekly to discuss key issues. With the enthusiastic sponsorship of Fred Benning, the project had great visibility and fostered cooperation among all the company participants.

System Design and Architecture

Scope

The project had two primary objectives, to find out about product profitability and about account executive profitability. The initial ABC study, conducted over a 12-week period, focused on four types of support costs: (1) branch costs, (2) G&A costs, (3) transaction processing costs, and (4) data processing and MIS costs. These four categories of expenses represented 50% of the total pool of nondirect expenses (see Exhibit 9-1).

Branch costs encompassed the occupancy expenses of Steward's seven branches where AEs and their support staff were located to serve their customers. G&A costs included headquarters administration,

Exhibit 9-1
NONDIRECT EXPENSES

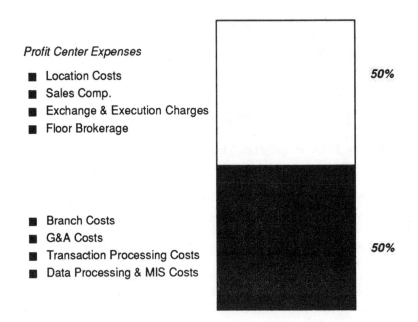

Profit Center Expenses

- Location Costs
- Sales Comp.
- Exchange & Execution Charges
- Floor Brokerage

50%

- Branch Costs
- G&A Costs
- Transaction Processing Costs
- Data Processing & MIS Costs

50%

accounting, finance, legal, compliance, internal audit, human resources, and some general marketing and sales administration costs. Transaction processing costs included telecommunications, office services, and brokerage operations, while data processing consisted of the costs related to Steward's outside data processing vendor as well as for all in-house development and operations. Early in the project, because of difficulty in obtaining accurate cost drivers, the project team decided to exclude from the analysis the expenses of telecommunications and quotation services, and the data processing expenses of the outside vendor. Thus, these expenses continued to be allocated based on ticket count and headcount as in the existing system.[1]

Definition of Products

At Steward, and at most financial service firms, profitability can be measured along many dimensions. Trading departments traded a variety of instruments and were responsible for execution and making markets. Account executives (AEs) bought and sold these instruments for their customers. These securities were bought and sold on the New York Stock Exchange (NYSE), NASDAQ (over-the-counter market), on multiple regional exchanges, in the "third market," and from firm inventory.

The ABC design team first had to agree on the definition of the product. Questions included:

- Is the product an instrument (security)?
- Is the product a group or collection of AEs who specialize or concentrate on certain securities?
- Is the product the division (e.g., if one group sells a customer an instrument that is traded primarily by a second group for hedging purposes, who gets the income and the related expense)?
- Is the product different if it is executed or traded differently (e.g., transactions can be executed on a listed exchange, traded over-the-counter, crossed in the "third market," or sold from inventory)?

The project team eventually attempted to answer three fundamental questions to guide the architecture of the ABC model and to define the product:

- What is a "product" for Steward?
- How does Steward want to manage its business?
- What was the level of detail of available financial information at Steward?

The Steward steering committee recommended that the project team use a product definition consistent with Steward's current product P&L, by product line. This definition would provide results that would be roughly comparable to existing reports and would also simplify the collection and analysis of expenses. The definition was derived from commissions credited to departments on the basis of instruments traded. It defined products as:

- Listed,
- OTC,
- Options/Futures,
- International,

- International Trading Group (ITG),
- Convertibles,
- Euro-Convertibles,
- Taxable Fixed Income,
- Corporate Finance.

Account Executive Profitability

A second model was developed to estimate account executive profitability. Sales management wanted to know the breakeven point for an AE to be profitable. An AE profitability model was expected to interest sales management in the ABC approach and further establish activity-based analysis at Steward.

Hierarchy of Activities

The ABC project team developed a new cost hierarchy for Steward. In manufacturing, costs are incurred at the unit and batch level. For Steward, the first level of the cost hierarchy was trades, with no distinction made between the unit and batch levels. The next level of the cost hierarchy was defined as customers. Regional branch offices and AEs existed to service customer accounts locally. Systems were developed and maintained to support customer activities and customer accounts. The upper two levels in the cost hierarchy were more traditional—product- and facility-sustaining.

Defining Activities and Activity Centers

Once the scope of the study and architecture of the model had been determined, the project team began to collect expense numbers from the four major categories of support resources. The expenses included salaries and related expenses, telephone, rent, supplies, and other overhead costs. These support cost center expenses then were assigned to activities performed.

Activity definition and expense assignment were developed by holding interviews with department heads and key employees to determine the major business processes performed in their departments. Few of these persons had been included in the early briefings about the ABC project. Also, many of the operating managers outside of the Accounting and Finance Department were not familiar with the expenses currently being assigned to their cost centers. Therefore, a great deal of informal education had to occur with each cost center manager during this data collection and activity analysis phase.

The project team asked department managers to enter data into activity matrices to indicate the approximate percentage of time employees in their departments spent on each activity. For example, the AEs estimated the portion of their time spent on maintaining existing accounts versus time spent prospecting for new customers. Exhibit 9-2 presents the activity matrix completed by the Accounting and Finance Department.

Some costs such as services provided by outside vendors were assigned directly to an activity. For example, Steward had a relationship with a vendor to provide technical analysis, economic analysis, and research information to its clients. This service was assigned directly to the "research" activity.

During the first stage of activity analysis, the team identified 140 activities. Because this number was too many activities for management to absorb, the team grouped the activities into 14 activity centers. Activity centers represented a group of activities with similar objectives or similar applications. They were:

- Sales & Support Activities,
- Sales Promotion Activities,
- Trade Comparison & Settlement,
- Account Maintenance,
- Human Resource Management,
- Legal & Compliance Support,
- AE Administration Support,
- Accounting Support,
- Data Processing Support,
- Investment Portfolio Support,
- Telecommunications Support,
- Trade Processing,
- General Management Support,
- Facility-Sustaining Support.

Initial Reaction to Activity Costs

After accumulating expenses by activities and activity centers, the project team shared the new information with Steward's senior management. President Fred Benning reacted favorably to the activity expense information.

Exhibit 9-2
LABOR ACTIVITIES ALLOCATION FORM

Cost Center: Accounting and Finance
Number: 951
Manager: Peter Van Harlen

Staff Members	Accounts Payable	Payroll	Payroll Plan Related	Commissions Payable	Subsidiary Accounting & Regulatory	Inventory Accounts	Regulatory Filings	International Accounting	Gold Book	General Accounting	Tax Planning, Compliance, Admin. Audits	Partnership & JV Accounting	Financial Analysis for Management	External Reporting	Office Mg. Mail Distr. Banking Leases	Total
1. Allen, Christine									90.0%	10.0%						100.0%
2. Belling, Michael								70.0%		5.0%	5.0%	10.0%	5.0%	5.0%		100.0%
3. Brown, Eliza	100.0%															100.0%
4. Chang, Cuoi									8.0%	27.0%			60.0%	5.0%		100.0%
5. Dreher, Shake										100.0%						100.0%
6. Frye, Albert		80.0%	20.0%													100.0%
7. Hansen, Sheri													100.0%			100.0%
8. Hart, Linda									73.0%	27.0%						100.0%
9. Hutchins, Marcine	100.0%															100.0%
10. Kine, Kimberly					5.0%	5.0%	20.0%	5.0%		25.0%		5.0%	25.0%	10.0%		100.0%
11. Lawson, Alan		90.0%	10.0%													100.0%
12. Lewis, Tamy						15.0%	80.0%			5.0%						100.0%
13. Lozano, Joseph											80.0%		20.0%			100.0%
14. Meso, David									25.0%	75.0%						100.0%
15. Neal, Lawrence						100.0%										100.0%
16. Park, William	100.0%															100.0%
17. Ross, Wendy										20.0%			10.0%			100.0%
18. Seeby, Ajay		10.0%	40.0%	20.0%						20.0%			10.0%			100.0%
19. Swink, Patricia	10.0%														90.0%	100.0%
20. Strayer, Dana							10.0%			20.0%			50.0%	20.0%		100.0%
21. Scott, Mary					100.0%											100.0%
22. Theiman, David				100.0%												100.0%
23. Van Harlen, Peter	10.0%	15.0%		10.0%	10.0%					20.0%			30.0%	5.0%		100.0%
Total Per Activity	9.8%	7.5%	2.4%	5.0%	4.7%	4.3%	5.0%	4.0%	6.9%	17.3%	7.2%	0.9%	18.5%	3.4%	3.1%	100.0%

It was helpful to know the real cost of performing certain functions. This information gave a cross functional view of our expenses. There is much more visibility to our costs when they are grouped into a few key activities than when they are buried as expense categories in cost centers.

Scott stated:

It was very helpful to have a detailed understanding of what activities the various units performed. But management still needs to understand clearly how costs are assigned to these activities. Otherwise they will doubt the profitability numbers when the activity costs are allocated to products.

Some administrative managers did not understand what expenses were in their unit's cost center and how overhead expenses were allocated. Next time we conduct an expense analysis, managers will take the allocation of their time to the various activities more seriously so the analysis will be more accurate.

Cost Driver Identification and Analysis

The project team proceeded to the next stage of analysis, to develop the cost drivers that would drive the activity expenses down to products. Again, the project team met with managers in order to discuss the best way to measure the demand for their activity. Many broker/dealers had assumed their resources were consumed simply by volume of transactions. There was a great deal of discussion about what caused certain costs to occur.

Many costs turned out to be not trade related. For example, MIS charges, formerly allocated by the number of transactions per product, were assigned based on programming time, mainframe CPU usage, hardware usage for PCs, reports run, and, finally, a trade-processing related charge.

Similarly, the expenses for the Operations Department previously had been allocated on a per trade basis. The ABC analysis revealed activities that were: (1) account related (retail versus institutional, margin accounts versus cash accounts) (2) product related (some products required additional activities depending on the industry settlement practices), and (3) transaction driven. Exhibit 9-3 shows examples of cost drivers selected for various activities.

For the next task, the team collected data for the activity cost drivers. Sometimes information was not available for the driver identified. In

Exhibit 9-3

EXAMPLES OF COST DRIVERS

Cost Center	Activity	%	Driver
LA Branch Sales	Listed Trades	70.0%	Direct to Listed
	OTC Trades	20.0%	Direct to OTC
	Technology Trading	2.0%	Direct to Technology Trading
Institutional Sales/Marketing	Develop Equity Clients	50.0%	# of Listed & OTC Trades
	Develop Corporate Finance Clients	50.0%	Direct to Corporate
New Accounts	Documentation for Noninst.	35.7%	# of Noninstitutional Accounts
	Institutional Acct. Maint.	64.3%	# of Institutional Accounts
Operations	P&S – Send out Confirms	2.7%	# of Customer Trades
	P&S – CXL/Correct	2.6%	# of Cancels/Corrects and Back-Dated Trades

those cases, an alternative driver was selected or sample data were gathered. Scott said, "We did not have the groundwork in our systems to provide the information for many of the selected drivers. We had to improvise to get rough approximations to the drivers we wanted. For future studies, we need to develop methods to gather information that better reflects actual resource usage."

Information for the drivers came from Steward's trade database (for transaction counts), Steward's account master (for customer/account drivers), human resource data, Accounting's monthly commission report by AE, and estimates by managers on how their employees spent their time. Black recalled:

> It was very difficult to quantify how much time the AEs spent on the various products. We had always allocated expense to the products based on the revenue an AE brought to the product. For the ABC study, we had to rely on interviews to drive the expenses. The estimated time spent was fairly close to the revenue percentages for most products, which was good. Otherwise, product managers might have said, 'Do me a favor and don't try to sell my product.'

There was a great deal of discussion about which transaction volume counts to use. Steward's trade database counted trades differently than Accounting's did. Accounting's trade numbers came from transaction counts as billed on the commission database, while the operational database generated trade counts on trades that required data input for settlement or crossing purposes. Another issue arose when the team realized that the database associated trades with the executing area rather than solely by product. Steward decided to add another field to its trade database to make future data more accurate.

Reviewing the Results

The team used the Profit Manager software to develop an activity-based profit and loss statement by product. The results were presented as preliminary to Steward's management. Because many in the core management group had not been formally trained in activity-based cost management, the presentation included a brief background of ABC and described its benefits over traditional cost accounting.

Much of the data had been collected and calculated quickly to conform with the 12-week schedule of the project, so the data were not 100%

accurate. This fact concerned Mary Scott and others in the Accounting and Finance Department. However, Scott made a decision, along with the implementation team, to present the preliminary data to senior management. She said, "Although I did not feel comfortable with the accuracy of the data that had been initially collected and processed, I realized that senior management would not get engaged in the study unless some tentative, preliminary results were presented to them."

Product Profitability

Senior management expressed some immediate skepticism but also some acceptance of the ABC profit and loss numbers. Exhibit 9-4 compares net earnings from the ABC analysis with net earnings calculated in the traditional system.[2]

Exhibit 9-5 shows the net earnings from the ABC analysis in much more detail. The revenues and expenses listed in the box at the top of the exhibit were treated as direct expenses and hence were outside the scope of the study. Exhibit 9-5 shows that the firm's internal portfolio and client management system is used only by listed and OTC securities trading. It also reveals that data processing resources are used very differently by the various products.

Exhibit 9-6 shows that the two most profitable products—high-yield securities and equities—were subsidizing the other Steward products. This result was true under both the traditional and the ABC calculation. Equities was the original and core volume business for the firm; high yield was a relatively new line of business for Steward. Net earnings were compared to revenues for each of the products, as shown in Exhibit 9-7. These results forced management to question the unprofitable international and convertible businesses and to identify ways to make those businesses more profitable.

Cost Hierarchy

The analysis clearly showed that costs were not driven simply by the number of trades performed. The cost hierarchy in Exhibit 9-8 shows the costs that were trade related, those attributable to maintaining an account or an AE, and those attributable to a specific Steward product. This view of the firm's cost structure helped Steward management to understand the significant investment cost of bringing out a new product and helped to change their view that costs in a brokerage firm were mostly "fixed."

Exhibit 9-4
TRADITIONAL P&L VS. ABC P&L – BY SELECTED PRODUCTS
YTD DECEMBER 31, 1990 ($000)

	Listed	OTC	Options/ Futures	Technology Trading	Convertible	Euro- convertible	Int'l	Taxable Fixed Income	Corporate Finance
Traditional Net Earnings	$37,952	$4,924	$11,192	$2,335	($223)	$1,135	($1,353)	$28,048	$199
Traditional Net Earnings %	45%	6%	13%	3%	0%	1%	–2%	33%	0%
ABC Net Earnings	$25,942	$784	$10,151	$804	($989)	$48	($2,328)	$27,414	($504)
ABC Net Earnings %	42%	1%	17%	1%	–2%	0%	–4%	45%	–1%
Change in Profitability	($12,010)	($4,140)	($1,041)	($1,531)	($766)	($1,087)	($975)	($634)	($703)
Change in Profitability %	–32%	–84%	–9%	–66%	343%	–96%	72%	–2%	–353%

Exhibit 9-5
TRADITIONAL P&L VS. ABC P&L – BY SELECTED PRODUCTS
YTD DECEMBER 31, 1990 ($000)

	Listed	OTC	Options/ Futures	Technology Trading	Convertible	Euro-convertible	Int'l	Taxable Fixed Income	Corporate Finance
Total Revenues	$69,832	$19,464	$17,133	$11,555	$5,705	$3,254	$7,245	$44,999	$7,758
Dividends Paid	$1,377	$14	$43	$0	$396	$15	$365	$0	$0
Total Interest	$401	$184	$159	$0	$2,242	$232	$1,313	$2,099	$0
Expenses & Sales Comp	$12,470	$6,808	$1,640	$2,652	$1,786	$535	$1,582	$1,384	$788
Location Costs	$3,731	$3,042	$1,072	$4,124	$684	$1,044	$1,959	$12,025	$6,056
Clearing House	$237	$0	$482	$118	$0	$0	$0	$0	$0
Exchange & Execution	$325	$264	$381	$30	$0	$0	$107	$0	$0
Conversion Fees	$0	$0	$0	$0	$0	$0	$771	$0	$0
Floor Brokerage	$6,275	$0	$1,168	$378	$162	$54	$672	$51	$0
Subtotal – Direct Expenses	$24,816	$10,312	$4,945	$7,302	$5,270	$1,880	$6,769	$15,559	$6,844
Profit Before ABC Expenses	$45,016	$9,152	$12,188	$4,253	$435	$1,374	$476	$29,440	$914
Activity Center Expenses									
Sales Office & Support Activities	$7,334	$3,835	$323	$1,230	$249	$191	$828	$656	$252
Sales Promotion Activities	$4,873	$419	$45	$36	$35	$34	$54	$36	$38
Trade Comparison & Settlement	$1,225	$681	$372	$342	$124	$100	$555	$197	$3
Account Maintenance	$236	$88	$33	$87	$10	$2	$34	$10	$0
Human Resource Management	$159	$105	$22	$29	$4	$23	$23	$59	$50
Legal & Compliance Support	$577	$435	$321	$333	$272	$306	$301	$271	$423
AE Administration Support	$373	$183	$68	$18	$20	$21	$14	$12	$15
Accounting Support	$363	$309	$203	$203	$204	$173	$256	$170	$169
Data Processing	$944	$526	$82	$316	$18	$10	$87	$114	$11
Portfolio Management Support	$928	$500	$0	$0	$0	$0	$0	$0	$0
Telecommunications	$372	$175	$36	$18	$16	$15	$30	$20	$28
ADP Trade Processing	$1,193	$640	$105	$406	$54	$23	$195	$37	$0
General Management Support	$196	$196	$196	$196	$196	$196	$196	$196	$196
Facilities Sustaining Support	$301	$276	$231	$235	$222	$232	$231	$248	$233
Total ABC Costs	$19,074	$8,368	$2,037	$3,449	$1,424	$1,326	$2,804	$2,026	$1,418
ABC Net Earnings	$25,942	$784	$10,151	$804	($989)	$48	($2,328)	$27,414	($504)
ABC Net Earnings %	42%	1%	17%	1%	-2%	0%	-4%	45%	-1%

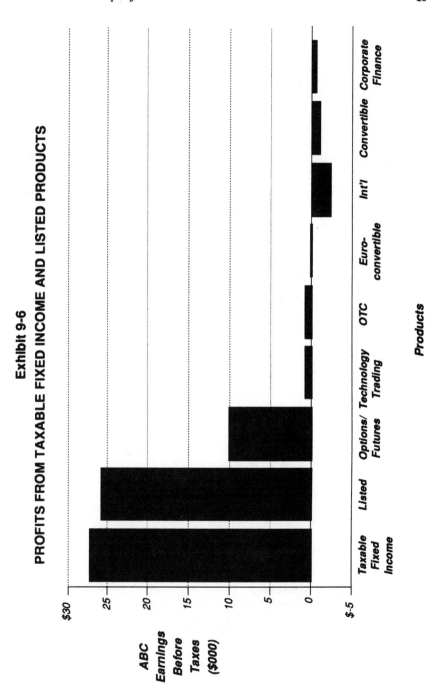

Exhibit 9-6

PROFITS FROM TAXABLE FIXED INCOME AND LISTED PRODUCTS

Cost Driver Analysis

Exhibit 9-9 shows that an activity such as settlement and comparison was used very differently, per dollar of revenue, by the different products. Complex products, such as international, with multiple currencies and locations for settlement, had the highest settlement costs.

Exhibit 9-10 shows the unit costs of selected cost drivers. The firm expected to use these unit costs as measures to drive performance improvement. For example, the cost driver analysis revealed the high cost of supplying the portfolio management system to account executives. The ABC analysis also provided Steward with the ability to measure performance and to identify where operating changes could cut expenses the most. For example, Exhibit 9-10 shows that exception

Exhibit 9-7
THE INTERNATIONAL AND CONVERTIBLES BUSINESS
TARGETED FOR PROFIT IMPROVEMENT

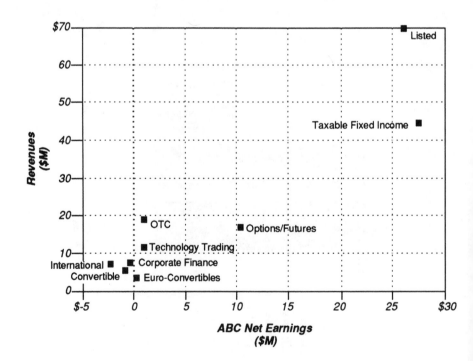

trades (transactions that had to be corrected or canceled and reentered) cost $8.57 or seven times as much to process as automated trades, which cost $1.23 per trade. This illustrated the high potential value from doing trades right the first time. Exhibit 9-11 shows in further detail the percent of exception trades by product.

In addition to concentrating on driving down the number of exceptions and the cost to correct errors, Fred Benning wanted to reduce the cost of processing the automated trades because those trades were the high-volume activity.

Exhibit 9-8
COST LEVERAGE AND TRADE

Steward Cost Hierarchy*

Facility Sustaining 24.1%
Product Costs 24.8%   Cost per Product = $1,155,000
Account/AE Costs 38.5%   Cost per Account = $235
Trade/Ticket Costs 12.7%   Cost per Ticket = $10

* Includes only ABC analyzed costs

Exhibit 9-9

PRODUCT CONSUMPTION OF COMPARISON AND SETTLEMENT COSTS

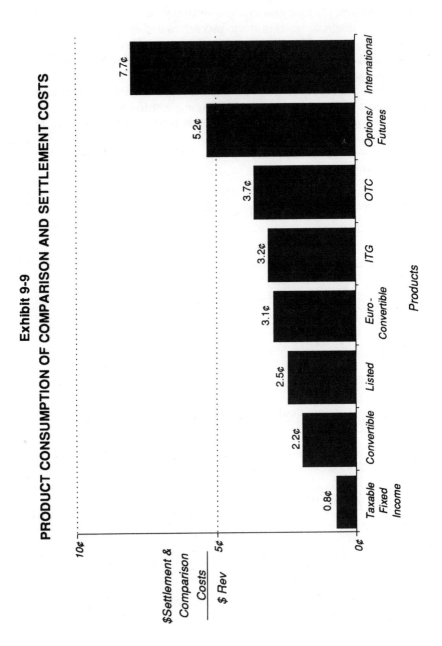

AE Profitability Results

P&L statements were produced for nine representative AEs—three of the top producers (based on commission dollars), three middle producers,

Exhibit 9-10
COST PER UNIT DRIVER

Activity Cost*	Drive	Cost per Unit
Portfolio Management System	# of AEs	$18,544.00
Registrations	# of AE Hires	$12,311.13
AE-Related Reports & Acct	# of AEs	$2,853.68
Human Resources	Headcount	$1,537.50
Telecom System Maintenance	# of Telecom Lines	$603.74
Human Resources	# of New Hires & Terminations	$370.25
Noninstitutional Acct Maintenance	# of Noninstitutional Accts	$12.92
Soft Dollars	# of Listed Trades	$11.29
Trade Comparison Exceptions	# of Exceptions	$8.57
Listed Research	# of Listed Trades	$6.62
Institutional Acct Maintenance	# of Institutional Accts	$2.99
Trade Comparison Automated	# of Trades	$1.23

* Includes only ABC costs

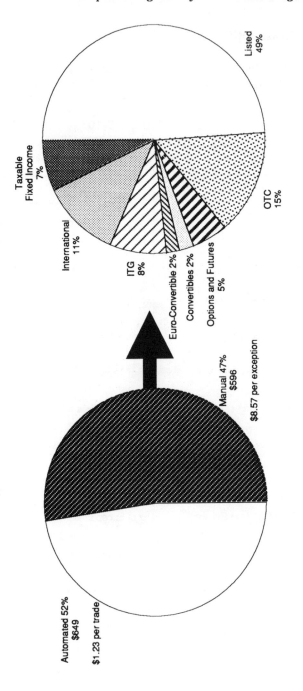

Exhibit 9-11
PROCESSED TRADE
EXCEPTION BASIS VS. AUTOMATIC PROCESSING

and three low-volume producers. Exhibit 9-12 is the P&L statement for a high-volume AE. The diagram in Exhibit 9-13 shows that the AE breakeven point depends on trade volume and AE branch location. Exhibit 9-14 shows the different percentage usage of activities and services among three AEs. For example, Ortland had the highest trade count, so his trade comparison and settlement and outsourced trade processing costs were much higher than those for the other two AEs. Hunter's clients used research information extensively, so his research expenses were high.

Management Acceptance of ABC Results

Fred Benning said the ABC results did not surprise him, but they triggered some organizational decisions:

I realized the core products—listed equity securities, listed options and futures, international, and over-the-counter securities—were not really separate businesses. We had thought of them as separate businesses, which led to a separate management structure and many arbitrary allocations. Now those products have been combined into a single equity profit center so that we can look at the profitability, in total, for those four products. The function of that group is to maximize the income of the sales force, not the income from four separate products. We have also decided to spin off ITG into a separate subsidiary. The better expense allocations helped us reach this decision.

I also found the P&Ls for the AEs quite helpful. I would eventually like the ABC system to treat each AE as an individual profit center. AEs, when they logged in a transaction at their workstations, would have their profitability and productivity calculated. This would get them to focus on who they are calling and what kind of returns they are generating. If we could implement this type of measurement system, we could eliminate a lot of administrative and managerial structure that costs money and occupies space. But it would be difficult to think about decentralizing like this without the improved measurement and accountability from an ABC system.

Larry Black was also enthusiastic about the AE profitability results:

The ABC study revealed the average breakeven point for an AE was $325,000 in gross commissions. This was a much higher number than we had assumed. Based on these results, I developed a ranking and classification of marginal or unprofitable AEs: (1) new hires—expect business to

Exhibit 9-12
STEWARD COMPANY ABC A/E P/L STATEMENT
ORTLAND ($000)

Revenues			
	Gross Commissions	$2,825	
	Trade Adjustments	76	
	Total		$2,901
"Direct Expenses"		$961	
"Indirect Expenses"		$674	
ABC Expenses			
	Branch Expenses	153	
	Sales Promotion	11	
	Trade Comparison & Settlement	92	
	Account Maintenance	2	
	Human Resource Management	1	
	Legal & Compliance Support	30	
	AE Administration Support	6	
	Accounting Support	9	
	Data Processing Support	68	
	Portfolio Management Systems Support	19	
	Telecommunications	3	
	Trade Processing	90	
	General Management Support	9	
	Facilities Sustaining Support	5	
	Total ABC Expenses	$498	
Total Expenses			(2,133)
Net Profit			$768

Exhibit 9-13
AE BREAKEVEN POINT

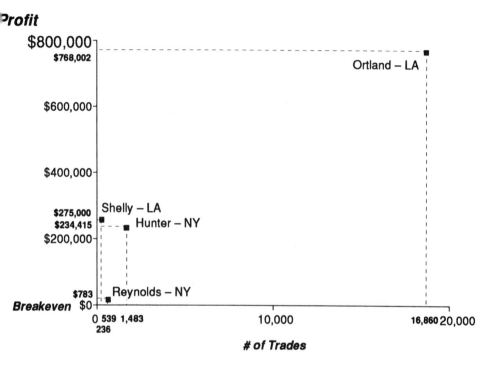

Profit

$800,000
$768,002

Ortland – LA

$600,000

$400,000

$275,000 Shelly – LA
$234,415 Hunter – NY
$200,000

$783 Reynolds – NY
Breakeven $0

0 539 1,483   10,000   16,860 20,000
236

# of Trades

grow in the future, (2) strategic—important linkage to other lines of business, (3) isolated—does special or unique trades, (4) all others. Unprofitable AEs who do not fall into one of the special categories may be asked to
leave. By looking at the activity expenses associated with each AE, I have
better insight into the avoidable expenses if an AE leaves.

In addition to having responsibility for the AEs, I manage the core products. ABC showed me which were the most profitable. The information,
while not entirely new, forced me to make a few decisions because it
focused me on what activities and products bring in revenue. The ABC
study also helped me think about the fee splitting issue—how much time
the AEs were spending on non-core products and how my department
should be compensated for that time commitment. Previously, we deducted
only 30% of the commission revenues to compensate the AE who generated
the business. The product manager received the other 70%. Now we've

Exhibit 9-14
HIGHEST RANKING ACTIVITIES
AS A % OF TOTAL ABC EXPENSES

	Ortland	*Hunter*	*Reynolds*
Sales Office and Support	31%	38%	49%
Trade Comparison & Settlement	19%	6%	4%
ADP Trade Processing	18%	4%	2%
Data Processing Support	14%	3%	1%
Legal & Compliance Support	6%	2%	2%
Portfolio Management Systems	4%	9%	12%
Soft Dollars, Research	2%	21%	7%
General Management Support	2%	5%	6%
Accounting Support	2%	4%	5%
AE Administration Support	1%	4%	6%
Facilities Sustaining Support	1%	3%	3%
Telecommunications Maintenance	1%	–	2%
Account Maintenance	–	1%	1%
Human Resource Management	–	1%	1%

assigned an additional 10% to the sales or execution department to support the additional activities they have to do to get the business.

Steward attempted to limit its losses in the international business by restricting the types of trades that would be allowed. Previously, the International Department had been using the firm's capital base for overnight trading and arbitrage, but this activity required a minimum complement of people in the United States and in Europe. The ABC study had revealed the high cost, in people, capital, and data processing, of performing international transactions. Senior management decided to minimize overnight trading and do international trades only for brokerage customers who would also generate the more profitable equity and OTC business.

Ron Knight, director of ITG, expressed skepticism about the initial results, however:

> I don't believe the allocation process was that accurate. Maybe the consulting team was not that familiar with our people and business and the interviews may have resulted in distorted information. For example, ITG received a high allocation of MIS costs. I believe the production and support of ITG is less expensive than the ABC analysis shows. Maybe negotiation with the unit when they are allocating resources and time would be a better way to get insight into the actual costs. That way, all parties involved could agree on the resources that are being provided and consumed. Another concern I have with the results is that they show the operational cost to process a manual trade is basically the same as the processing of an electronic trade from our automated trading system. I can't really believe that is the case.

Despite some questioning of the numbers, the ITG business was spun off into a separate subsidiary after the initial ABC study had been completed. Knight admitted:

> The ABC study played a major role in the decision to spin off ITG. The analysis forced us to take a more detailed look at product line P&Ls. The review showed that the ITG business had little in common with all the other product lines we offered.Within ITG, I have begun to assign revenues and assets to individual products. This has already led to a decision not to support a particular product that was heavily analytic and demanded a fair degree of assets and other support resources.
>
> Managers are also now poring over their monthly P&L statements much more carefully. The monthly statements have not yet changed to the ABC format, but managers now believe they can better understand and affect the assigned expenses. Before, our overhead charge for G&A seemed like a management slush fund. We now see the actual components of the expenses for the first time and understand our costs better. We can make better decisions about outsourcing certain support services and whether we want to offer certain products or provide certain services.

ABC Aids in Understanding Expenses

Andrew Bane, chief administrative officer, said:

> I liked the rationale for ABC but some of the number collection strategies

were flawed. For example, the team pulled some of the data from our front-end database. However, the product codes on the database are based on the executing area rather than actual product that is traded. This means revenues are not always linked with expenses if we use that product code. Also, the database trade count numbers are different from the ones the finance group has used, which caused some inconsistencies. I believe we can gather better, more accurate drivers in the next iteration. The study did cause us to begin to look at the activities needed to perform a function rather than at the actual expenses incurred by an organizational group.

Mary Scott described her reactions to the study:

Obviously, I was already very familiar with the expenses and who used what services, so I was not that surprised. But I did find it interesting to see how MIS expenses were assigned. Expenses in MIS had increased significantly over the past years and it was not clear to me who benefitted from the growth in systems resources. ABC helped to reveal this large infrastructure and that it is not free. We can now see how different parts of MIS are used by AEs and products, and have a basis for judging the value of this resource to them. The product P&Ls also got management's attention. Some liked the numbers and were happy, but others challenged the study's results. Some of the costs had been assigned equally to all products, which led to some distortion of the numbers. For example, ITG was a new product and had only been in existence for four months.

As chief financial officer, Scott saw additional benefits from the ABC study, stating:

The study helped senior management see what issues the Accounting and Finance departments had been struggling with to assign costs. ABC got everyone involved in the financial exercise to see what expenses related to different activities and products. Senior management got a sense of the nature of the challenge. Actually, with the information the cost accounting group had available to them, they were doing a great job. ABC helped us all realize that to do a better job we needed to invest more in systems.

Where is ABC Going at Steward?

When asked about next steps, Fred Benning replied:

The ABC analysis should be able to give us a profile of account profitability.

We have 1,600 major customers. I suspect that 1,100 of these are marginal or unprofitable and 500 are profitable, of which only 50 are really important to us. We need to know if our services are only worthwhile when they are mispriced and Steward loses money on the transaction. AEs are paid commissions on each trade they make, whether the trade is profitable or not. Account profitability will show us who we're making money on and to which customers we can add value.

Also, ABC should help everyone in the company have a better understanding of how the company's financials work. In the past we have kept headcount growth down in operations and accounting by applying technology. Support people and AEs will need to behave more like business partners and understand the impact their activities and costs have on the organization. The ABC profitability approach will definitely keep everyone more focused on the bottom line.

Larry Black concurred. "I, too, would like to see profitability by account. Now that we have a better understanding of where our costs are, the next key step is also to look at where we can reduce costs."

Ron Knight said he would like to use the information to make decisions on new products:

We have never known the costs of getting into new businesses. ABC should allow us to make better decisions about how to use our key asset—capital. When analyzing new projects, we can also look more carefully at their impact on manpower needs and profitability potential. It will generate a lot more discussion about profitability, not just about how new ideas can lead to more revenues.

Andrew Bane said the ABC study made him more determined to get the costs assigned more accurately to the various areas.

I see us spinning off the operations and administrative units into a separate department and then selling these functions to the units on a price basis. This will force these services to offer competitive services and prices. ABC will give us the information we need to make this happen.

Next Steps

Steward was starting to integrate the ABC methodology into their monthly financial statements. Several systems issues had to be solved to facilitate timely and accurate collection of data. The firm had hired a staff person in the Finance Department to work full-time on ABC database issues.

In the next iteration of the ABC model development, the group refined the activity analysis and gathered more accurate cost driver data. The project group also expanded the scope of costs covered in the ABC analysis to include all telecommunication and quotation expenses and did a more accurate assignment of MIS expenses received from the (outsourced) data processing vendor. Mary Scott summed up the progress to date. "I think we have just begun to realize the value that ABC can provide us. Fred Benning wants to use the ABC-based profitability report next year to drive compensation. That will get everyone to pay a lot of attention to the numbers!" she said.

Notes

[1] In a subsequent update of the model, these expenses were driven more accurately down to individual products and AEs.

[2] The ABC-calculated profitability for all products was lower than with the traditional P&L approach because the ABC analysis could drive many more expenses, such as branch expenses, to products than could the traditional method. Steward's management, in addition to noting the breakeven nature of many of its products, also observed significant shifts in the relative profitability of its products. For example, the traditional P&L showed listed trading and Euro-convertible trading as almost equally profitable, while the ABC analysis showed that the profit margin on listed trading actually was more than 10 percentage points higher than for Euro-convertible.

Chapter 10

Slade Manufacturing, Inc.: Hudson Automotive Parts Company

Executive Summary

In early 1990, the management group at Hudson Automotive Parts Company (HAP) found themselves in an unenviable position. On one hand, their customers, primarily the Big 3 automobile manufacturers, were in the process of reducing their supplier bases, which meant intense pressure to be cost and price competitive. On the other hand, Slade Manufacturing, Inc. (SMI), HAP's parent company, was in dire need of short-term cash flow from its operating divisions. At the time of the activity-based costing project, the parent company was in the final stages of an aggressive growth and diversification strategy, which was accomplished primarily through highly leveraged acquisitions. In this turbulent environment, Slade's management selected Hudson Automotive Parts Company to be the pilot site for implementing activity-based costing. HAP, one of Slade Manufacturing's larger operating companies, historically had been a source of cash for the parent company but recently had experienced declining profits and cash flows. The activity-based costing implementation effort produced three different types of benefits:

- The ABC analysis produced more accurate product costs and gave management new insight into the actual cost of producing particular products and serving specific customers. The implementation effort validated management's view that "all customers were not created equal" and provided invaluable leverage during difficult negotiations with an important Big 3 customer.
- Division management gained insight into the underlying cost drivers of their business. In particular, the ABC analysis highlighted the cost of maintaining older, fully depreciated capital equipment and perishable tooling. ABC analyses also highlighted

the costs of quality and guided management to pay more attention to prevention and appraisal activities to reduce failure costs.

- Finally, ABC data served as a key input for developing a new quote system. Today, quotes are developed for customers based on activity-based product costs. Division management recently used this new system to quote a major bid (in excess of $30 million) to an important customer.

Company Background

Slade Manufacturing, Inc, a Fortune 500 company, is a conglomerate of manufacturing companies whose sales range from $30 to $150 million. SMI was founded in the early 1900s as a processed goods manufacturing concern. Throughout its history the company grew primarily through acquisition. By 1990, the company was organized into three primary business groups: Automotive, Industrial, and Machinery (Exhibit 10-1 outlines the Slade Manufacturing, Inc. business unit structure).

In early 1990, Slade Manufacturing's corporate management was completing its aggressive growth and diversification strategy. However, its automotive businesses, which contributed more than 40% of corporate revenues, were facing a significant slowdown in business to

Exhibit 10-1

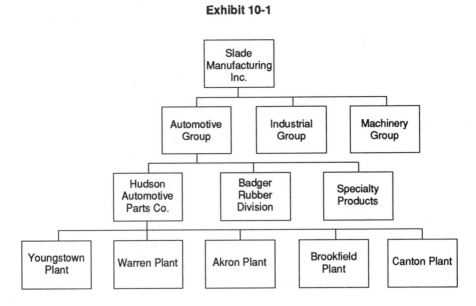

levels well below breakeven. In addition, the company had taken on a significant amount of highly leveraged debt, primarily "junk bonds," to fund its acquisitions during the latter half of the 1980s. In order to alleviate the high cost of debt service, it was critical for management to restructure this junk bond debt through more traditional financing sources such as equity and bond markets and banks. Unfortunately, these traditional sources were not so readily available as a result of the continuing savings and loan bailout crisis and the overly aggressive lending practices of the 1980s. Management would need significant improvement in its short-term cash flows to avoid a restructuring that might include more than just its junk bond debt.

Slade's management critically evaluated the cash flow contributions of all operating units and directed division presidents to improve financial performance immediately. Bill Carlisle, Slade's controller, recognized the demanding competitive requirements facing all divisions, but particularly the automotive divisions, and wanted to be prepared to compete in this environment. Carlisle maintained:

> The automotive industry is unique, a completely different ball game compared to markets in our Industrial or Machinery Groups. It's critical that you understand your costs in the automotive marketplace. Yet, in a number of our Automotive Group companies we have no idea what it really costs to make our products. Without this knowledge, we cannot compete effectively as an automotive supplier. Across the Automotive Group our cost systems were not up to par. It was an area we really needed to improve—and that's what first led us to ABC.

Aware of the weak financial performance of several of its operating companies, and with shareholders and institutional investors eager for a debt restructuring plan, management took a hard look at internal operations. Slade Manufacturing's long-term strategies depended on the cash-generating capabilities of its relatively autonomous, financially erratic operating companies. Senior Slade managers demanded short-term cash flow from division presidents as well as clearly defined plans to improve longer-term profitability.

Slade Manufacturing Automotive Group

Automotive Group sales of approximately $410 million are highly concentrated among the Big 3 U.S. automotive manufacturers, with one customer representing the greatest part of revenues. Slade Automotive

Group competes against a variety of domestic and transplanted companies to supply component parts to automotive assembly companies. Competition for this business is intense, with success determined primarily by quality, price, and delivery reliability.

During the past 20 years, growth in the Slade Automotive Group was sustained through acquisition of small family-owned manufacturing companies. Over time, the Automotive Group evolved to become a conglomerate of highly autonomous, completely decentralized manufacturing companies that competed in a variety of automotive industry segments. Business lines included: stampings, fuel systems, electrical assemblies, engine components, transmission components and assemblies, and rubber products. As the Automotive Group acquired companies, management made a conscious decision to rely on the expertise of local operating company management teams. Relatively few organizational changes were made when a company was acquired, and few corporate policies or standards were implemented.

The decision to run acquired companies in a decentralized, autonomous fashion shaped the operating philosophies, company cultures, and management practices across the Automotive Group. At the plant level, managers and employees considered themselves employees of the local company; they perceived little connection to Slade Manufacturing, Inc. Signs and displays at Automotive Group plant sites often displayed the local company's name and logo more prominently than Slade Manufacturing, Inc.

The independent cultures of Automotive Group companies manifested themselves in a variety of ways. Labor contracts were negotiated on a company-by-company basis; responsibility for negotiations and contract administration rested with local company presidents. Each company conducted purchasing, research, application engineering, and testing activities independently. Accounting practices and performance reporting systems were also unique to each company. Cost systems ranged from simple, single-basis overhead allocation systems to "sophisticated" multistage mainframe systems.

With their much higher share of Slade's overall business, the performance of the individual Automotive Group companies was now key to the corporation's success. Slade corporate executives were acutely aware of this fact. At the same time, they recognized the significant organizational impediments they would encounter when trying to realize the large-magnitude, short-term performance improvements they needed.

Historically, corporate had minimal involvement at the business unit or plant level. Any initial attempts to standardize management information systems and performance reporting had met resistance. In the words of Jim Carpenter, Automotive Group president:

> We've always allowed the companies to operate autonomously—it's been the company president's business to run. But today we have a different environment. Cooperation from our company presidents is essential. The only way we will succeed is with their support. Unless performance improves, and soon, our presidents may get some 'help' from corporate. In fact, a year from now we may not have a presence in all the markets where we compete today.

Activity-Based Costing: Initial Motivation

Slade Manufacturing's move toward more automotive-oriented businesses raised the need for improved cost systems across the corporation. Carlisle, Slade's controller, recognized the unique competitive dynamics in the automotive industry and foresaw the need to improve cost systems in all the Automotive Group companies.

As a first step, Carlisle hired Larry Martin in July 1989 to fill a newly created position, controller for the Slade Automotive Group. Carlisle gave Martin one mandate: improve cost accounting systems across all Automotive Group companies. Martin also was instructed to earn the respect of operating company presidents and establish links between corporate and the local company levels. These relationships were to lay important groundwork for performance improvement initiatives that would follow over a longer horizon.

Prior to assuming this position, Martin had worked for a large public accounting and consulting firm, where he had been exposed to activity-based costing concepts. Martin spent his first few months on the job familiarizing himself with Automotive Group company operations. He commented on the state of affairs he found in the operating companies.

> Things were a mess out there. Company-level controllers were viewed as bean counters rather than as resources to the company presidents. In some cases this perception was justified. Our controllers and plant accountants 'ran the numbers' and published financial reports with little regard for business issues or the needs of operating managers. Reports were late, numbers didn't tie, and formats were unintelligible. At best, we provided accounting data but definitely not actionable management information.

During his first eight months, Martin met continually with the various operating companies to become familiar with the group's operations. After this orientation, he met with Carlisle to develop a plan of action. Martin recommended activity-based costing as the tool to accomplish his short and longer-term mandates (to improve cost systems and to establish relations between operating companies). Martin explained:

> Given the state of affairs in the operating companies and the urgent need to improve performance, we didn't have the time or resources to start with a clean slate. Developing and implementing entirely new accounting systems would require mainframe computer systems and cash resources we didn't have. Such a strategy would have demanded a full-time commitment of skilled people we could not afford.
>
> Another option was to fix the problems with our existing accounting systems. That seemed like an equally daunting task. It would require computer systems and programming skills on a order of magnitude similar to the clean-slate approach. And quite frankly, given what I'd read about the limits of traditional accounting systems, it seemed somewhat like rearranging chairs on the deck of the Titanic.

In the end, Carlisle and Martin decided that a stand-alone PC-based ABC system was the best alternative. The PC system could operate independently of the many inadequate plant-level systems, and implementation would require less pure "systems" skill. Carlisle and Martin were both familiar with ABC principles and agreed that external research and some internal assessments would be required. Together, they devised their preliminary implementation plan.

Hudson Automotive Parts Company

Carlisle and Martin selected Hudson Automotive Parts Company, the largest company in the group, as the short-term target for implementing activity-based costing. Pretax profits had stagnated after two successive years of improvement. Any significant improvements in Hudson's operating performance would yield important short-term returns to the company as a whole.

Hudson was historically a profitable operation, with pretax profits ranging from a high of 12.8% in 1986 to a low of 1.5% in 1989 (Exhibit 10-2 presents HAP financial data). Hudson's plants produced a wide array of machined products for use in automotive applications. Products included gears, flanges, pinions, and metal housings, manufactured at five facilities in northeastern Ohio. Hudson's competitive position depended on purchasing and machining cast metal components at lower conversion cost than their competitors' cost would be.

Hudson employed approximately 1,400 people in its various plants. The work force at HAP facilities was unionized and highly experienced. Employees averaged 20 years seniority, always in the same facility and generally within the same department. Wages were comparable to those in other manufacturing companies in the area, and employee turnover had not been a problem. Relations with local unions were cordial. The company had not experienced organized strikes or work stoppages. Production facilities were between five and 25 years old and had been maintained well. Process technologies ranged from state-of-the-art machinery to fully depreciated, high-maintenance equipment. New equipment had been acquired when justified by financial analysis. Old equipment remained in service as long as it performed adequately. No significant improvements or capacity additions were planned.

Exhibit 10-2
CONSOLIDATED OPERATING STATISTICS

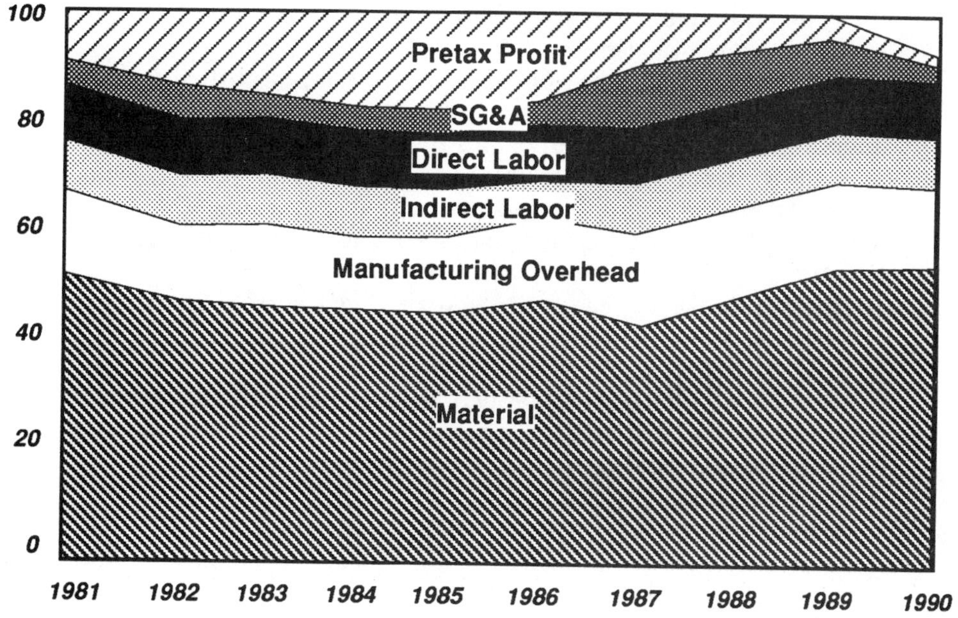

Competition in Automotive and Auto Parts Markets

Throughout 1989 and 1990, U.S. automotive original equipment manufacturers (OEMs) encountered lower overall production volumes because of a sluggish U.S. economy and a continuing loss of market share to imports. The industry downturn was exacerbated by the increasing production of Japanese transplants operating in the United States. North American production of foreign models increased dramatically despite relatively soft sales volumes for the industry overall.

New car production rose slightly in the third quarter of 1990 but only when compared to low year-earlier levels. The fourth quarter saw sharp cutbacks in production—even lower than the dismal fourth quarter of 1989. Fourth-quarter reductions were sparked by higher oil prices and uncertainty following Iraq's occupation of Kuwait.

Auto parts companies generally produce for three market segments: original equipment manufacturers (parts and accessories for new autos); replacement or aftermarket parts and accessories; and nonautomotive products. OEM sales are the backbone of many large manufacturers' businesses, although most of the companies also produce parts for the higher-margin aftermarket. Key success factors for parts makers include the demand for new vehicles, retention or expansion of contracts with the Big 3, and the ability to obtain profitable new contracts from Japanese transplant manufacturers.

Parts makers tend to specialize in producing components that require a high degree of skill and efficiency, an area in which they have a cost advantage over the parts divisions of auto companies. The parts companies can spread their capital outlays over several contracts and generally operate with lower labor costs than the OEMs. The parts makers, however, do not enjoy this same cost advantage against other independent parts suppliers, who generally operate at cost parity.

The introduction of new, pricier, and more sophisticated systems on cars represented one favorable trend for some parts makers. Increased demand for safety options was another plus. Automakers found that customers were willing to pay for more sophisticated and safety-related options. Motorized seat belts, driver-side passive restraint systems, and antilock brakes were of particular interest to prospective buyers.

Increased pressures from domestic automakers presented formidable challenges as well. Big 3 producers demanded improved quality and lower production costs. At the same time, domestic producers were rationalizing their supplier bases, sourcing parts from fewer, more technologically capable suppliers. In return for price concessions, the Big

3 promised closer relationships with suppliers and participation in the design process.

Excess capacity in the industry also affected parts makers. U.S. parts makers competed with approximately 300 foreign parts companies that were establishing factories in the United States to supply Japanese transplants. The factories under construction were capable of producing parts well in excess of Japanese transplants' needs. These foreign-owned facilities already were competing actively for parts contracts from the U.S. Big 3. The parts market was relatively fragmented but consolidating. Market competitors ranged from small second-tier suppliers to divisions of first-tier Fortune 500 companies such as TRW, Eaton, Federal-Mogul, Rockwell International, Dana, United Technologies, ITT, and Arvin Industries.

The Big 3 manufacturers had placed intense pressure on their suppliers in the late 1980s, and this pressure was intensifying in early 1990 at the time of the ABC implementation project. HAP was confronted with the prospect of signing supply contracts with Big 3 customers that committed the company to annual price reductions over the course of a contract. In addition, the contract provisions called for annual material, efficiency, and productivity savings. Hudson could share in 50% of the savings during the first contract year; all savings for the remaining four years were to be "passed on" to the customer.

Previous experience with these supply agreements showed a predictable pattern. The overall product line grew over the life of the contract, with a dramatic increase in the number of low-volume products. Prices were unaffected by the product line proliferation because management used a standard cost system as an estimating and product pricing tool. The management group rationalized the product changes and modifications by maintaining that "at least these products provided an outlet to spread the company's fixed costs."

At the same time, however, HAP management recognized that the give-backs were killing their margins. As one said, "Essentially, the Big 3 customers were taking our margins. We weren't realizing any efficiency gains yet we had to pass on the contractually specified savings to our customers."

ABC at Hudson Automotive Parts

In this environment of intense external competitive pressure and increasing cash flow and profitability demands from corporate management, Slade Automotive Group and Hudson Automotive Parts

Company weighed the cost and benefits of implementing activity-based costing as a management tool. Carlisle and Martin met with the HAP management team to discuss the benefits of implementing ABC. In March 1990, Larry Martin met with the HAP president and his staff to discuss activity-based costing. His presentation was not received enthusiastically. In fact, HAP management expressed considerable skepticism about the value of implementing ABC and questioned the timing, given prevailing business conditions. Further, HAP managers, like those at other autonomous operating companies, were not particularly impressed with this unanticipated and uninvited offer of "help" from corporate staff.

The HAP reaction caused Larry Martin to regroup and devise another course of action. He was determined to demonstrate the benefits of ABC in terms that would persuade the HAP management group. Martin understood ABC concepts and was frustrated that his first attempt to sway HAP had failed. After some thought he realized that actual experience, above all, carried weight with operating company managers. Martin reasoned that he would need someone experienced in ABC to convince Hudson management to implement the new approach. But this was no small task because ABC was a relatively new concept, and few companies had actually implemented an ABC system.

Martin worked through industry relations, professional accounting associations, and contacts at his prior employer's to identify an experienced ABC practitioner. In April 1990, he met Jon Curran, a consulting partner with a large public accounting firm. Curran had implemented activity-based costing in a variety of manufacturing companies and brought experience and credibility that might persuade Hudson's management team. Subsequently, Curran met with HAP management and discussed the wide range of industries and issues where ABC had proved valuable.

Martin's plan proved successful. The breadth and depth of examples that Curran related during the meeting persuaded HAP management that ABC was a powerful management tool. But Hudson managers were concerned about the human and cash resources required to implement the ABC system.

After some discussion, Martin and Carlisle reached an agreement with HAP management. One HAP plant site would serve as a pilot location for an ABC implementation effort conducted under the guidance of an outside consulting team. In return, Slade Manufacturing would share one-half of the cost of the consulting fees, and Larry Martin would serve as a full-time resource for the 16-week engagement.

Selecting a Pilot Site

Carlisle, Martin, and HAP management, in a subsequent meeting, selected the HAP Youngstown plant as the pilot site for the ABC implementation effort. Youngstown was selected for several reasons:

- Its importance to Hudson Automotive's financial performance made the plant a likely candidate. HAP was experiencing a decline in revenues and margins. The Youngstown plant represented about 25% of HAP's revenues so profit improvements at this plant would affect HAP's overall performance significantly.
- After a period of sustained unprofitability, the Youngstown plant had shown improved financial performance (see Exhibits 10-3 and 10-4). Activity-based costing would help to build on recent performance improvements.
- Several key business issues provided a "mandate" to understand cost dynamics at the Youngstown plant. A large-dollar, five-year contract was due to be negotiated with a customer, and ABC data were regarded as fundamental to developing a competitive bid on the contract.
- A key customer was threatening to "revoke" the Youngstown plant's preferred supplier rating.
- Finally, the plant had experienced a dramatic proliferation of new but apparently "margin-contributing" parts in recent years.

Youngstown Plant

The Youngstown plant produced a broad line of machined metal products in nine product families and 63 end items. Product families at the facility included: gears, armatures, pinions, covers, flanges, valves, supports, housings, and filters. Sales of one product line—gears—accounted for approximately 36% of the company's revenues (see Exhibit 10-5 for sales across the nine product families). The production volumes varied enormously across the 63 end items, ranging from under 100 units to several million units per year.

Youngstown's 20-year-old production facility contained approximately 150,000 square feet of space. Proprietary process technologies and specialized assets were used to produce machined products. Processes spanned a wide continuum, from automated and relatively machine-intensive operations to manual and direct labor-intensive operations. Machinery in the Youngstown plant was highly specialized and

Exhibit 10-3
YOUNGSTOWN PLANT SALES 1988–1990
(in millions)

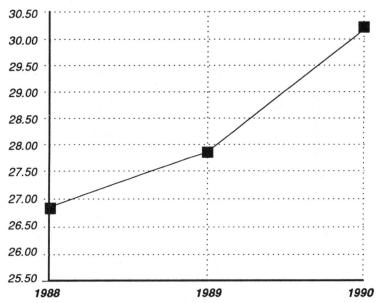

product-line specific. Products manufactured at Youngstown were exclusively for Youngstown plant customers. No interfacility transfers were made to other HAP sites.

Gears, the high-volume product, were manufactured in several discrete process steps. Machined steel, the primary raw material, was received through a central receiving department. Next, steel components were inspected for visual and measured characteristics. Steel parts were delivered to manufacturing departments upon requisition from a production scheduler or the department foreman. Steel components proceeded through a series of eight distinct manufacturing operations to produce a finished gear.

Each of the products was manufactured in a self-contained work cell. In-process inspectors made visual and measured checks to gears at selected stages of these eight manufacturing steps. Statistical process control data were collected and monitored on some of the high-volume products.

Youngstown employed approximately 300 direct hourly employees;

Exhibit 10-4
YOUNGSTOWN PLANT COST STRUCTURE

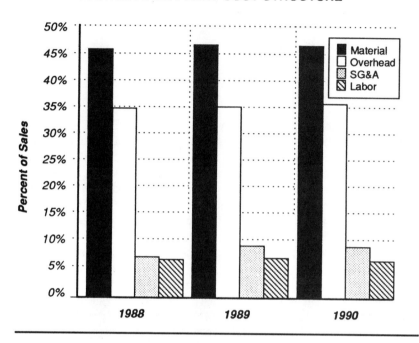

Exhibit 10-5
YOUNGSTOWN PLANT SALES BY PRODUCT LINE

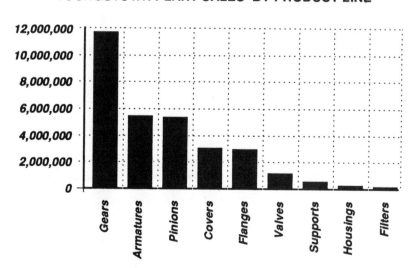

another 125 were employed in indirect support functions such as quality inspection. Skilled trades and other direct hourly employees were represented by a local chapter of a national union. The plant production required a broad spectrum of employee skills. These skills ranged from those possessed by highly trained tool-and-die craftsmen to the less skill-intensive jobs of assembly operators.

Initiating the ABC Project

Martin arranged a meeting in May 1990 with Bud Cramer, the Youngstown plant manager, and his direct reporting staff, to "sell" them on accepting the offer for an ABC pilot implementation at the plant. Martin was more than a little concerned about this meeting. He was not sure how the plant staff would respond. He had worked hard to build his credibility at the Youngstown plant over the past few months, and he hated to diminish the progress he had made. He also remembered the difficult "sell" at HAP.

Martin liked to say, "You rarely get a second chance to make a good first impression."

Jon Curran and Larry Martin presented ABC at the plant staff meeting, and Martin was extremely satisfied with the results. The plant team expressed fewer reservations than had the HAP management group. In fact, the concepts and proposed working arrangement were well received by the management group. Plant Manager Bud Cramer described his feelings:

> We were under intense pressure to improve quality and performance. Corporate was looking for more margins and cash flow while our customers wanted price reductions. We knew that we were struggling with our cost accounting system. It spit out numbers that weren't consistent with our intuition, but we had no other choice. Then along comes the ABC project team and they tell us our intuition had been right!
>
> As I look back, timing was another important factor in our decision process. We were facing a large dollar bid on a contract for our biggest customer. We'd seen the results of past bids based on standard costs, and we weren't happy at all. The ABC system promised more accurate costs. It would give us another tool that promised answers consistent with our intuition.

At this first plant-level meeting, Cramer gave approval for the implementation effort to begin immediately.

Implementation at HAP Youngstown Plant

A project steering committee was established. It included:

- HAP President Scott Springer,
- HAP Manufacturing Manager Tom Tarka,
- HAP Vice President Finance Brian McKeon,
- HAP Vice President Purchasing Lisa Smith,
- HAP Vice President Sales & Marketing George Laflin,
- Youngstown Plant Manager Bud Cramer,
- Consulting Partner Jon Curran,
- Consulting Senior Manager Stan Blaylock.

Working with Cramer, Springer, and the consultants, Martin formalized the role of the steering committee at a first meeting. The group would guide the ABC effort, providing input to the project team at a mid-project meeting. The group also would participate in a hands-on final meeting to analyze recommendations and determine and authorize subsequent actions. Martin established the project team at the plant and defined the team members' roles. The project team included Larry Martin, Bud Cramer, and Nick Gamble, the Youngstown plant accountant. In addition the consulting firm supplied Jon Curran, Stan Blaylock, and Eric Meyers, a staff consultant.

Larry Martin served as a full-time resource and project leader. In this role, he coordinated team meetings, participated in cost driver interviews, and marshalled the resources required by the project team.

Nick Gamble committed 60% of his work week to the project. His responsibilities included entering data into the ABC model, creating the ABC product file, and developing download files for data such as expenses and activity cost driver quantities, already available from the plant's information systems. Bud Cramer invested approximately eight hours per week in the ABC initiative. He conducted cost driver interviews, scheduled meetings, and acted as a sounding board for project team ideas.

The consulting team was involved throughout the study, most extensively as trainers and process facilitators. Consultants helped in the cost driver interviews and worked with the team to develop the architecture for the ABC model.

The project team began by holding several meetings to define a set of activities that would capture the business functions at the Youngstown plant. These activities were developed based on an activity dictionary provided by the outside consultants that documented more than 250 activities performed in manufacturing enterprises. Based on several lengthy discussions, the Youngstown plant project team selected 140 activities. They were published in an activity dictionary tailored specifically for the Youngstown plant. Exhibit 10-6 illustrates representative activities from the Youngstown dictionary.

The project team organized meetings with the Youngstown plant's indirect work force to raise awareness of the project objectives throughout the plant and to present basic ABC concepts. The team also distributed the plant activity dictionary during the meetings and asked employees to complete an activity survey that profiled their time commitment in each of the activities listed in the dictionary. Employees also were asked to record factors that influenced their time

Exhibit 10-6
ILLUSTRATIVE ACTIVITY DICTIONARY

G10   *Buying – Raw Materials and Parts* – Arranging for the purchase of raw materials and parts that will be consumed or used in the production processes. Excludes miscellaneous shop tools and supplies.

G11   *Buying – Shop Tools and Supplies* – Arranging for the purchase of shop tools and supplies.

G12   *Expediting – Incoming Shipments* – Advancing vendor shipment to the company of a specific item. Excludes expediting of production and/or shipments to customers.

G13   *Incoming Inspection – Products* – Inspecting and validating the quality and quantity of all company finished goods received from vendors.

G14   *Contract Administration – Purchasing* – Preparing, administering, and auditing contracts and buying agreement covering material and other procurement situations.

H00   *Creating Products and Services* – Activities needed to determine and document all information required to specify what the final product will be. For the most part, this activity group includes the creative activities of the business that pertain to products and services offered to prospective customers.

H01   *Product Planning* – Determining or specifying products consistent with marketing strategy, analyses of competitive products, and marketing research studies.

H02   *Competitive Products Evaluation* – Performing technical evaluations of competitive products and their performance characteristics.

H03   *User Research* – Assessing the impact of the various environments on products and vice versa. Relating that impact to the various environmental statutes, ordinances, and laws. Includes product-environmental testing effort.

H04   *Patent/Trademark Research* – Exploring, discovering, analyzing, and determining new or different parts, products, or processes.

commitments. For example, Elizabeth Scalise, a production supervisor, spent 15% of her time developing production schedules. She indicated that the number of schedule changes was an important factor that affected the amount of time she devoted to this activity. The activity data were accumulated in a database and served as a key input when the project team devised the structure of the Youngstown plant activity-based costing model.

Thirty additional individual interviews were conducted with Youngstown plant employees to discuss business issues and possible cost drivers for the model. Each interview lasted approximately 45 minutes. The employees were asked to profile cost issues that were important at the Youngstown plant. Answers included having more accurate product costs to support competitive bids and measuring the costs of quality: prevention, appraisal, and failure. These sessions also provided a forum to uncover cost drivers. Participants were asked to review the "factors" listed on their activity survey forms and to develop quantifiable cost drivers for each activity listed. Sample cost drivers included: number of engineering change notices (ECNs), number of orders expedited, number of purchase orders generated, and number of parts per assembly.

Selecting Activities and Activity Centers

The project team began to select activities for the ABC model. Assigning each production process to a separate activity center was a fairly obvious decision. Plant departments and assets were exclusively dedicated to the nine distinct plant product families. Nine production activity centers were established to parallel these production areas.

Support activities proved more challenging. The team's choices were constrained by two factors: the sense of urgency that surrounded the engagement (driven by impending bids on various contracts) and cost driver data availability. Ultimately the project team defined 11 support activities to highlight key business processes at the plant. Exhibit 10-7 depicts production and support activities.

The project team envisioned several uses for the information from the 20 activity centers. First, the structure would reveal to management the expenses incurred for each of the nine production machine centers. The production machine activity center information also could serve as a starting point for more extensive analysis. Plant management could investigate the factors at each production activity center that led to its usage of resources such as utilities, indirect labor, shop supplies, or maintenance.

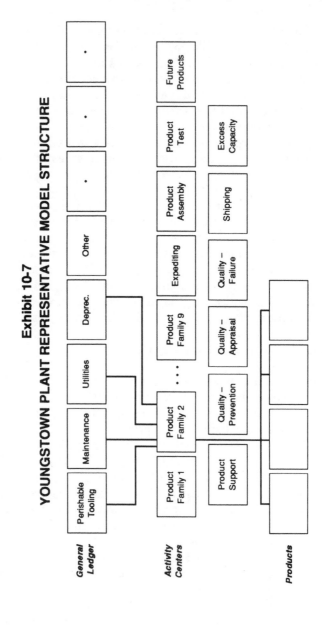

Exhibit 10-7
YOUNGSTOWN PLANT REPRESENTATIVE MODEL STRUCTURE

Cost drivers for the production activity centers included: number of releases by finished product, number of machine hours, number of operations, and the materials-handling cost driver (the sum of receipts and shipments for a finished product). Exhibit 10-8 illustrates the activities, cost drivers, and product costs for the activity center where "cover" products are manufactured.

The project team had to reject certain choices for support activities. For example, the project team wanted to define a materials-handling activity. Management viewed materials handling as a nonvalue-added activity but could not quantify its cost with a traditional cost system. They wanted the ABC model to identify, collect, and analyze such nonvalue-added costs.

The project team found, however, that the number of materials-handling moves was not tracked at the Youngstown plant. Without a quantifiable cost driver, these costs could not be linked to specific products at the plant. Lacking a good cost driver, materials handling was not established as a separate activity in the Youngstown model. Instead, materials-handling resources were assigned to products based on a surrogate cost driver equal to the sum of the number of shipments plus receipts for all components of a specific end item. While this driver was not perfect,

Exhibit 10-8

YOUNGSTOWN PLANT REPRESENTATIVE
MODEL STRUCTURE

Activities/ Expenses	Perishable Tooling $208,731	Maintenance $48,381	Utilities $73,776	Deprec. $330,703	Other

Selected Cost Drivers

Cover Products Activity Center		
Value-Added Driver		$88,359
Number of Releases by Finished Product		2,654
Number of Machine Hours		563,860
Number of Direct Labor Hours		31,227
Number of Operations		73,736
Finished Product Receipts + Shipments		16,633

Products	Part #1 $561,401	Part #2 $147,773	Part #3 $46,563	Part #4 $46,563

the team decided it was the best available proxy for the number of material moves within the plant.

Similarly, maintenance was considered but eventually dropped as a candidate for a separate activity center. Establishing maintenance as a distinct activity center would require identifying a cost driver that could link maintenance activity to specific products. Lacking such a driver, actual maintenance expenses were collected as a budgetary expense item and driven down to the nine production activity centers. In turn, these costs were driven to products based on the number of machine hours a product consumed within its respective activity center.

ABC Model Architecture

Four aspects of the system architecture were particularly interesting:

- Customer-specific product codes,
- Future products activity center,
- Excess capacity activity center,
- Separate cost-of-quality activity centers.

Customer-Specific Product Codes

Products at the Youngstown plant were discrete and specific to individual customers. Each of the 63 products was coded by: customer, product line, volume (high, medium, or low), and production state (launch or development products, production products, and after-market service products). This coding system enabled the Youngstown plant management to generate reports that provide insight into customer profitability as well as the traditional analysis of high- versus low-volume products and profitability across launch, production, and after-market products.

Future Products Activity Center

A future products activity center was created to accumulate costs associated with new product development. The team foresaw two benefits to this design choice. First, management would have its first real view of the cost of future product development. Conventional data could associate engineering salaries with this activity but could not capture all the expenses associated with product development. Assigning activity expenses to future products would enable management to see the manufacturing engineering and quality control man-hours and expenses, such as gauges, airfare, outside consultants, and tests, associated specifically with new product development. Second, the expenses driven to the future product activity center would not burden today's product costs.

The decision to separate development costs for future products from today's product costs was not without controversy. Nick Gamble contended that excluding these costs meant ignoring the requirement to generate funding for this activity in today's product prices. Gamble reasoned that today's products should reflect new product development costs in the Youngstown plant's pricing decisions.

Bud Cramer disagreed, maintaining that new product development efforts had little to do with today's product lines. In the auto industry, components for new car programs often required entirely new tooling and process technologies and, occasionally, even new program-specific plant facilities. This fact meant that supplier bids were received and awarded based on competitive prices: development costs were incurred only after a contract was awarded.

Ultimately, several additional factors swayed the team's decision. First, most product development resources were located at division headquarters. Accurately tracing these costs to Youngstown plant products would require a time-consuming survey of product engineers, and the demands for completing the project within 16 weeks did not give the project team the luxury to perform this additional task. Also, the team recognized that, if desired, HAP product development resources could be tracked to Youngstown products in a subsequent ABC implementation effort, when time pressure was less severe. In addition, engineering resources at the plant level represented less than 1% of the overhead costs that would be driven to Youngstown plant products.

Finally, the team reasoned that the activity center approach represented a significant improvement from current practice. Currently, plant-level development costs were spread (with other overhead costs) across *all* products, based on direct labor hours. And development costs incurred at the corporate site were not allocated to products at all. For analytical purposes and in management decision making, these development costs were assumed to be 11% of sales for all products. For estimating purposes, this 11% burden rate was added to product cost estimates provided by the standard cost system.

Given these factors, even though the team acknowledged that the short-term ABC approach would be less than ideal, the system still would treat these costs sensibly. Individual products would not bear development costs; yet these costs could be accumulated and analyzed at the product family level using the ABC model.

Excess Capacity Activity Center

Management at the Youngstown plant concluded that existing products should not be burdened with costs related to excess capacity. Excess capacity was attributable to management decisions not related to specific products or product lines. In this case, industry-specific factors led management to maintain extra capacity at the Youngstown plant.

The cyclical nature of the automotive industry makes it common practice (and often a competitive prerequisite) to plan for surges in demand. This phenomenon is particularly acute at automotive component manufacturing plants. Component manufacturers are at the end of the supply chain so that small changes in final consumer demand can lead to dramatic schedule changes at the automotive component level. For example, a relatively small 2% to 3% increase in orders from retail car dealers can produce a 5% to 10% increase in the build plan at an automotive assembly plant. As the intermediate participants in the supply chain ramp up production schedules, changes in parts and components plants may increase 10% to 15% in response to the 2% to 3% increase at the retail level. In this environment Big 3 customers prefer to have their parts suppliers operate below full capacity levels. The prohibitive costs of shutting down an assembly plant give automakers a strong incentive to mitigate any risk of unnecessary downtime caused by parts shortages. Given these industry dynamics, the Youngstown facility regularly operated below its weekly theoretical capacity. Unused shifts in each week were available to meet unexpected increases in customers' demands.

By creating an excess capacity activity center, the ABC model provided an "outlet" where these costs could be accumulated without being driven to products. For example, assume the periodic expense on a machine is $3,000 per period. Assume further that this machine runs 10 out of a possible 15 shifts per week (i.e., at 67% capacity). If no activity center is created to accumulate excess capacity costs, the products that run on the machine each period are assigned the full $3,000 of expense. By creating an activity center to accumulate the excess capacity costs, only 67% ($2,000) of the $3,000 expense is assigned to products. The remaining $1,000 is assigned to the excess capacity activity center.

This treatment helps to quantify the cost of management's decision to reserve some excess capacity and prevents this decision from distorting the cost of products actually produced. Nick Gamble, the Youngstown plant accountant, commented on his initial reservations about this treatment:

> I was most concerned with how this decision fit with GAAP. After a lot of discussion with the consultants, we came to understand two important considerations. First, GAAP didn't matter in the short term. We didn't plan to use ABC costing for external reporting. Its primary purpose was for management decision making.
>
> In addition, over the long term, we could always use a facility-sustaining driver, like number of units produced, if we wanted to spread the costs accumulated in the excess capacity activity center down to all the products.

Cost-of-Quality Activity Centers

Over the preceding year, the Youngstown plant's largest Big 3 customer had experienced recurring problems with the plant's products. The customer now was threatening to revoke the plant's preferred supplier quality rating. Youngstown plant management soon would be faced with a full-scale supplier quality review.

The ABC project team decided to develop separate activity centers for measuring the costs of quality prevention, appraisal, and failure. The team expected two separate benefits from this decision. In the short term, the activity-based cost of quality data might demonstrate to the customer that Youngstown was developing new procedures to highlight the importance of improving quality at the plant. In the longer term, the quality data would provide insights into quality costs at the activity and functional group level. These data could be used to improve resource allocation decisions within the plant to improve quality. For example, Bud Cramer could reallocate indirect employees across prevention, appraisal, and failure-related activities depending on cost and customer needs.

The project team identified activities in the plant's activity dictionary that would be included in each of the three cost-of-quality activity centers. Concurrently, they analyzed the expenses associated with these activities so that indirect resources and actual expenses could be assigned to the prevention, appraisal, and failure-related activities. For example, rework and scrap expenses were categorized as failure expenses. The expenses accumulated in each activity center then were associated with specific products using cost drivers. Specifically, quality prevention costs were driven based on the number of variable gauges for a given product, quality appraisal costs were assigned using the number of test operations, and quality failure costs were associated using the amount of machine scrap dollars.

Results of Activity-Based Costing at Youngstown

Sixteen weeks after its inception, the ABC implementation effort culminated with a final steering committee meeting in Youngstown. HAP President Scott Springer and other steering committee members attended the session. The project team reviewed the work performed over the course of the project and described its model structure choices. Finally, the team presented activity-based product cost data that highlighted the cost impact of several key variables, including product volume, complexity, and the use of new versus fully depreciated assets.

ABC data provided new insight into the cost and profitability of specific products and customers. Management acted swiftly and aggressively, based on analysis of the ABC data. Initiatives were launched to address both strategic and operational issues.

A joint HAP and Youngstown plant management team scrutinized the ABC cost data at the customer and product level. Exhibit 10-9 shows the

Exhibit 10-9
YOUNGSTOWN PLANT SALES AND PROFIT ANALYSIS

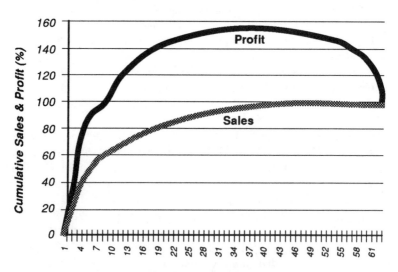

Number of Part Numbers

sales and ABC profit contributions across the Youngstown product line. The analysis revealed the usual ABC pattern of 30% of the products representing 80% of sales volume and 150% of total profits. Based on the ABC information, the task force developed recommendations for HAP President Scott Springer.

Springer tested the group's assumptions and pressed the task force to think through the implications of its recommendations. Springer provided an invaluable balance to the plant and HAP-level perspectives. He recognized the importance of certain Big 3 customers across HAP businesses and, further, to the entire Slade Manufacturing Automotive Group. After a series of meetings, a detailed action plan was developed for approaching each customer.

Several customers were asked to collaborate on ideas to reduce specific activity costs. HAP and Youngstown task force members reviewed historical ordering patterns and lot sizes with these customers and explained the resulting costs. The discussions between the task force and customers proceeded in a productive and cooperative fashion because of the availability of defensible data about operations. Customers agreed to actions that, for particular products, would lead to reduced materials-handling costs, fewer expedited orders, and longer production runs.

The Strategic Impact

The results of implementing this action plan were profound. In some cases, customers agreed to substantial price increases; in others, products and customers were eliminated from the plant's production mix. The net effect was reduced complexity and increased profitability overall. Price increases alone yielded $1.2 million in incremental revenues. Commenting on the strategic impact of ABC, Bill Carlisle, Slade Manufacturing's controller, noted:

> One of the biggest differences that ABC made was to build our confidence during negotiations. Today we don't crumble when confronted by a customer demanding price improvements. We're not afraid to take the business to $80 million if there's no negative impact on the bottom line.
>
> ABC also made us more aggressive in bidding for new business that we believe our competitors are not costing and pricing correctly.

One specific example demonstrates HAP management's commitment and new confidence in the ABC information. As already mentioned, Bud

Cramer and the Hudson Automotive management team were faced with a difficult quote for a major customer. The customer was requesting a price reduction applicable for the remaining three years of an existing contract. The gear products covered by this contract accounted for a significant percentage of Youngstown's sales. HAP was supplying a majority of the customer's requirements for this gear family, with the remainder from one competitor.

HAP Youngstown used the newly developed ABC system to estimate the cost of the products covered in the quote. Based on this information and a subsequent, more detailed analysis, the management team determined that the products were already highly unprofitable. They decided to quote a *higher*, not lower, price for the remaining years of the contract, despite the customer's request for a price reduction. The competitor was awarded the contract for the remaining business.

At first, Hudson's decision may have seemed ill-advised, to have risked and lost a substantial volume of business when many of the costs assigned to the contested products under the ABC analysis were not avoidable in the short run. But Hudson realized substantial short- and long-term benefits from this decision.

In the short term, Slade turned a family of unprofitable products into earnings contributors because it did receive the higher bid price for the gear products during the first of the three years remaining on the contract while the competitor tooled up for production. Once the competitor began volume production it was locked into the lower bid price for the remaining two years of the contract.

Hudson Automotive reaped long-term benefits from the decision as well. HAP Youngstown already had been awarded a contract to produce the next generation of gears that eventually would replace the products they "lost" to the competitor. "Losing" the bid enabled the management group to focus more resources on next-generation products for this important customer. At the same time, the competitor's resources presumably now were committed to activities that supported production, at low prices, for current-generation products.

ABC Data at the Operating Level

On an operating level, division management is using the ABC data to understand the cost of maintaining capital equipment and perishable tooling. For example, prior to the ABC implementation effort, management did not associate the cost of perishable tooling with any particular product or customer. Today, management uses ABC data to track the cost of tooling and can associate tooling dollars with specific machine centers and products. The new data enable management to control tooling costs through cost trend analysis across product families and machine centers.

Maintenance data provided similar operating level benefits. Youngstown management uses ABC model data to track maintenance resources committed to specific machine centers. These data support replacement versus repair decisions for plant assets. They also have justified a major preventative maintenance program at the plant.

An example will help illustrate these maintenance-related improvements. Management at the Youngstown plant believed that supports were a highly profitable product family. ABC data revealed that supports were, at best, marginally profitable. Upon investigation, the management team found that the profit reductions were caused by the large maintenance costs for the machines that were used to produce support products.

Pursuing the maintenance cost issue further, managers discovered that machine operators in the support production area regularly set up and ran the production equipment at the highest possible run speeds. The machine operators were paid on a piece-rate incentive system, and they liked to bet that high-speed production would not cause a breakdown during their shift. The piece-rate system had another counter-productive effect. In the event that support production equipment required maintenance, operators would reroute support products to other available production machines. Often these machines were not designed to manufacture the specific support, yet operators would produce the supports there in order to meet their piece-rate requirements. Based on these findings, management at Youngstown revised the piece-rate incentive system. In the year that followed the ABC implementation effort, maintenance costs in the support production area declined by 28%.

Quality improvement efforts also benefitted from the ABC project's efforts to capture the specific costs associated with quality. These data motivated management to improve product quality by reallocating more resources to prevent poor quality for high-volume products. Quality failure costs on high-volume products dropped by 13% in the year following the ABC effort because of the reallocation of resources to prevention and appraisal activities. Finally, HAP management developed a sophisticated quote system that uses the ABC data to help estimate product costs. George Laflin, vice president, Sales & Marketing, described past efforts to estimate product costs.

We never really trusted the numbers from our standard cost system, so we developed ways to work with or around the data it provided. When preparing a quote we continuously made adjustments to the standard cost estimates. Gear M28076 is a good example. Under the traditional system, the standard cost for material was $3.00 per unit, direct labor was $.50, and overhead was $2.00, for a total standard cost for the product of $5.50.

For the actual quote, we used $4.75 as the unit cost since we estimated that automation would reduce direct labor by $.15 per unit and the overhead would be reduced at the 400% plantwide direct labor burden rate. That logic brought us to assume overhead would be $.60 less per unit, leading to our revised cost estimate of $4.75. Obviously, the ABC data bring a lot more rigor to our bidding model and analysis.

George Laflin and his Sales & Marketing staff are using the ABC model to develop quotes on new business. In the new bidding model, standard costs still are used for labor and material cost estimates. But the ABC-based system uses overhead cost rates that correspond to the actual expenses incurred in production and support activity centers. Fundamentally, the system provides a "similar to" model. When a quote is received, Laflin and his colleagues first assess which current product family is similar to the quote received. Next, they calculate an average unit overhead cost for each production and support activity center. The sum of these average unit overhead costs is added to standard direct labor and material cost estimates. The result provides the base case for developing a unit price and quote.

The Youngstown ABC model is being updated quarterly by the plant accountant, Nick Gamble. At the plant level, model data are used to analyze customer and product profitability, within a specific ABC model run and across model runs. Data also are analyzed to identify historical trends in product costs and costs per unit of cost drivers.

Since implementing ABC at Youngstown and a second pilot site, HAP has developed ABC systems for eight additional plants. All HAP plants are using their ABC systems actively for quoting, managing customer relationships, and directing process improvements.

Chapter 11

KRAFT USA

Executive Summary

A vice president in the Operations group, Donald Benson, explained the recent enthusiasm for activity-based management at KRAFT:

> ABM acceptance was more of an evolution than a revolution. It was a concurrent development, but until we saw its link to quality, it was alone in the finance group. We now see that it links well with our TQM initiatives. Total quality works easier and better when it can be linked to ownership of activities. If we are to empower ownership of processes at the factory floor, we have to give managers and employees good information about their operations.

KRAFT USA (KRAFT) embarked on an ABC study in early 1990, in conjunction with an intensive Performance Measurement study. Previous internal and external studies had demonstrated the weaknesses of the existing cost accounting and performance measurement systems in providing management with information to respond to rapidly changing business conditions and intense competition.

Jim Smith, a regional controller, stated, "The need for better cost information was driven by our product line complexity and proliferation and intensified competition with a trend toward niche markets and decreasing product margins."

Consumer demand for variety and health conscious foods and the growing strength of competitors had caused KRAFT to rethink its market strategies and review operational control performance measures. Len Grant, an Operations vice president, claimed:

> Our forecasts indicate a flat overall market. We plan to hold on to our existing share by proliferating our product line. We will need to understand the cost of this strategy and how to manage and control these costs. Currently,

the costs of product proliferation are 'recognized' but not 'appreciated' because we don't have effective means of communicating the story.

Two plants that had cream cheese product lines within the Operations unit were selected to pilot ABC to compare product costs between the two facilities. All manufacturing costs were reviewed on an ABC basis. Costs such as customer service and research and development were not included in the study.

The ABC and performance measurement projects were independent of each other. Both were slowed (although at different times) by the Philip Morris merger in December 1988, which changed many management positions. According to a plant controller and ABC project team member, "Change in management caused us to be about a year behind. Still we continued."

Both projects continued but with a limited budget. During this time, the performance measurement team developed a prototype currently being tested at a plant, and the ABC team developed front-end activity databases and reviewed product costing software options other than PC-based. Both methodologies are being tested in tandem at one plant.

Resulting ABC product costs at the first two pilot plants were not significantly different from traditional cost. High-volume products remained virtually unchanged overall. The cost of very low-volume products increased approximately 5%. Smith was not overly concerned that significant cost differences were not uncovered, stating that "comparisons between costs derived from a direct or variable cost system and costs derived from an ABC approach are difficult to make." Many of the notable cost differences were found in milk products because the traditional system did not segregate receiving and handling milk as a cost to be assigned only to milk-based products.

Even without sharp differences in product cost data, senior managers were still enthusiastic about the project. Don Benson of Operations explained:

> ABC identifies where you add value—in procurement, in conversion, and in distribution—to the production process. Traditional systems do not provide this insight. The new information sets priorities for my attention. Before, we did it intuitively.
>
> Also, we are now examining the total costs of the new product introduction process. We are extending our analysis back to all the activities we do in the product development phase to bring new products successfully to market.

Other relevant comments included:

The data showed that we were overpricing long-run items and underpricing short-run items. I was not surprised at the result, just at the amounts. We take a major hit with our shorter runs, especially with run loss that averages five to six percent on short runs but only one percent on long runs. The existing cost system calculates product costs assuming an average run size for all runs.

After the changes in management and the lag in the project's timing, the ABC project has been revived and now is being implemented at a third plant with the hope that it can be linked to the performance measurement model. But ABC project member Tom Bertram summed up the current status very simply. "We've gotten to the numbers but have taken no actions. It has raised some eyebrows, but it won't be sustained over time unless others get involved." (See update in Epilogue.)

Company Background

KRAFT USA is one of seven business units of KRAFT General Foods (KGF). The group was acquired by Philip Morris Companies Inc. in 1988. KRAFT began as a small cheese operation of J.L. Kraft in Chicago in 1903. It currently employs more than 14,000 people in 123 locations, with revenues exceeding $4 billion.

KRAFT is one of the most recognized and respected names in the food industry, with the leading market share in five of the 25 top-selling food categories in the United Sates. It has products in six major food categories:

- Cheese products;
- Viscous products, such as mayonnaise & Miracle Whip;
- Prepared dinners;
- Pourable salad dressings;
- Margarines and spreads;
- Barbecue sauce.

Large competitors include Con-Agra in the dinners market and Borden Foods in the dairy products market. Private labels are becoming growing competitors. Customers vary from small grocers to institutional food makers.

Currently, KRAFT operates 15 processing plants and 10 natural cheese plants, which supply the processing plants. Products include macaroni and cheese dinners, cream cheese, dips, salad dressings, process cheese, natural cheese, and mayonnaise.

The company attempts to be highly responsive and innovative to meet consumer needs and preferences. This strategy has not been easy due to the continuously changing marketplace. Most recently, KRAFT has been deploying leading-edge technologies to develop reduced fat products to meet consumers' concerns about fat and cholesterol.

KRAFT made major investments in the late '80s to improve quality and productivity, to position themselves for the '90s. Donald Benson noted, "We embarked on total quality five years ago. In addition to quality programs, some plants and product lines were consolidated or relocated during the late '80s."

KRAFT's major operating units are:

- Retail cheese marketing,
- Grocery marketing,
- Operations,
- Specialty products marketing and manufacturing,
- Sales & sales operations,
- Marketing services.

Improving Measurement Systems

In early 1988, KRAFT Operations instituted a productivity program to encourage cost-savings projects. Prior to 1988 a "cost savings report" was generated quarterly as a post-cost savings metric. The finance group within Operations modified this concept by adding financial measures, and the report became known as the "KRAFT Productivity Program" (KPP).

Two different cost standards for variable costs were established within KPP: frozen or "billed-out" standards, and operating or "currently attainable" standards. A productivity report measured operating against frozen costs. A performance report measured actual against operating standard costs. Fixed (period costs) were expensed each month but measured against a planned amount. In addition, "waste accounts" were established for such expenses as unsalable goods, faulty goods, and obsolescence (also measured against a planned amount). KPP proved useful as an initial attempt at measuring productivity savings but also served to highlight significant weakness with the management accounting system. A project tracking system (PTS) was developed to augment the KPP program, as the accounting system did not provide enough information.

Jim Smith, regional controller, commented, "The KPP reports trapped cost savings but did not identify the reasons why those savings occurred nor offer any insights that would help to further reduce cost or waste. They did not support a continuous improvement philosophy. Further, accountants could understand the reports, but not users."

Smith had joined KRAFT in 1987 just before the merger. The goal of his Operations finance group was to give people data they could use. It was felt that the current cost system was ineffective because it tried to be all things to all people—a financial reporting system, a performance measurement system, and a product costing system.

Smith and Tom Bertram, the other regional controller at the time, began reading various books and articles on cost management and performance measurement topics. In the summer of 1988, they organized an offsite management conference and invited consultants to participate in discussions of topics such as ABC, performance measurement, and continuous improvement.

Performance Measurement Study

The finance group (within Operations) requested approval for a performance measurement study from Operations management in order to improve and monitor key measures that could drive cost out of the business. The project was approved under joint sponsorship of Production and Finance management.

KRAFT's Operations unit initiated the performance measurement project in early 1989. While designed to focus primarily on performance measures, the project team recognized the linkage between ABC and performance measures through the use of "cost drivers." Smith recalled, "We really didn't understand the drivers of our business. We saw ABC as providing a link to those drivers."

But because of the immediate need to improve productivity, the initial study focused only on performance measurement, with ABC deferred to a later study. The specific objectives of the performance measurement study were:

- Obtain a detailed assessment of the existing performance measurement/cost management system,
- Identify cost drivers and performance measures,
- Identify opportunities for improved information,

- Assess the linkage of performance measures with KPP,
- Assess the impact of using activities as the basis for performance measures,
- Identify necessary modifications to information systems,
- Address the feasibility of implementing activity-based costing,
- Ensure the integrity of performance measures with critical success factors for Operations.

The performance measurement study identified 128 performance measurements for a manufacturing plant. These metrics were ranked by importance and priority. The project team selected 18 measures as key performance indicators (KPIs). The team also recommended reporting levels and suggested systems modifications. The regional controllers, Smith and Bertram, recalled:

> Giving people data that they could use was an innovation. KPIs were only one part of the cost management system we needed. The measurements were classified into three hierarchical levels. The line level was the lowest, which rolled into a supervisory level, which rolled into a plant managerial level. People would see data detailed or summarized for their level. But we weren't able to gather the data and measure them at the time. We presented a timetable to get the measurements implemented, but the merger put everything on hold.

In December 1988, KRAFT USA was acquired by Philip Morris. Many changes ensued, especially at senior management levels. Projects such as the performance measurement study lost sponsorship and were put on hold. Within a few months, however, the performance measurement team gained approval to continue its efforts, and it began to develop a KPI system for the Garland, Texas, plant.

The goals of the KPI system were identified. They were to:

- Collect relevant data,
- Provide relevant measures,
- Link to plant goals and objectives,
- Support continuous improvement philosophy by tracking data over time.

The system design methodology began by identifying business functions. The team then mapped the KPI measures to these functions. Data modeling was used to depict the flow of data to the measures. A KPI project team member recalled,"The process was very interactive. We wanted to build a system to match the way the supervisors wanted to run their businesses. Our data collection efforts were built off the shift report they were already using." Using the shift report as the main data source greatly reduced the amount of training that would have been required if brand new forms had been designed to capture data.

The performance measurement system used the following prototype measures:

- Line effectiveness,
- Production service level,
- Overweights,
- Percent line downtime,
- Output per line hour,
- Soybean oil filling yield,
- Total plant output per total man-hour,
- Output per standard direct labor man-hour.

Project resources were limited, however, and the project progressed slowly. By late 1991, only a prototype of the Performance Measurement system had been designed, and it was still being tested at the Garland plant. The system is scheduled for completion at Garland by the second quarter of 1992.

The Need for ABC

As the Performance Measurement study progressed, Smith continued to see the need for improved product cost information in the areas of operational control and strategic decision making. He also believed that ABC had a value beyond just product costing. Smith argued that ABC would enable the finance department to provide information useful for both operational and strategic decision making. It would facilitate operational control by:

- Establishing targets linked to strategies;
- Comparing actual to targeted performance;
- Promoting efficiency, productivity, and learning.

It would support strategic decision making by determining:

- Which products and markets are profitable and why,

- Which resources should be used,
- Which business processes should be used,
- What capital should be purchased.

KRAFT's traditional cost accounting system, a detailed standard direct cost system, was adequate for satisfying the company's external reporting requirements—to value inventory for external financial statements and to assist in regulatory agency reporting. The direct standard cost system applied variable expenses to products on a per pound and per line hour basis. Period or fixed manufacturing costs were allocated to product groups and then applied to products within groups by production tonnage.

Bertram recognized that "our traditional cost systems satisfy our external users but are antiquated for our internal users. The system does not provide key operational measures, such as first pass yields, and results are only available to managers two weeks after the close of an accounting period."

Smith concurred with the inadequacies of the existing standard cost system:

> It does not provide timely and detailed information for operational control purposes. Nor does it properly allocate costs to products or product lines for strategic decision making. The cost system in place is based on line hours and pounds produced. Limited analysis of indirect, fixed, or distribution costs is performed.
>
> Managers needed better cost information to cope with our increased product line complexity and proliferation, the strengthened competition we were facing, especially in niche markets, and the decreasing product margins we were experiencing. We also have the knowledge that the competition is already implementing ABC programs. We also saw ABC as an opportunity for Operations Finance to shift from having an external reporting focus to being a proactive business partner of the units we were supporting.

Getting Started

In July 1989, Smith, Bertram, and an outside consulting group presented an ABC overview session to senior finance management from KRAFT and General Foods operating divisions. KRAFT General Foods Finance sponsored the meeting, introduced the session, and provided closing remarks. Smith recalled this meeting.

Back then, most people still viewed ABC as purely a product costing technique. They believed it to be just another way of allocating costs. I probably should have focused their attention on cost behavior patterns that get revealed, using the unit, batch, product-sustaining, and facility-sustaining hierarchy, and on the linkage of TQM to the structure of activities and business processes, rather than on product costing.

Preparing the Organization

In late 1989 (one year after the merger and several months after the initial performance measurement efforts), senior management approved a proposal to implement ABC on a pilot basis to test its applicability to the KPI program and to determine whether ABC could respond to KRAFT's need for better product costing information. The project was to be performed with the assistance of outside consultants. Bertram commented on the project's initial support. "I don't believe senior management could see the benefits of ABC yet so we were funded to go forward but with only a small budget," he said.

Scope and Sites of the ABC Project

The scope of the two projects included only manufacturing costs. Nonmanufacturing areas, such as Customer Service, Sales, Marketing, and Research & Development, while part of the longer-term objectives for ABC, were excluded from the initial analysis because they were outside Operations Finance's organizational responsibility. People from these areas had little to no involvement in the initial ABC projects.

Two plants, Beaver Dam and Springfield, were chosen to pilot ABC because both had cream cheese product lines. By developing models for two facilities that produced the same product lines, the project would be able to compare product costs in the two plants. Springfield was chosen because Tom Bertram had become controller there and could assist with the buy-in process.

Beaver Dam and Springfield

At the time of the study, the Beaver Dam facility employed approximately 200 persons and produced approximately 34 different types of cream cheese products. All overhead costs for the 1989 year were included in the ABC study.

Springfield is a multiproduct facility, which produces approximately

266 products. The facility employed approximately 1,000 persons at the time of the study.

Garland

The ABC project was placed on hold from the completion of the Springfield project in late 1990 to spring 1991, mainly because of further changes in management after the merger. Smith commented on this delay, saying, "I feel we lost a year's worth of time overall. However, Operations management had the foresight to continue and still gave me a small budget to keep the project alive." During the year, ABC project members remained busy completing and finalizing the activity dictionary, reviewing ABC software options, and building front-end activity data spreadsheets.

In mid-1991, the project team began to implement ABC at the Garland, Texas, plant, which also had served as the testing ground for the performance measurement initiative. The implementation of ABC at Garland, with possible linkage to the performance measurement system (currently still in development) is seen as a prototype to be used at other plants, but no formal plan exists at this time to link the two initiatives.

Objectives of the ABC Project

The project team defined specific objectives for the ABC pilots:

- Identify key cost drivers.
- Compare traditional product cost to ABC product cost.
- Compare product costs between plants.
- Compare ABC process implementation between the plants. How easy or difficult is the ABC implementation process in a larger and more complex plant (Springfield) versus a small focused facility (Beaver Dam)?
- Evaluate any differences in ABC architecture between the plants (such as in the definition and selection of activities, activity centers, and cost drivers).
- Evaluate ABC software model as a management tool.

Longer-term objectives for the ABC effort included:

- Link ABC study to main operating system, such as Prism Advanced Costing Module (MRP II system).

- Apply ABC methodology to KRAFT USA headquarters administration costs.
- Expand the ABC methodology to other KRAFT facilities, KRAFT General Foods (KGF) facilities, and KGF headquarters costs.

Timing of the ABC Implementations

The ABC implementations began in January 1990. Beaver Dam, the less complex plant, was the first site to be investigated. Beaver Dam is a small focused plant producing cream cheese products in a fairly simple manufacturing environment. Springfield is a large, complex plant producing a rather full line of products. The Beaver Dam project began in February 1990; results were presented three months later in May 1990. The Springfield project began the following month, in June 1990, with results presented seven months later, in January 1991. By late 1991, the third ABC project had been approved for the Garland, Texas, plant.

The Project Team

Jim Smith (now director, cost systems and analysis) provided leadership for the project team. For the first project, Beaver Dam, a team of financial experts was assembled. As the project expanded into Springfield and, more currently, into Garland, resource personnel were added to the project team, with a mixture of financial and nonfinancial backgrounds.

Over time the team has included, in addition to Smith:

- Tom Bertram, controller for the Springfield plant. He provided the knowledge of current operations and its informational needs at the plant level.
- The manager of cost analysis, who acted as the project manager for the ABC implementations at Beaver Dam and Springfield.
- Several cost analysts with manufacturing accounting backgrounds, assigned to the project.
- The controller at Beaver Dam, who provided support and assistance to the project.
- A quality analyst with a cost background, who joined the ABC team just prior to the start of the Garland implementation. Prior to being a quality analyst, she had been a cost analyst at the Champaign plant. Her experience, including extensive

involvement both with a plant-level cost system and with a plant's quality program, proved an excellent fit for ABC work.

- Two external consultants, who provided expertise gained from previous ABC engagements. They assisted mainly in areas of project management, model design, and data gathering. Toward the end of the Beaver Dam implementation, one of the external consultants, Steve Gotherd, was hired by KRAFT as manager, cost systems, to support ongoing implementation of ABC at the company.
- A senior business consultant from the information systems group, who joined the ABC team during the Garland implementation. His background in systems design assisted the team on automation techniques. The information group also is involved in the performance measurement initiative at Garland.

The approximate percentage of time devoted by team members to the ABC projects is shown below.

Beaver Dam
- Jim Smith, project leader, Finance—25%,
- Plant controller—25%,
- Accounting analyst—50%,
- Manager of cost analysis—50%.

Springfield
- Jim Smith, project leader, Finance—25%,
- Tom Bertram, plant controller—25%,
- Accounting analyst—75%,
- Manager of cost analysis—50%.

Bertram commented on recent changes in the composition of the project teams. "Today we have dedicated ABC resources; in the first two projects, we did it as part of our everyday job assignments," he said.

Training the Project Team and Management

The ABC team attended a two-day training session on ABC implementation, conducted by the outside consultants, in January 1990. The focus was to understand how to implement ABC. The training covered Harvard case studies (Siemens, John Deere, and Kanthal), ABC model design structure, and specific Beaver Dam detailed implementation steps. Additional training sessions were conducted on an individual basis for others who joined the team subsequently.

In addition to the training for the project team, many awareness sessions were held to help KRAFT management understand the benefits and uses of ABC and to heighten enthusiasm. Because of the Philip Morris merger, sponsorship at the VP level changed during the course of the project, so that a greater emphasis on educating new managers about the project was needed. According to Bertram, "Management changes delayed completion of the projects by about a year."

Many awareness sessions were held, often repeating similar presentations to previous management groups. Steve Gotherd recalled, "It was a lengthy education process. We can't fault the people for their lack of enthusiasm. Everyone was focused on coping with the merger."

System Design and Architecture

The ABC team used the following methodology for both initial sites (examples are from Springfield study):

1. Define activities,
2. Analyze nonlabor expenses,
3. Analyze activity,
4. Group functions and subfunctions,
5. Define resource cost drivers,
6. Define activity cost drivers,
7. Load data and calculate product costs, and
8. Analyze and present results.

Define Activities

The project team interviewed the managers of each of the following areas:

- Logistics;
- Quality control;
- Human resources;
- Plant accounting;
- Asset (inventory) management;
- Production management;
- Business unit managers for dinners, process cheese, cream cheese, natural cuts, and Di Giorno;

- Sanitation;
- Maintenance;
- Manufacturing engineering.

The ABC study focused on overhead costs. Direct labor was *not* included in the interview process. Standard direct labor rates from the company's existing cost system were used to apply direct labor to products.

Activity Dictionary

During departmental interviews, the team created a list of activities by group. The team then developed a definition for each activity that became incorporated into an "activity dictionary." The dictionary was circulated to the management group for suggested changes and approval. Steve Gotherd commented on this process, which took longer than anticipated:

> Obtaining consistent and understandable activity definitions among everyone was not an easy task. All managers had to agree on and understand an activity definition before the ABC team could go forward. The project team had to spend extra effort with the managers defining and explaining activities. Ultimately, the dictionary was completed and approved.

With the definitions established, department managers identified the percentage of time each of their employees spend performing each activity. The data were collected and aggregated using Lotus spreadsheet programs designed by the team. According to Steve Gotherd, "This also was a very time-consuming task. We knew long term we would want to automate it." (Subsequently, the ABC team automated the process using the Paradox database language, to be discussed later in this case.)

The initial activity dictionary was extensive and very detailed, containing approximately 225 activities. The number of activities defined for each functional area included:

- Logistics—25,
- Quality control—39,
- Human resources—9,
- Accounting—11,

- Asset management—15,
- Business unit managers—25 per product line area,
- Sanitation—6,
- Maintenance—7,
- Engineering—13.

Mapping General Ledger Dollars to Activities

The existing general ledger accounts, such as Quality Control Salary and Expenses, captured expense information at a highly aggregated level. The plants did not have subdepartmental reporting. The project manager had to spend several weeks to trace general ledger expenses down to departments and responsibility centers.

To be consistent with KRAFT's internal reporting groupings, each department's costs were split into three categories before being driven down to activities: (1) management payroll, (2) hourly or staff payroll, and (3) nonpayroll expenses (i.e., supplies).

Analyze Nonlabor Expenses

The team analyzed all nonlabor and machine-related expenses so that they could be assigned to 20 to 30 separate machine groups. The machine groups were determined based on similar processes being performed. Among the expenses assigned to the machine groups were: (1) depreciation, (2) energy expenses (electricity, water, etc.), (3) maintenance costs, and (4) replacement and spare parts. Grouping expenses by machine groups provided management with a more accurate view of the costs of operating the machinery and equipment in any given area.

Analyze Activities

Three separate classifications of activities were established: (1) by activity hierarchy, (2) by value analysis, and (3) by activity center analysis.

Hierarchy Analysis

The team classified each activity as unit, batch, product-sustaining, or facility-sustaining. The classification of batch-related costs, however, proved difficult. In food processing, "batches" exist throughout the plant but differ greatly at each phase of the process. Looking back on the hierarchical analysis and subsequent results, Gotherd felt that "the benefits of this analysis to KRAFT were, from a practical perspective, minimal."

But Smith disagreed. He stated, "The activity cost hierarchy clearly reveals different cost behavior patterns. This type of analysis would have helped me convince my management that ABC was not just a product-costing exercise."

Value Analysis

The ABC team attempted to rank activities by their "value-added" contribution to the company, (e.g., high, medium, low). But the team soon learned how difficult it was to classify activities as having little or no value and decided that a value classification was not an important objective for their ABC systems. The value ranking has not been used in any study, and Gotherd believes that such a ranking will be difficult to use at KRAFT.

Activity Centers

The team grouped the 225 activities into activity centers based on production lines and other support areas. Approximately 45 activity centers were designed for each site. Every production line was defined as its own activity center. This definition provided visibility to activities such as quality control, sanitation, supervision, maintenance, training, planning/scheduling, and general administration at each production line. Each of the four product areas (cream cheese, natural cuts, process cheese, and dinners) had between six and nine production lines.

Activity centers were established for activities relating to warehousing, raw material management, central quality control, and additional processing areas in the plant. A facility-sustaining activity center also was established for the nonproduct-specific activities such as plant maintenance and insurance. The facility-sustaining activity center contained approximately 20% of the plant's overhead costs. Activity centers relating to quality included:

- Prevention: activities related to safety and training;
- Appraisal: activities related to testing;
- Failure: activities related to detecting failures, both internal and external detection.

By monitoring these categories over time, management hoped to see increases in prevention activities cause a sharp drop in the cost of failure activities.

Group Functions and Subfunctions

Plant management wanted to view activities at a higher level than activity centers. The team defined functions and subfunctions. All activity centers (described previously) were called subfunctions. Similar subfunctions (activity centers) then were grouped into a broader term called functions.

This grouping made it easier for plant management to view and interpret the data, as well as to illustrate functional activities that occurred across departments. For example:

- Function: manufacturing control and monitoring;
- Subfunction: pourables line 1;
- Activities: line changeovers, production supervision, sanitation supervision, and relief.

Define Resource Cost Drivers

The department managers helped to define the resource drivers used to drive expenses to activities and activity centers. The managers determined the best drivers to represent their department's work effort accurately by production line or activity center. The managers' involvement in this process helped to establish their buy-in on the ABC model structure.

Eighty first-stage, or resource, drivers were required to drive expenses to the extensive number of activities—225—and activity centers—45. The combination of 225 activities and 45 activity centers resulted in more than 2,300 cost pools. This detailed delineation of activities to specific production lines gave the ABC model its high level of precision but required a substantial amount of data preparation time to quantify the resource drivers.

Some of the resource drivers used included:

- Supervision time,
- Breakdown hours,
- Maintenance part usage,
- Number of maintenance work orders,

- Sanitation supervision time,
- Case volume,
- Training time,
- Cleanup time,
- Capital project dollars,
- Number of changeovers,
- Line hours,
- Number of SKUs,
- Maintenance supervision time,
- Amount of salvage,
- Line mechanic hours.

Define Activity Cost Drivers

The ABC team identified ideal (conceptually accurate) activity cost drivers to assign activity costs to products. The team found themselves constrained, however, by the limited information readily available. Often surrogate or substitute drivers had to be used. To help with future ABC updates at both Beaver Dam and Springfield, the team informed plant management about the unavailable data so that they could be collected in the future.

Bertram explained a typical compromise: "For our distribution costs, we used pounds shipped as our cost driver. But we know it should include a complexity factor of some kind. We will need more cross functional support to get that information."

Most (60% to 70%) of the activity cost drivers turned out to be volume (unit-level) based. Examples of cost drivers and the percentage of activity dollars driven include:

Cost Driver	Beaver Dam	Springfield
Line hours	29%	42%
Pounds of product	20	17
Labor hours	9	6
# of batches	9	--
# of tests	--	7
# of pallets	7	5
# of cases	--	5

Exhibit 11-1 shows a more complete list of activities and cost drivers.

Bertram commented on the activity cost drivers, saying, "Almost a whole new set of cost drivers were identified when compared to the

Exhibit 11-1
PARTIAL LIST OF COST DRIVERS AND ACTIVITIES

Cost Driver	Activities
Line Hours	Maintenance
	Depreciation
	Sanitation
	QC Supervision
Pounds of Product	Expediting
	Purchasing
	Salvage
Labor Hours	Production Supervision
	Training
Number of Cases	Material Handling

performance measurement study. Yields, however, were still key for both purposes."

Load Data and Calculate Product Costs

The data (general ledger dollars, activities, resource and activity cost drivers) were loaded into an ABC software tool, and product costing was run. Approximately 200 product IDs were costed. The data were reviewed for accuracy before starting the analysis.

Analyze and Present Results

The ABC team analyzed the results and designed a presentation with the original project objectives in mind. The complexity of the model (2,500 cost pools, 80 resource drivers, and 200 products) added to the difficulty. A complex model results in greater detail and precision but can often make it onerous to analyze and present in a meaningful form, especially to managers not completely familiar with ABC concepts.

The ABC project team on its own analyzed the data and made presentations to various management groups: (1) KRAFT USA Operations management, (2) Production vice presidents and plant managers, (3) KRAFT USA financial level, and (4) KRAFT General Foods senior management.

Role of Consultants

The role and assistance of the consultants changed during the Springfield implementation because of budget constraints placed on Smith. Also, the ABC team had gained experience on the first pilot, and the outside consultants were felt to be not as necessary in the Springfield project. Most of the outside assistance at Springfield was used to help design the ABC architecture.

Near the conclusion of the Springfield implementation, KRAFT ran out of funding for the external assistance. Thus, the ABC team had no external assistance in the ABC analysis, roll-forward plan, or evaluation of what had been accomplished, though this lack was not viewed as a major problem. The ABC team made the final presentation to Springfield management in January 1991.

Software Automation

The ABC team wanted to automate the time-consuming steps of implementing and using an ABC system. A senior business consultant with a background in systems design joined the team for this purpose. The systems department also is involved in the performance measurement initiative at Garland.

The ABC team, guided by systems personnel, set out to create a front-end tool for both the ABC model and the PM system. The resulting front-end tool was written in Paradox and called process activity costing tool, or "PACT" (see Exhibit 11-2). Inputs to PACT included general ledger account data, job-related information, and activity questionnaire responses. Outputs produced included the activity dictionary, functional and cross-functional listings, and export files for ABC software systems and AS/400 applications. Steve Gotherd explained:

> PACT is an activity dictionary in Paradox that takes the lowest level of our initial ABC study, breaks it down into detailed tasks, then aggregates the activities up to a managerial level. We can take PACT to any user at any plant. Some plants may differ slightly, but those changes can be accommodated easily.

The team plans to use department activity questionnaires from PACT to compile all activity data (see Exhibit 11-3). The PACT database contains all employee information (including labor rate, job/grade information, department), general ledger data, activity data (including

Exhibit 11-2

PARADOX ABC FRONT-END TOOL

Inputs:

■ Departments/Business Units
■ Business Process Information
■ Activity & Task Definitions
■ G/L Account Information
■ Labor Hours & Standard
   Department Rates
■ Job/Grade Information
■ Activity Questionnaire Responses
■ Activity/Business Process Linkage
   Information

Outputs:

■ Functional & Cross-
   Functional Hierarchy
   Listings
■ Activity Dictionary
■ Department Activity
   Questionnaires
■ Activity Cost Reports
■ Cost of Quality, Special
   Project, Business Process
   Cost Reports, and the like
■ Export Files for ABC &
   AS/400

Exhibit 11-3

ACTIVITY-BASED COSTING
ACTIVITY RESOURCE USAGE QUESTIONNAIRE

Location: Garland   Department: Accounting   Dept. #: 220   Date: October 15, 1991

Grade level: _____
Employee Name: _____   Job Title: _____
Employee Name: _____   Job Title: _____
Employee Name: _____   Job Title: _____

Directions:
1. Complete name, title, and grade level information above for all employees represented on this form.
2. Estimate the % of time spent on each activity in the activity listing provided below. If an activity does not apply, simply leave the % Time column blank.

Activity	Description	% Time	Activity	Description	% Time
Accounting – A/P	Analyze Lost Discount Report		Administrative – General	Coordinate Department Activities	
	Enter Vendor Action Notices			Corporate Reporting	
	Generate KPIP Reports			Daily Troubleshooting	
	Manually Match POs w/Receipts			Departmental Filing	
	Update KPIP System			Departmental Reporting	
	Verify Invoices			Mail Distribution	
				Meetings	
Accounting – Closing Routine	Enter ARJBs for Milk & Cream			Miscellaneous Reports	
	Enter Faulty into System			Monthly "Letter of Comments"	
	Enter Holdover into System			Outbound Mail Preparation	
	Make KPIP Adjustments			Routine Paperwork Processing	
	Perform Journal Analysis			Secretarial Duties	
	Perform Variance Analysis			Service FAX	
	Perform Yield Analysis			Service Xerox	
	Post L&E Activity Entries				
	Post Miscellaneous Journal Entries				
	Reconcile Clearance Accounts				
	Report KPP Savings				
Accounting – Product Costing	Forecast Material Prices				
	Maintain BOM				
	Maintain Direct Labor Standards				
	Maintain Efficiency Standards				
Accounting – Production	Enter Overweights into KOOA				
	Enter Scheduled Downtime in KOOA				
	Enter Unscheduled Downtime				
	Reconcile Production & Distribution			Total	100%

definitions and business process linkage). The ABC team can custom design the questionnaire for each department through on-screen options.

Data from PACT are formatted for downloading into the ABC software. In addition, PACT provides activity cost reports, activity dictionary listing, and special reports such as cost of quality and business process costs. As mentioned previously, PACT also provides information to be used for performance measurements.

New Design Feature: Supply Chain Function

The Garland implementation includes a new design feature: the supply chain function. This function is a business-level process of an organization, such as procurement or customer administration. In KRAFT's case, to obtain business process level or what they refer to as supply chain function, similar functions (described previously as containing one or more subfunctions) are grouped into one supply chain function. Supply chain functions already identified at the Garland plant are procurement, conversion, and distribution. Activity information is organized at the supply chain function and function level to benefit plant managers by making the data more meaningful and useful to them (see Exhibit 11-4).

Findings and Results

The most substantive conclusion of the two pilots was to prove the feasibility of ABC concepts at KRAFT. Senior management now acknowledge the potential insights of ABC for the business, thus paving the way for future implementations. The results of the pilots went beyond calculating improved product costs, one of the stated initial objectives. For example, management valued the insights on how activities affected their product costs.

Product Cost Analysis

The recalculated ABC overall product costs were not significantly different from KRAFT's traditional costs. However, individual items were found to have wide savings in costs when traditional costs and ABC costs were compared. This finding was not unexpected because the activity cost drivers were somewhat similar to the allocation bases used by the traditional system. High-volume products remained virtually unchanged overall. The cost of low-volume products increased about 5%.

Exhibit 11-4

PROCESS COST FOR THE PERIOD 01/01/91 TO 12/21/91

PRODUCT XYZ

Supply Chain Function	Function	Sub-function	Activity	Total Cost	Cost/ Case
Procurement					
—	—	—	—	—	—
Conversion	Manufacturing Control & Monitoring	Pourables Line 1			
			Line Changeovers	$ 480.00	$ .006
			Production Supervision	560.00	.007
			Sanitation Supervision	176.00	.002
			Relief	660.00	.009
			—	—	—
			Pourable Line 1 Summary	$ XXXX	$ XX
		Pourables Processing	—	—	—
			Mfg. Control & Monitor Cost Summary	$ XXXX	$ XX
	Resource Control				
	—	—	—	—	—
	Quality Analysis				
	—	—	Conversion Cost Summary	$ XXXX	$ XXX
Distribution					
—	—	—	TOTAL LABOR COST FOR THE PERIOD	$ XXXX	$ XX

Smith was not surprised at these results and went on to explain:

> True comparisons between direct traditional product cost (using just variable overhead) and a 'fully' costed ABC cost would be unfair. Therefore, a fully absorbed traditional cost was created by allocating fixed costs to products using volume basis and was compared to ABC. This is an inherent problem in comparing a direct cost to an ABC cost.

The ABC model, however, did provide direct visibility to activities by production line. This information was new to KRAFT because it never had departmental cost information. Bertram commented on the product cost revisions, "As expected, small volumes were undercosted. And our food service bulk business was undercosted. This product line had been deliberately subsidized by the company when it was first introduced."

The largest changes in product costs occurred in products that contained milk. Smith noted, "Prior to ABC, all the activities associated with purchasing and receiving milk had been spread to all products. With ABC, only those products which actually used milk, such as 'lite' products, received an allocation of the special milk-handling activities."

Exhibit 11-5 describes changes in product costs for four products. Products Two and Four are more costly due to the direct assignment of milk overhead costs. Management thought these two products probably would turn out cheaper under ABC because it would undo the traditional

Exhibit 11-5

PRODUCT COST IMPLICATIONS
MILK INTAKE RESOURCES (PER CASE)

Product Description	Traditional Costing	ABM Costing
Product One-Cream Cheese	$.060	$.055
Product Two-Cheese	.090	.110
Product Three-Cream Cheese	.090	.085
Product Four-Cheese	.145	.185

■ Traditional method absorbs cost by using total weight case

■ ABC method assigns costs by the amount of milk required

■ Cheese products call for more milk in their formula because milk has less fat content than cream

Exhibit 11-6
ILLUSTRATIVE DATA

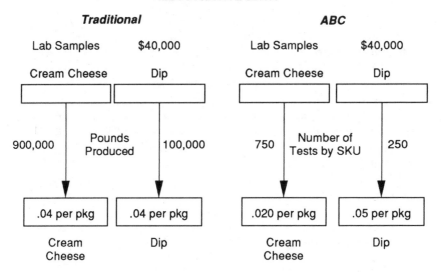

arbitrary allocation method that allocates costs on a weight basis.

Some expenses were assigned differently because activity cost drivers replaced pounds for assigning indirect costs. Exhibit 11-6 shows the results of changing a cost driver from pounds produced to number of tests performed. Because of the different intensities for testing, Product Two's testing costs increased by 25% whereas Product One's testing costs dropped by 50%.

Transfer Price Decision

The ABC results supported a change in a transfer price for certain cream cheese products. In contrast to the traditional costing method, ABC showed a significantly higher cost for these products, based on special activities performed for them. Smith stated, "Changing the transfer price for some cream cheese was a fairly easy decision since we had been considering it even before the study."

Activity Visibility

KRAFT managers traditionally see departmental salary expense, such as for the Quality Laboratory, as only one aggregate line item in the general ledger. With ABC, the activities of departments, such as raw materials and finished goods testing in the Quality Laboratory, become visible. Managers then can see the cost of activities performed within their area of responsibility. In addition, the new activity cost drivers, such as number of raw material and finished goods tests per product, supplement the traditional allocation bases of pounds and production-line processing hours. Using these cost drivers enables management to see more precisely how various activities affect cost behavior.

Exhibit 11-7 shows the new departmental data featuring activity and cost driver information. Smith stated, "Operations managers loved this new data. It was so much more informative then their traditional labor and expense reporting."

Using an arbitrary department as an example (see Exhibit 11-8) the team showed how activity information could be used when making decisions on such issues as the cost of quality or cost of carrying inventory. To obtain cost of quality data, departmental quality reports have been developed (see Exhibit 11-9). Activities within each department have been segregated by the type of quality-related activity: prevention, appraisal, and internal and external failure. In addition to the listing of activity cost, the report calculates a quality performance ratio—the prevention costs divided by the total cost of the remaining quality-related activities.

Management Acceptance

The new operating management at KRAFT Operations now supports activity-based cost management at KRAFT. An engineering director stated:

> We make many decisions based on calculated product costs. But the previous product costs were far removed from actual plant operations. They were calculated by accountants who used lots of allocations. We have not maintained a good engineered base of standards.
>
> The biggest gains from ABC will come from helping us to gain control over materials flows. For example, vendor certification and testing of incoming materials increase overhead but yield great benefits in improved materials usage and reduced scrap. The existing cost system doesn't allow us to see the sensitivity of product costs to yield improvements and better materials usage. ABC should enable us to shift from *ex post* cost reporting to *ex ante* cost modeling.

Exhibit 11-7
COST OCCURRENCE
ABC VS. TRADITIONAL ACCOUNTING INFORMATION

Labor & Expense Report

Line Item	Amount
Laboratory	$650,000
Benefits	250,000
Totals	$900,000

ABC Report

Activity	Amount	1st Stage Cost Driver	2nd Stage Cost Driver
FG Testing	$200,000	#FG QC Tests	Line Hours
Lab Maintenance	70,000	#FG QC Tests	Line Hours
Milk Tests	130,000	100% QC Sust	Milk Usage
Process Testing	400,000	#FG QC Tests	Prod Volume
Raw Material Tests	100,000	100% QC Sust	QC Ingr Test
Totals	$900,000		

Exhibit 11-8
USES OF ACTIVITY INFORMATION

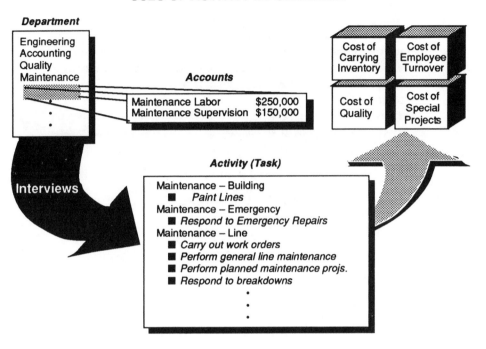

Another team member commented:

We have one accounting system that tries to do everything for everybody. This doesn't work. ABC gives us the opportunity to develop specialized systems.

The data showed that we were overpricing long-run items and underpricing short-run items. I was not surprised at the result, just at the amounts. We take a major hit with our shorter runs, especially with run loss that averages five to six percent on short runs but only one percent on long runs.

The existing cost system calculates product costs assuming an average run size for all runs. But with all our new SKUs, it's hard to run only long runs. And if we make too many long runs, we risk running out of some product codes.

The engineering director added to this point.

Two types of changeovers were identified in the ABC process; simple size changes and more time-consuming cleaning changes between products. The cleaning changeovers require the sanitation department assistance. We are continually trying to assess whether to increase batch size to reduce the changeover costs per pound or decrease the batch size to decrease the inventory carrying costs. ABC could help us make that decision. At present we don't have adequate data to help us make the appropriate trade-offs.

We have one accounting system that tries to be everything for everyone —performance measures, financial accounting, and cost accounting. Vari-

Exhibit 11-9
ABC EXAMPLE OF DEPARTMENTAL
COST OF QUALITY REPORTS

Department X Cost of Quality Report – *November 1991*	
Prevention Costs	
Safety Training	$
Formulation	$
Sanitation	$
Total Quality Support	$
Total Quality Training	$
	$A
Appraisal Costs	
Testing – Finished Goods	$
Quality Audits	$
In-Process Testing	$
Sanitation Audits	$
Internal Failure Costs	
Inventory Control – FG Unsalables	$
Handling Faulty	$
Handling Salvage	$
Material Losses	$
External Failure	
Product Recall Support	$
Cost of Stockouts	$
Consumer Complaints	$
	$B
Quality Performance Ratio	A/B

ances at the plant are too aggregated and too late. We need better measures. In our business it's too easy to blame productivity problems on raw material problems: it becomes a black hole of excuses. We need to understand our overheads.

Senior operating managers now were expressing strong enthusiasm for the ABM project. Donald Benson explained:

ABC identifies where you add value, in procurement, in conversion, and in distribution, to the production process. Traditional systems do not provide this insight. The new information sets priorities for my attention. Before, we did it intuitively.

Also, we are now examining the total costs of the new product introduction process. We are extending our analysis back to all the activities we do in the product development phase to bring new products successfully to market.

Len Grant, another Operations vice president, shared his views on the role for ABC:

Our forecasts indicate a flat overall market. We plan to hold on to our existing share by proliferating our product line. We will need to understand the cost of this strategy and how to manage and control these costs. Currently, the costs of product proliferation are 'recognized' but not 'appreciated' because we don't have effective means of communicating the story. Our current strategy emphasizes flexibility and first-to-market, but our existing cost systems don't capture the costs, the economics, of these strategies. As a consequence, we don't optimize our entire system. We don't understand the trade-offs that should be made across the entire supply chain, so we suboptimize within functional responsibilities.

In the food business, the retailer now has the clout. He has taken over power from the manufacturer. The retailer makes demands that increase our costs-to-serve, but he doesn't pay higher prices. So our marketing department comes to Operations and tells us what the customer demands and what we have to deliver, but none of us knows the cost consequences from these new requirements.

Donald Benson continued:

Total quality and activity-based costing will be critical for future success and competitive advantage in the food industry. We will need to understand what really creates value in the marketplace and what it costs. Future value may arise more from operations: procurement, conversion, and distribution, rather than from brand management. But we have now taken all the slack out of existing operations. Any future improvements will have to occur by restructuring activities.

Benson and Grant were asked how their conversion to ABC occurred. Benson replied:

ABM acceptance was more of an evolution than a revolution. It was a concurrent development but until we saw its link to quality, it was alone in the finance group. We now see that it links well with our TQM initiatives. Total quality works easier and better when it can be linked to ownership of activities. If we are to empower ownership of processes at the factory floor, we have to give managers and employees good information about their operations.

Still, for the past two years we have been in a major cost-cutting mode and we had only limited funds for new initiatives. I tried to nurture Jim Smith's and Steve Gotherd's efforts, but I agree that senior management hasn't really been out in front of the ABM effort. Frankly, we focused primarily on cost reductions while maintaining a minimal ABC effort. Also, we recognized that ABM could not get too far without major systems enhancements that were not yet in place.

During the project, we were kept adequately informed through occasional briefings from the operations controller about the Beaver Dam study.

Grant stated:

My exposure has been limited. But now it's our challenge and opportunity to understand how we can accelerate and expand the process, especially in our new or restructured plants. But we won't feel the full benefit until ABM is rolled out beyond Operations into all of KRAFT USA. So far the Sales organization supports ABM only in theory, and even that is only at the vice president level currently.

Benson added:

ABM will likely have its highest impact in multiproduct facilities that produce many products for a variety of distribution channels: retail, institutional, and food service. At present, the economics of these plants is distorted by massive and arbitrary cost allocations. After an ABM analysis, I expect to see that there are some products we definitely should not be manufacturing and some other products that we should be committing many more resources to. We should be able to use ABC to decide on which facility should manufacture particular products for each market. We will be able to watch the impact of proliferating SKUs and the necessary link to process improvements. ABM should affect our long-term decisions on which businesses KRAFT should be in.

Benson and Grant were asked where resistance to ABM would likely occur. Benson replied, "The major business heads in Marketing will likely protest when they see the cost of SKU proliferation. The Food Service Business already shows low margins. ABM may reveal that this business is really a major loss for us." Grant stated, "A Marketing person now looks at some private label business to be breakeven on a variable cost basis. How will these products look when all relevant costs are applied to it?"

As to what might have been done differently to accelerate the ABM process, Grant stated, "I wasn't in this position when those decisions were made, but now I wish that more resources had been committed to the effort so that the information would be available to me now." Benson admitted, "There were so many changes occurring in the late 1980s, we probably couldn't have managed any more change on top of what was already occurring."

Grant added, "...unless ABM was positioned then as a change mechanism or a change facilitator."

Scott Simon had been appointed recently (March 1991) to controller, Operations. He reviewed the ABM project from his new perspective:

Jim Smith was clearly frustrated in early 1991 by the lack of senior management support. ABM was viewed as a exercise for the finance people to play with. I asked Jim about what he saw from the project. He emphasized significant changes in product costs but, more important, the new insights into manufacturing processes, giving visibility to the things we do that drive the cost of products.

I now see ABM as giving us the information to link processes to organizational units. An activity becomes the unit of analysis. We can ask, "What process does the activity support and who owns the activity?" We will measure costs, the use of financial resources consumed, at the activity level. This will provide a good way of measuring our progress toward our total quality goals to improve processes.

Better product costs will also provide links to the economics of our business. We will be able to identify the costs that will go away if we stop making a product. Down the road, it gives us possibilities for zero-based budgeting, also a better mechanism for managing our risk exposure.

I feel that senior management in Operations has now really gotten interested in ABM. But it is a big task that has to be done in parallel with many other systems initiatives we have underway. We will have to decide whether ABM is a real-time or a point-in-time system. Should it be stand-alone or integrated with our PRISM production scheduling and inventory management system?

Smith will also need to produce some demonstrable short-term 'wins.' People are intrigued by the early surprises, such as the higher costs for our milk-based products, but no major decisions or actions have been taken yet.

Future

The future of ABC at KRAFT begins with the Garland plant, especially in its possible tie to the performance measurement system. KRAFT recognizes that the spread of ABC throughout KRAFT USA, particularly beyond the Operations unit, will be a slow and careful process. Gotherd provided his vision for future implementations of ABC:

Personal computer-based models are good for study purposes and for pilot projects, but you can't share data very well with PCs. Plants and corporate need to access similar data. I looked at an AS/400 software product recently. It's a process-oriented MRP system that lets you allocate costs to product class. I loaded all the Beaver Dam data into it. It lacks some features, such as business processes. But I envision that it will fit nicely with our long-term needs. I would like to see ABC as part of our MRP and inventory control system, with a box [terminal] at every plant.

There will probably always be a need for the PC-based prototype model. You need to understand your businesses first. But eventually, I believe people need to bring the ABC data into their main systems in some fashion.

On whether ABC and performance measurement data will become part of the same system, a KPI project team member replied:

Conceptually, yes. In practice, probably not. The cost drivers determined for performance measurement and ABC are not entirely consistent. A linkage between the two systems will require some consistent measures.

The ABC team member from the systems group commented:

> The model should be designed to address plant-level issues. Therefore, it is critical to get the involvement of the plant manager and his staff. We want to build something that the plant managers would use willingly. This prototype will also have a link to total quality.
>
> Looking ahead, we would like to pare down the number of cost drivers identified. We would like to identify ten to twenty key cost drivers and concentrate on gathering that information.

Steve Gotherd sees ABC as a continuous process:

> ABC should become part of a plant's performance gauge. It should link to its nonfinancial measures—such as unplanned downtime by line or cycle time. It should also hook to the quality system—for example, the percentage of vendor inspections. By improving quality, costs will follow.

Jim Smith believes that the new cost system will enhance the TQM process and be simplified due to technology advancements:

> The opportunities for a new cost system are stronger than ever. KRAFT's commitment to TQM requires us to understand our business better—ABC supports this understanding. Also improved technology and enhanced information systems will help to simplify the ABC process.

Epilogue

Recent discussions with ABC advocate Jim Smith highlighted a few principal decisions management has made regarding future use of ABC within KRAFT.

To begin, Smith described a key decision regarding ABC software options:

> After much discussion and with significant budget constraints playing a major role in the decision, it has been decided that KRAFT USA Operations will pursue a PC solution in the short term as its ABC tool. Later, the ABC solution will be linked to the underlying manufacturing control system.

Also, KRAFT is broadening its view of ABC from a plant perspective to a business process perspective.

Because of two new ABC champions from Operations the implementation of ABC will follow an holistic business view for the entire cream cheese business along the entire supply chain. The project is on track to be completed by mid-1993. Activities will be analyzed in the R&D area, Operations, and Marketing & Sales to gain a business perspective as opposed to a plant-by-plant roll-out of the concept. Truly, after several years of studies and inconsistent management support, KRAFT USA Operations has the management commitment to make ABC a functioning system. The project will culminate in an implementation of a system, not simply a 'study.'

And most exciting to learn, Smith described how KRAFT management has begun to use the data:

In addition, the concept is being used to support a major product line resourcing decision. Further, specific plans are in place (and action is being taken) to link TQM and KPIs with ABC. Staffing of the teams now includes an engineer with significant TQM and ABC experience.

Chapter 12

Analysis of ABC Models: Design, Structure, and Findings

This chapter summarizes the ABC models developed at each of the eight sites. It focuses on the structure of the models—activities, cost drivers, and cost objects—as well as on the resources required to develop the models.[1] The discussion also will include the insights management received from the activity-based models and the actions contemplated or already taken based on these insights. We refer to this aspect of an ABC project as the *analysis stage*. The analysis stage involves "getting to the numbers" and interpreting them for management insight and potential actions.

In several organizations, however, operating managers were not taking actions based on the newly revealed numbers, at least at the time of the field visits. We believe that the reasons for delay in taking action were influenced more by the way a project was organized and supported than by the design or structure of a particular ABC model. We highlight this issue in the subsequent chapter, where we focus on the *action stage* of an ABC project. The action stage requires that organizations make the difficult transition from attaining insights from an estimated ABC model to having managers act upon these insights, making decisions that will lead to higher organizational profitability. Thus, the current chapter concentrates on developing and analyzing the activity-based model, including model scope and resources required. The next chapter describes the organizational processes for the action stage so that the insights from an activity-based cost model are translated into effective action leading to higher profits.

Model Scope

In the initial effort, none of the eight sites developed a complete model of all organizational expenses. But in aggregate, the eight sites covered models of manufacturing operating expenses, marketing and selling

273

expenses, distribution expenses, and general corporate overhead expenses. Therefore, by aggregating across the models developed in the eight sites, we can start to see how an enterprise-wide, organizational, activity-based model can be implemented, and the nature of the decisions that would be supported by such a model.

The eight case studies occur in quite different settings.

Production and Marketing Cost Analysis for Manufacturing Companies

- Farrall Corporation: two plants of a manufacturer of filters and housings;
- Monarch Mirror Door: two plants of a private $70 million manufacturer;
- AMD: the Malaysian assembly and test facility for a $1 billion semiconductor company;
- Slade: Youngstown plant of a $120 million automotive components division of a $700 million manufacturer;
- KRAFT: two processing plants of a very large food company.

General & Administrative Cost Analysis for Service Organizations

- Steward: a regional institutional brokerage company;
- ARCO Alaska: controller's department (175 people).

Distribution Cost Analysis

- Williams Brothers Metals: a privately held metal fabrication and distribution company.

Production and Marketing Expenses

AMD, Slade, and KRAFT focused on analysis of manufacturing expenses for product costing and profitability. This application was the original focus of activity-based analysis and contributed to describing the procedure as activity-based "costing" (ABC). Even in this now traditional application, these three projects still emphasized the role for activity costing and analysis to stimulate process improvements in manufacturing operations.

Farrall and Monarch also analyzed factory-related expenses but extended their activity-based analysis to include the assignment of marketing and selling expenses to major market segments and individual customers. Thus these two projects illustrate the growing trend for an activity-based model to be more comprehensive by incorporating all organizational expenses, not just those arising in manufacturing operations.

Links to Continuous Improvement Activities

All of the manufacturing companies explicitly recognized the linkage of ABC to their companies' formal quality initiatives. The model designs typically included specific activities and activity centers to collect information on quality-related expenses. Monarch identified a specific benefit from its activity-based model—that it became a certified supplier to a major customer. A manager said, "ABC helped to quantify our world-class manufacturing processes and the results from our TQM program. Sears rewarded us with vendor certification, an unexpected benefit from our ABC efforts."

Farrall's factory manager became "sold" on activity-based management when he saw the strong relationship to his plant's quality management efforts. He states, "The ABC model gave our people the right numbers [on quality] for the first time. It helped us identify the price of nonconformance and tied in 100% with our quality improvement program."

At AMD, the manufacturing department already had implemented JIT cells for the high-volume simple products in assembly and test even though its existing traditional cost system could not support this decision. ABC demonstrated that the product costs for the standard high-volume products that ran on the JIT cells were significantly lower than traditional costs. It also proved that the low-volume complex military products were significantly more expensive than previously thought. In the words of a local production manager, "ABC provided cost information that acted as a feedback mechanism to validate manufacturing improvement programs. Plant management felt that now they had a cost system that would measure the impact of batch level activities on product costs and provide a more accurate picture of assembly and test costs for different products."

Slade was encountering severe quality complaints from its largest customer, and its preferred supplier quality rating was in danger of being revoked. Slade's ABC project team defined specific activity centers to collect the costs of prevention, appraisal, and failure. This information was expected to demonstrate to the customer that Slade had recognized the problem and was in the process of correcting it. Slade used the cost of quality data to redirect resources from failure to prevention activities. Management assigned more resources to quality prevention for high-volume products, and quality failure costs dropped by 13% in the following year.

For KRAFT, the entire ABC project was justified to support its key performance indicator program. Jim Smith, the ABC project leader at KRAFT, felt that activity-based costing was needed to support the performance measurement project. Smith believed that ABC had a value beyond just product costing. He argued that ABC would enable the finance department to provide information useful for both operational and strategic decision making. For operational control, ABC information would:

- Establish targets that are linked to strategies,
- Compare actual to targeted performance,
- Promote efficiency, productivity, and learning.

A senior operating executive at KRAFT noted the strong linkage between activity-based costing and the company's TQM and improvement activities:

> Total quality and activity-based costing will be critical for future success and competitive advantage in the food industry. We will need to understand what really creates value in the marketplace and what it costs. Future value may arise more from operations: procurement, conversion, and distribution rather than from brand management. But we have now taken all the slack out of existing operations. Any future improvements will have to occur by restructuring activities.

Another operating executive described how he became converted to ABC's role in the organization:

> ABC acceptance was more of an evolution than a revolution. It was a concurrent development, but until we saw its link to quality, it was alone in the finance group. We now see that it links well with our TQM initiatives. Total quality works easier and better when it can be linked to ownership of activities. If we are to empower ownership of processes at the factory floor, we have to give managers and employees good information about their operations.

Thus, managers in each of the five manufacturing companies saw strong synergies between their activity-based costing program and their organization's TQM and performance improvement initiatives.

General, Administrative, and Distribution Expenses

As already mentioned, Farrall and Monarch, in addition to developing an ABC factory expense model, also developed an ABC model to analyze marketing and selling expenses so that they could calculate individual customer and market profitability. Steward and ARCO Alaska extended the applications of activity-based management to the general and administrative expenses in financial service organizations, with Steward also developing a model for account executives' marketing and selling activities. Williams Brothers Metals focused on an activity-based model of the company's distribution expenses.

In summary, the eight sites illustrate how activity-based models and management can encompass all aspects of a company's value chain:

- Purchasing and procurement,
- Operations,
- Marketing and selling,
- Distribution,
- General and administrative expenses.

Model Structure

We analyzed each company's activity-based model based on three key structural components:

- Measurement of costs of activities and business processes,
- Measurement of cost drivers,
- Measurement of product and customer costs and profitability.

Activity and Business Process Costs

The implementing companies found that one of the quickest benefits from the ABC analysis was the restructuring and mapping of an organization's expenses from functional categories and departments into activities performed by the organization's resources. Existing general ledger systems in companies collect expenses by departments or responsibility centers. Within each functional department or responsibility center, expenses are classified further by account type: wages, salaries, benefits, materials, utilities, depreciation, data processing, and so on. The ABC project teams at the eight sites generated activity and business process costs within several weeks of initiating the project, though not all project managers shared this information in a timely fashion with their project sponsors or senior executives.

In each study, senior managers reported that the activity and business process costs revealed, for the first time, the costs of the activities their organizational units were performing. They expected to use this information for decisions on:

1. *Outsourcing*. Steward already (prior to the ABC study) had out-sourced much of its data processing department. The ABC study was expected to continue this examination of shifting administrative functions to external parties. ARCO Alaska was considering reorganizing or shifting some of its processing tasks, such as accounts payable, outside the Alaska group or to a site in the "lower 48 states" where labor was cheaper.

2. *Eliminating*. ARCO Alaska financial services decided to cease doing some expensive reports or processes of low value.

3. *Improving*. Many of the sites reported that seeing the amount spent on activities stimulated cost reduction activities. For example, Farrall's operations manager immediately attacked materials-handling costs; Monarch's operations manager investigated the causes for the high downtime costs from older machines; Williams Brothers Metals was examining the credit and collection costs in the customer administration business process; ARCO Alaska was concentrating on the high costs of processing accounts payable; Steward, after seeing the seven times higher cost for exception trades, placed priority on getting trades right the first time.

The number of activities used at each of the eight sites (see Exhibits 12-1 and 12-2) ranged from the simple (only a few activities defined) to the complex (several hundred activities). The short-term benefits and insights obtained from the models were not related systematically to the complexity of the model developed.

Activity Centers

Several of the sites, especially those that had defined a large number of activities in their ABC model, chose to group activities in more aggregate activity centers or business processes. This grouping reduced the information burden on senior managers and enabled them to view their organization across functional boundaries. In a complete analysis, the activity center/business process analysis could identify and collect expenses for all processes along the company's value chain. The business processes defined by various sites are shown on the next page.

Exhibit 12-1
PRODUCT MODELS

	AMD	Farrall (Riverside)	Monarch	Slade	Kraft	WBM	Steward	ARCO
Numbers of Models	3	1	2	1	1	5	1	1
Number of Activities	62	213	180	140	225	175	140	308
Number of Activity Centers (Business Processes)	62	21	74	22	45	15	67	22
Number of Cost Drivers (2nd Stage)	38	38	42	12	7	18	25	8
Number of Cost Objects (Products, Fields)	1,440	2,936	4,700	63	200	23	9	14

Exhibit 12-2
CUSTOMER/SALES MODELS

	Farrall (Riverside)	*Steward*	*Monarch*
Number of Activities	79	55	75
Number of Cost Drivers (2nd Stage)	16	8	19
Number of Cost Objects (Customers, A/Es)	213	15	7,000

Farrall	*Steward*	*Williams Brothers*
Procurement	Sales & Support	Order Processing
Materials Handling	Sales Promotion	Inventory Mgmt.
Production Centers	Trade Settlement	Distribution Mgmt.
Inventory Mgmt.	Account Mgmt.	Customer Mgmt.
Quality	Human Resources	Sales & Marketing
Sales & Marketing	Legal & Compliance	Support Services
General & Admin.	AE Administration	Truck Loading
	Accounting	Equipment Maint.
	Data Processing	Packaging
	Investment Portfolio	Materials Handling
	Telecommunications	Transfers
	ADP Trade Proc.	
	General Mgmt.	
	Facility-Sustaining	

Slade	*KRAFT*
Production Centers (9)	Production Centers
Product Assembly	Warehousing
Product Test	Raw Materials
Product Development	Quality Control
Production Support	Facility-Sustaining
Expediting	-Plant Maintenance
Quality—Prevention	-Insurance
Quality—Appraisal	
Quality—Failure	
Shipping	
Excess Capacity	

The activity centers defined at Slade had several interesting features. First, Slade grouped all its excess capacity costs in a separate activity center. Because of the high variation in automotive parts business, plus a recent downturn, Slade had significant excess capacity. Slade's managers recognized that the excess capacity related to management decisions for surge capabilities, not to the production of existing products. The excess capacity activity center enabled the managers to identify excess capacity costs specifically, without having them driven down to become part of product costs.

A second innovation was to define an activity center (product development) to collect the expenses related to the development of future products. Slade's managers concluded that today's products should not bear the costs of future product development; these costs should be accumulated separately for subsequent project profitability analysis. Third, Slade, like several other sites, defined activity centers to accumulate expenses in the established "cost of quality" categories: prevention, appraisal, and failure.

The general usefulness of activity and business process costs came as somewhat of a surprise to managers. At many of the sites, managers viewed activity-center costs as a valuable but serendipitous by-product of the activity-based analysis. Perhaps they had thought that ABC produced only different product cost information. They had not expected the insights that would be gained by identifying the activities performed by support resources and determining the costs currently incurred to perform these activities. Managers expressed satisfaction with seeing their expenses accumulated and reported by business processes that cut across traditional departmental lines. Several of them commented:

> The information gave a cross functional view of our expenses. There is much more visibility to our costs when they are grouped into a few key activities than when they are buried as expense categories in cost centers. [Steward]

> Activity analysis confirmed what we thought. Activities are the driving force of our costs. Now we can see how our activities contribute to the bottom line. ... What we can control is our exploration activities and our costs. Activity-based analysis detects inefficient activities, helps us streamline activities which are not competitive, and shows us low-value activities we can eliminate. [ARCO Alaska]

> The activity analysis gave us information we can act on. For example, I had no idea how much double handling was going on. And maybe we should spend more money on prospecting new business. [Williams Brothers Metals, owner/manager]

> Managers loved this new data. It was so much more informative than their traditional labor and expense reporting. [KRAFT]

At Slade, division management used the activity data to track the cost of maintaining capital equipment and perishable tooling. The data enable managers to control tooling costs through cost trend analysis across product families and machine centers. The expenses driven to the maintenance activity have stimulated a preventive maintenance program at the plant and informed decisions on replacement versus repair for older equipment. Also, the three quality-related activity centers supported a decision to allocate more resources to prevention activities, especially for high-volume products. This commitment to prevention already had produced a 13% reduction in quality failure costs for the high-volume products within one year of the study.

Activity Classification

Contributing to the insights from the activity analysis were the several types of activity classifications used by the sites, including cost hierarchy and value ranking.

Cost hierarchy. Most of the sites used some form of the activity-based cost hierarchy in which activities are classified as unit, batch, product-sustaining, or facility-sustaining.[2]

Farrall Corporation was surprised that only 23% of expenses related to unit-level activities. The hierarchy analysis demonstrated that business expenses were much less volume sensitive than had been calculated by the traditional cost system. As an immediate benefit, operations managers could shift their priorities from improving unit-level activities (reducing direct labor and buying faster-running machines) to improving batch activities (faster setups, more efficient materials movement) and product-sustaining activities (greater design commonality for products).

Monarch saw that more than 20% of its operating expenses were product-sustaining, indicating the high cost it was paying for its recent proliferation of products and customers.

AMD discovered that most of the activities at its test and assembly facility were not unit related. Fewer than 50% of activities were driven by variables proportional to the volume of production. This insight was expected to shift improvement activities at the site from increasing processing speeds to improving the efficiency of or eliminating the need for batch and product-sustaining activities.

Steward, using a cost hierarchy developed specifically for its financial services business, saw a large portion of expenses associated with individual customer accounts and account executives. Previously these expenses had been driven to products based on number of transactions. This insight helped management to understand the significant investment in capital and manpower required for adding new products and the high cost of having hundreds of low-volume customers who traded in low volumes or used low-margin products.

Williams Brothers Metals developed a unique hierarchy for its distribution business. Orders—groups of metals—were defined as the lowest or unit level; shipments or movements of products or orders were defined as batch activities; "product-sustaining" activities referred to maintaining dedicated machines or product management; and "facility-sustaining" activities represented general plant and corporate management expenses unrelated to individual products or orders.

With 22% of expenses accumulating in the facility-sustaining category, the company could see the high cost of conducting its current level of business activity at four separate locations. But a majority of costs (62%) related to orders, shipments, and movements and varied with levels of business activity. The project leader indicated the impact of this finding, saying, "People were amazed at the results. We would have expected more fixed (facility) costs rather than unit. Virtually all costs can be controlled and managed to volume—much more than we had thought."

KRAFT also found that most (60% to 70%) of the factory activities were volume or unit-level driven. One project member felt that the hierarchical analysis offered limited benefits to plant management, but the project manager disagreed. He felt, "The activity cost hierarchy clearly reveals different cost behavior patterns. This type of analysis would have helped me convince my management that ABC was not just a product-costing exercise."

The Farrall study developed a cost hierarchy for marketing and selling expenses. Farrall sold to customers in four distinct market segments: (1) distributors for the home appliance division, (2) distributors for the leisure division (3) distributors for the new housing division, and (4) direct sales to original equipment manufacturers (OEM).

In the marketing and selling expense hierarchy, individual customer orders for specific products were defined as the lowest level. Distributors and customers were at the next level; sales representatives, who were responsible for a group of distributors and customers, at the next level; and the four major market segments at the highest level. The hierarchical structuring of marketing and selling activities enabled Farrall's management to develop a contribution margin approach to customer, sales rep, and market segment profitability.

In all cases, project managers found that the activity-based hierarchical analysis gave them significant insights about their cost structure behavior and the types of activities that created demands on indirect and support resources. These insights, however, were confined mainly to people closely involved with developing the activity-based model. The hierarchical structure of costs and its implications for managerial decision making had yet to be communicated, much less internalized, by senior operating managers. Thus, the action implications flowing from the hierarchical structure of costs had yet to be exploited in the eight companies.

Value ranking. Several of the sites found the value classification of activities informative. ARCO Alaska defined two codes for each activity: a value code (high, medium, low) to reflect the activity's role in supporting the individual group's mission; and a reason code (regulatory, contractual, management request, business unit request, other) to reflect why the activity was performed or who requested it. Only 4% of the activities were classified as of low value to a group. In retrospect, the project leader realized that the criterion used was too restrictive because it did not attempt to make clear whether an individual group's mission created value for the entire organization. The project leader stated:

> On the next study, the value ranking will be done, not on the individual group's mission but on the Controller's Group's mission as a whole. The next assessment should be made on whether the activity directly supports the generation or protection of company assets or cash flow—and that's all. Using this criterion, the percentage of low-value activities would be a lot higher and more meaningful to us.

The reason code analysis revealed that most activities performed by the finance group were management requested, not regulatory or contractual. Further, most of the low-value activities were management generated. A finance person reflected, "In theory, we should only be doing low-value activities which we are legally or contractually bound to perform. Therefore, we want the low-value activities to be made up of almost all contractual and regulatory activities."

The Farrall project team generated a five-category classification of activities (low, low-medium, medium, medium-high, and high) based on each activity's importance for the company's objectives and mission and for providing value to customers. The project leader recalled, "This was a painful process. Everyone had a different definition of what's valuable to them. The concept, however, tied closely to our quality program, and it got people's attention."

Farrall project people believed, at the end, that the value analysis gave them some insight into the business but otherwise had not provided much benefit.

Monarch and Williams Brothers Metals coded each activity on a

9-point scale, with a 1 representing No Value Added: an activity that shouldn't be performed (making errors or correcting errors) and a 9 representing High Value: an activity that adds value to the product and/or the customer. In both companies, about 16% of activities received scores below 5, indicating a "necessary evil that could be improved" or eliminated entirely without jeopardizing customer satisfaction. The companies were establishing target improvement teams to focus on improving or eliminating these low- to medium-value activities.

AMD, in contrast, eventually made a deliberate decision not to value rank activities. An initial attempt consumed a large amount of time and proved highly controversial. The plant manager decided that any efficiency improvements should focus on high-cost activities, regardless of whether these activities had been coded somewhat arbitrarily in his mind as of high or low value.

Cost Driver Analysis

Many of the sites reported that measuring cost drivers proved to be the hardest job in the study. In the Steward study, the lack of cost driver information led to excluding two key expense categories—telecommunications/quotations services and the outside vendor's data processing charges—from the initial ABC study. A follow-up study was being performed to develop the cost drivers for these two large resource categories. Even for the resource categories included in the study, the project leader indicated the difficulty of collecting accurate cost driver information: "We did not have the groundwork in our systems to provide the information for many of the selected drivers. We had to improvise a lot to get even rough approximations to the drivers we wanted."

Some senior managers at Steward lacked confidence in the study's findings because of the rough approximations used. One said, "I don't believe the allocation process was that accurate. ... I believe the production and support of [my unit] is less expensive than the ABC analysis shows."

Despite these reservations, Steward managers still gained considerable insights from the cost driver analysis. The cost of exception trades was revealed to be seven times higher than the automated trades for which no corrections were required. The cost driver analysis also showed the high cost of supplying account executives with an analytic software service. Operations managers expected to use the unit cost driver rates as measures to drive performance improvement.

In the Slade study, the lack of adequate cost driver information prevented the project team from implementing two desired activity centers: materials handling and maintenance. The project team recognized that both materials handling and maintenance varied significantly among products and machines but had no quantifiable cost driver available for either activity. Consequently, these expenses had to be spread to products by proxy drivers that, while adequate for the initial product-costing objective of the study, were not sufficiently accurate to permit more detailed activity or performance measurement analysis.

For the Farrall study, the project team learned that moving and purchasing materials varied significantly by the type of materials. Rather than conduct detailed studies of these activities, the team estimated weighting factors for the materials-handling and purchasing activities cost drivers to reflect the degree of difficulty of moving or purchasing individual parts and materials.

Farrall expected to use the cost driver rates as benchmarks to compare costs for similar processes in other units or companies and to serve as targets for continuous improvement programs. Of particular note, the study revealed the high costs of engineering changes ordered by customers. This information was expected to encourage sales applications representatives to conduct more informed discussions with customers and to promote ways to reduce the cost of performing customer-requested changes. The high cost of batch-level cost drivers, for scheduling, shipping, and creating work orders, was expected to change decisions on minimum acceptable order sizes. The individual machine-hour cost drivers also revealed the economics of newly purchased, flexible machines versus older, slower, and less flexible machines, which was one of the primary goals of the ABC study.

At Monarch, because data were unavailable for many of the "ideal" cost drivers, the project team frequently had to substitute surrogate cost drivers. Extensive effort was required to collect even the surrogate cost driver information. Much of it was contained in separate databases and required considerable programming effort or manual collection to access and collect. For example, the ideal cost driver for materials movement would identify and measure the path followed by each product, information available from a product routing. But Monarch did not have a product routing file. The team created a surrogate driver, the number of machine centers in which a product was processed. The logic for this surrogate driver was that a product using several machine centers would be moved more often than one processed only in a single machine center.

Monarch's difficulties in accessing cost driver information were mirrored in AMD's experiences. Team members had to perform extensive programming to extract data from multiple databases. When such data were unavailable, they sampled data to get typical cost driver profiles by products. Among the key cost drivers used were number of line items scheduled, number of quality problems encountered, and number of times a product fell below a critical yield level.

Williams Brothers Metals, like Farrall, used weighting factors in its cost drivers to reflect relative difficulty of handling, loading, and delivering different metal products. Similar to the other sites, WBM expected that it would have difficulty finding cost driver information in its existing databases. In contrast, however, WBM found that almost all of the cost driver data were accessible on machine-readable databases. "We had no idea that the original site was maintained on a transshipment record. The MIS group provided valuable assistance in extracting data from the existing systems."

One key project member recalled the cost driver analysis: "When we started, we didn't know what was available in the systems. Designing cost drivers was a big deal. You really need to have good systems in place before you start an activity-based management project." The selected cost drivers at WBM created controversy among senior management. One owner/manager rejected the findings of the study [that his two largest products were unprofitable] by blaming the cost drivers:

> The product profitability was built on assumptions which are completely wrong. For example, the number of orders was used to drive Sales & Marketing costs to products. That's crazy. One order can take five minutes, another five days. Those differences should be built into the model.

At ARCO Alaska, some confusion existed initially between what some of their people came to call activity drivers and cost drivers. Their activity drivers were the fundamental forces that could explain the reason why the activity existed at all (e.g., policies, contracts, regulations) or that generated the demand for the activity (such as the price of oil influencing the amount of oil exploration). The cost drivers required for the ABC model, however, explained how cost objects (products, customers) used the different activities.

Even with this definition clarified, the project team still had difficulty collecting the cost driver information because the activities were performed by staff people in the Controller's Group who did not keep detailed records of how often they performed various tasks. Eventually, the project team relied on subjective estimates that supervisors provided when they first defined their various activities.

Products and Customers

All of the sites ultimately wanted to drive their organizational expenses from activities to individual products, customers, or other cost objects. For the manufacturing companies the definition of product or customer was generally straightforward.

Farrall

For Farrall, getting improved estimates of product and customer cost and profitability was the primary goal for the ABC study. With its organizational separation between manufacturing and marketing/sales, more accurate and detailed product costs were expected to become the basis for setting transfer prices. The Riverside, California, consumer products facility had proliferated its product line, offering more than 700 varieties of filter elements (varying by element type, color, size, and customer specification) and 25 housing lines with 10 to 15 versions per line. Increased competition and declining profitability had created a demand for knowledge of how product diversity was influencing manufacturing and support costs.

The ABC study indicated that the low-volume, complex products tended to be much more expensive than had been calculated by the existing standard cost system. The ABC model provided a "bill of activity costs" for each product, enabling managers to see the costs of procurement, inventory carrying and management, materials handling, inspection, shipment, and setup for individual products. This information was expected to lead to changes in decisions about the production scheduling, design, mix, and pricing for the division's products.

The Consumer Products Division of Farrall provided its customers with extensive technical and sales support. The company wished to assess whether broad classes of customers used more in customer support resources than they paid for in the net contribution margins of products purchased. The analysis showed that the most profitable 10% of customers generated about 230% of the organization's profits. Most customers were at or near breakeven, but the least profitable 20% of customers had losses that accumulated to 150% of the division's profits. Analysis of individual customer profitability yielded few surprises. Large-volume customers who had been doing business with Consumer Products for many years were quite profitable. Newly acquired customers or small customers, for whom generous credit terms and extensive sales and technical support were provided, were found to be unprofitable.

Because Sales & Marketing personnel had not been extensively involved in the design and execution of the study, they had yet to react or take action on these findings (more on this later). In Farrall's U.K. division, Sales & Marketing had been more actively involved in the study and were more enthusiastic about the early findings. They said, "It can be used right away to support our day-to-day [customer management and] discount decisions."

Monarch

Monarch, like Farrall, was critically interested in the cost and profitability of its many products and customers. From its founding in 1962 as a focused producer of mirrored doors, the company had grown internally and through acquisition so that it now had four different product lines, each with extensive variety and customized versions, sold to customers in five diverse market segments: (1) building materials outlets, (2) mass merchandisers, (3) new construction, (4) OEM, and (5) international. This proliferation of products and customers had led to high indirect and support expenses. The national sales manager acknowledged, "Our manufacturing costs are low but are offset by our selling and distribution costs. Our competitors are more regionally focused and don't have the high selling, general, and administrative costs that we do."

Monarch looked to the information from the ABC study to influence its strategies on which products and markets to emphasize, which to abandon, and which to improve.

The study showed that, particularly at the facility where a large number of custom products were made, a surprisingly high proportion of expenses could be identified with the number of products manufactured and the number of customers served (i.e., product- and customer-sustaining expenses). The main and most urgent finding was the low profitability of several market segments. The company saw that mass merchandisers purchased very low-margin products and likely never could become high-profit contributors. The international and OEM markets, with modest sales, were at or below breakeven. The project sponsor indicated, "Since the ABC implementation, we have developed and initiated an exit strategy for the OEM market and have held off any attempt to grow our international market. The ABC data put certain decisions on the table. We now had data to support our discussions."

AMD

The cost objects in AMD's assembly and test facility in Penang, Malaysia, included 120 different packages in the assembly area and 1,200 different devices in the test area. The analysis showed large differences in products' assembly and test costs from what had been reported by the existing traditional cost system. Low-volume products, especially those produced in many batches and that required significant product-sustaining activities, had much higher expenses assigned.

Because only a portion of total product manufacturing costs are incurred at the Penang assembly and test facility, no actions could be taken immediately at the product level based on these findings. Rather, the large distortions in the traditional cost system revealed by the Penang ABC project provided managers with justification for extending the study to the company's wafer fabrication facilities, an effort that was in progress at the time that interviews were conducted at the company. The company expected to implement ABC-based transfer prices for all manufacturing operations by the end of calendar year 1992. At that time, managers would be using ABC-derived cost information for design and product mix decisions.

Slade

Product costing was the primary objective of Slade Manufacturing's activity-based model. Severe price pressure from automobile OEM customers plus heightened demands for product variety and customization had led to proliferation of product lines and low profitability. Slade piloted activity-based management at its key Youngstown plant, which produced nine product families and 63 individual products. The activity-based model found that 30% of the products, representing 80% of the sales volume, generated 150% of the profits. The middle 60% of products were marginal or breakeven, and the least profitable 10% of the products lost 50% of the profits. This finding mobilized management into action. In the year following the development of the ABC model, 13% of the customers and several production items were eliminated, and 20% of the service parts were phased out of production. This rationalization of products and customers reduced complexity and enhanced the division's profitability. For other products, price increases yielded $1.2 million in additional revenues.

Slade translated its activity-based model into a sophisticated quoting system that determined costs by calculating the demands on six overhead resources for each customer-requested product quote. The controller described the impact of ABC at the division by saying:

> ABC has built our confidence during negotiations. Today we don't crumble when confronted by a customer demanding price improvements. ... ABC has also made us more aggressive in pursuing new business—we're aggressive on bids for products that we believe our competitors are not pricing correctly.

The Automotive Division was using its more accurate product costing data strategically. It deliberately refused to accede to an important customer's request for a significant price reduction for the last three years of an existing contract and eventually lost the business to a competitor. Slade's managers recognized that producing for three years at the lower price would be highly unprofitable. Slade was able to enjoy higher prices for the period until the products were transferred away, it freed up capacity to develop and bid for profitable next-generation products that would be produced when the existing products left, and it locked a major competitor into committing a significant part of its capacity to an unprofitable contract.

The three service organizations in the study had more difficulty in defining their products or cost objects. Once an acceptable definition had been reached, however, these companies' interest in the cost and profitability of their products and customers matched that of the manufacturing companies.

Steward

The Steward project team debated whether its products were the financial instruments they traded, the account executives who performed the trading, or the market in which a security was traded. The team decided to build one model defining products based on the existing P&L reporting structure for the type of instrument traded: listed equity security, OTC, option/future, international, convertible, fixed income, technology product. A second model was built in which the product (cost object) was the account executive (AE).

The financial instrument cost and profitability model showed that only two products—equity securities and high yield securities—were profitable. The remaining securities were breakeven or showed significant losses. Based on these results, the company cut back on one product line—international—almost immediately and reorganized its product responsibilities to increase the focus on profit improvement. Four previously independent products—listed equity securities, listed options and futures, OTC, and international—were combined into a single equity profit center, and the sales force was directed to maximize the contribution from this collection of products. A recently formed investment technology group was spun off into a separate subsidiary so that its unique features could be managed and sold independently. The new director of the Technology Trading Group stated:

> The ABC study played a major role in the decision to spin off the Technology Trading Group. The analysis forced us to take a more detailed look at product line P&Ls. The review showed that this business had little in common with all the other product lines we offered. Within the Technology Trading Group, I have begun to assign revenues and assets to individual products. This has already led to a decision not to support a particular product that was heavily analytic and demanded a fair degree of assets and other support resources.

The AE profitability study showed that AE support costs were much higher than had been believed. Many of these costs had been allocated arbitrarily by the previous system, down to individual trades. The director and head of the equity department was enthusiastic:

> The ABC study revealed the average breakeven point for an AE was $325,000 in gross commissions. This was a much higher number than we had assumed. Based on these results, unprofitable AEs who do not fall into a special category [new hire, important link to other product lines, or special/unique trades] may be asked to leave. By looking at the activity expenses associated with each AE, I have better insight into the avoidable expenses if an AE leaves.

Steward's CEO envisioned the ABC study being extended down to individual AE and customer profitability:

> I would eventually like the ABC system to treat each AE as an individual profit center. AEs, when they logged in a transaction at their workstations, would have their profitability and productivity calculated. ... If we could implement this type of measurement system, we could eliminate a lot of administrative and managerial structure that costs money and occupies space. But it would be difficult to think about decentralizing like this without the improved measurement and accountability from an ABC system. ...

The ABC analysis should [also] be able to give us a profile of account profitability. We have 1,600 major customers. I suspect that 1,100 of these are marginal or unprofitable and 500 are profitable, of which only 50 are really important to us. We need to know if our services are only worthwhile when they are mispriced and [we] lose money on the transaction. AEs are paid commissions on each trade they make, whether the trade is profitable or not. Account profitability will show us who we're making money on and to which customers we can add value.

The ABC analysis also was expected to lead to more informed discussions about the introduction of new products. As the new division head of the Technology Trading Group said:

We have never known the costs of getting into new businesses. ABC should allow us to make better decisions about how to use our key asset—capital. When analyzing new projects, we can also look more carefully at their impact on manpower needs and profitability potential. It will generate a lot more discussion about profitability, not just about how new ideas can lead to more revenues.

ARCO Alaska

The project team at ARCO Alaska also had extensive discussions about the appropriate definition of its "products." Initially, the team thought it would use the company's product definition, barrels of oil. But this definition was not relevant for the output of the controller's department, the organizational unit studied at the site. The team recognized that most of its output could be classified as facility-sustaining for individual oil fields, so the owner and operator of each field was identified as a separate "product." In addition, exploration projects, division management, and company management were defined as "products" because they created a demand for and presumably benefited from the controller's department activities.

ARCO Alaska's ABC product cost analysis showed, not surprisingly, that the largest oil field generated the highest percentage (32%) of costs. Of more surprise, the second highest cost object turned out to be the division's management, not one of the other fields or corporate management. In other words, more than one-fourth of the controller's department activity expenses were to serve internal, not external, purposes. One manager, upon seeing these results, commented, "I found the cost object analysis interesting. I never knew precisely how much time our group spent for one field versus another. This information will be really helpful in evaluating where to direct resources in the future."

The controller's department was limited, however, in taking action based on this information because its activity expenses were only a small fraction of the total activity expenses incurred for the various cost objects, such as the producing oil fields. To get managers to take action, the sponsor noted:

> In order to view what the total resources used by the fields are consuming, a full-scale analysis must be done. For example, the systems department costs are not included here, and they probably vary greatly between the fields. ... To change the demand from outside users requires executive support and a bigger activity-based analysis study. Until that happens, cost object analysis will not include fully loaded costs to make meaningful decisions.

But another manager in the department believed:

> Clearly, cost objects become more meaningful the higher you are in the organization. Our controller's department is just a small piece of all the costs demanded by the fields. But with a complete activity analysis for the Alaska company, field management could use the cost object data to better understand how operational demands affect controllership activities and costs.

Williams Brothers Metals

At Williams Brothers Metals, the project team rejected defining each specific cut, length, and width of metal as a specific product. This approach would have created thousands of products and required data collection and analysis much more extensive than envisioned for the initial project. After speaking with product managers, the team chose to treat each of 23 product classes as the cost object for the study. Pricing and most decision making occurred at this product class level, not at the level of individual cut, width, and length.

The ABC analysis indicated that the products shipped as mill direct were the most profitable. Such shipments incurred almost no inventory and materials-handling costs. This finding, however, caused management to question the value-added of their distribution business if their most profitable products bypassed most of their internal processes. The analysis also showed that most product classes had both low revenues and low contribution margins. Management had not yet internalized this message and had yet to contemplate, much less act upon, this finding. They were still arguing about the cost drivers and other methods used to generate product cost and profitability.

Project Resources

Resources required to develop an activity-based model include:

- Internal personnel,
- Outside consultants,
- Time,
- Data,
- Software.

Exhibit 12-3 summarizes some of the resources used at the eight sites.

Project Resources: Internal Personnel

With one exception, each of the sites had its own project team do the bulk of the model development: interviews, formal and informal data collection, running the model. The Farrall project was sponsored by Jay Hansen, corporate controller, who had received support and approval from the company CEO for the project. The project manager was Robert Spears, controller of the Riverside facility where the ABC model was being developed.

The project team was led by John McCarthy, who came from the site's cost accounting group, and also included representatives from information systems and the corporate staff (to explain existing corporate cost allocations to facilities) and a minor input from senior sales executives. Spears supervised the project himself; an interfunctional steering committee was not used.

At Monarch, Mike Laney, the vice president of finance, was the overall project sponsor and project leader. Laney generated the initial enthusiasm and support for the project, monitored the project, and provided advice on the overall architecture and conceptual design. The corporate treasurer served as the team leader at the first site, Chatsworth. He helped to resolve issues or problems that developed during the implementation and helped to make key decisions as they were needed. The Chatsworth project team included on a full-time basis: one person from Finance familiar with the existing costing system and the product and bill of material files, and one person from Information Systems with experience working with the Operations Department. At the second site, Tupelo, the project team included one Finance person familiar with the general ledger and current costing system, one person from Information Systems, who had previously worked in Production

Exhibit 12-3
PRODUCT MODELS

Site	Duration[2]	FTEs[3]	Role for Outside Consultants[1]		
			Facilitate[4]	Analysis[5]	Create Change[6]
AMD	4	2.5	3	3	0
ARCO ALASKA	2	2.5	5	4	1
WILLIAMS BROTHERS	8	2.0	3	3	0
STEWARD	3	0.25	5	5	0
KRAFT	6	2.5	3	1	0
MONARCH	6	1.5-2.0	3	3	0
FARRALL	8	2.0	3	3	0
SLADE	4	2.0	4	4	3

[1] The role for outside consultants will be coded on a scale from 0 to 5:
       "0": zero involvement in a particular task
       "1": low involvement
       "3": medium involvement, and
       "5": active involvement.

[2] Duration is the estimated time, in months, to estimate and analyze the organization's first ABC model.

[3] FTEs represents the Full-Time-Equivalent company people involved in the ABC project over its duration. Several of the companies, particularly Steward, used outside consultants extensively to help in the model development process, which reduced the required commitment for internal people.

[4] Facilitate includes initial training and awareness seminars, design of ABC model.

[5] Analysis includes interpretation and presentation of results and development and presentation of recommended actions.

[6] Create Change involves spurring the organization into action; developing an agenda for and facilitating organizational commitment, decision making, and action.

Planning, and one Operations person with an engineering background who was familiar with the product and bill of materials files.

The sponsor and project leader for the AMD project was Vic Lee, group controller. Lee worked closely with the vice president of Far East manufacturing in gaining corporate support for the project. The Penang project team included seven people, drawn from different functional specialties. The project manager was the section head of the repair and maintenance area of the test facility and had extensive operations experience. The other team members had backgrounds in industrial engineering, product engineering, quality analysis, MIS, and cost accounting. Management deliberately chose a large multifunctional team because they believed that active participation of members from all operating areas would be critical to the success and implementation of the project. The AMD project was performed under the supervision of a steering committee that included Vic Lee, the plant director, the plant controller, and all operating department managers. The steering committee resolved major issues that arose during the project.

At Slade, the sponsor for the ABC project was Bill Carlisle, Manufacturing's controller. Carlisle, concerned about the distortions from the company's traditional standard costing system, hired Larry Martin to be controller for the Automotive Group with a specific agenda: to improve cost accounting systems for all Automotive Group companies. Carlisle and Martin worked together to get corporate approval and support for the project. They selected the largest company, Hudson, within the Automotive Group, as the pilot site for an ABC project.

The steering committee for the ABC project included from Hudson Automotive the company president; the manufacturing manager; the vice president, finance; the vice president, purchasing; the vice president, sales & marketing; the Youngstown plant manager; and the engagement partner and senior manager from the outside consulting firm. The steering committee would guide the overall ABC effort, provide input to the project team at a mid-project meeting, and participate in a hands-on final meeting to develop recommendations and plan the next steps.

The ABC project team was led by Larry Martin, the Automotive Group's controller, who worked full-time on the project. Other members included the Youngstown plant accountant (60% of the time) and the plant manager (who conducted cost driver interviews, scheduled steering committee meetings, and acted as a sounding board for the project team's ideas).

The KRAFT project was sponsored and led by Jim Smith, regional controller (at the time) in the company's Operations Group. Smith initiated the project with the assistance of Tom Bertram, a plant controller, as part of a broader company effort to develop key performance indicators. Smith served as project manager. At the Beaver Dam and Springfield pilot sites, the manager of cost analysis served as project leader, under the guidance of Bertram, the Springfield plant controller, and assisted by the Beaver Dam controller. Other team members included people with backgrounds in cost accounting, quality, and systems. No steering committee was formed at KRAFT. The lack of a steering committee was both an indication of and a contributor to senior management's limited support and commitment.

At Steward, the ABC project had strong senior management support, ranging from the chairman and CEO through the chief administration officer, the head of the core equity business, the vice president, accounting and finance, and the chief financial officer. As will be described subsequently, the actual work was performed by outside consultants, but the project was under the continual supervision of a steering committee consisting of the chief administration officer, the vice president accounting and finance, and the chief financial officer

ARCO Alaska's project was initiated and sponsored by Dan Casey, company controller, who was transferred to another job shortly after the project started. The project continued even in Casey's absence, with the results and recommendations presented to his management team at the completion of the project. The project was performed only on expenses incurred in the Controller's Group, so, unlike the other sites, only financial people were involved.

The co-project leaders were the supervisor of headquarters accounting and an internal business consultant for one of the major operating fields. The steering committee, consisting of the managers of General Accounting and of Financial Reporting and Analysis, was created to guide the project, to wrestle with issues as they arose, and to approve all design decisions. Two summer interns did the detailed project work. The management team established a demanding seven-week deadline to complete the project because of the limited availability of the interns and the desire to have the information available for the upcoming budgeting process.

Williams Brothers Metals' ABC project was generated, sponsored, and led by Jim Curry, the vice president of finance. Curry selected a manager from his finance department to be the project leader (she stated that she had never even heard of ABC until Curry assigned her to lead the project). Another finance person was assigned full-time to the project, and MIS personnel assisted on an "as-needed" basis. No steering committee was created for the project.

To summarize, senior financial people played a critical role at all of the eight sites examined in this study. With the exception of the brokerage company, Steward, where the motivation for the project came from the company CEO, the motivation and sponsorship at all the other sites arose and was maintained in a finance group. Most of the project teams, however, drew upon people other than those from the finance group to staff the project teams, with the main contributors coming from MIS and Operations. Project steering committees were used at four sites—AMD, Slade, Steward, and ARCO Alaska. As will be discussed in the subsequent chapter, management actions were most noticeable at Slade, Steward, and ARCO Alaska, suggesting that steering committees may play a vital role in gaining management understanding, acceptance, and commitment to the activity-based cost management approach.[3]

Project Resources: Outside Consultants

At most of the sites, the outside consultants played a facilitating role. They conducted initial training and awareness seminars, both for the project sponsors and senior management team and for the project team itself. They helped the project team structure the interviews and assisted in transferring both the hard data from the company's databases and the soft data from management interviews and estimates into the PC-based activity-based software model. Finally, they generally assisted in the data analysis and preparation of reports and presentations to the project sponsor and senior management. But the bulk of the day-to-day work was performed by the company's internally staffed project team. For example, at Slade Manufacturing, the outside consultants were involved throughout the study but mostly as trainers and facilitators. They played their most active role during the cost driver interviews and when assisting the project team in designing and developing the ABC model architecture. At KRAFT, the consultants assisted in project management, model design, and data collection. One of the consultants eventually was hired to support ongoing ABC implementations.

Steward Brokerage, because of limited personnel availability, used its outside consultants to develop and analyze the activity-based model. The extensive use of outside consultants at Steward required that the company make only a modest time commitment (0.5 FTE) to model development and analysis and perhaps led to a shorter project duration (three months). Normally, the extensive use of outside consultants for model development and analysis could lead to resistance in the organization in accepting the estimates, analysis, and action implications from the model. For Steward, however, the strong sponsorship of the project by the CEO and the active communication between the consultants and the company's steering committee negated this tendency. As will be discussed in the following chapter, senior managers at Steward accepted the validity and implications of the model and acted quickly, based on the new information.

Project Resources: Time

Exhibit 12-3 presents the time in months required for a complete activity-based model development and analysis. The shortest time, two months at ARCO Alaska, was motivated by the availability of two summer interns who did the data collection and model development. The short time also was facilitated by the extensive use of outside consultants in model development and analysis. ARCO Alaska's activity-based project also had the most limited scope of the eight sites: only the activities of the Controller's Group of 175 people were analyzed.

The next shortest project time occurred at Steward. Full-time outside consultants performed all the data collection and analysis functions, which helped to reduce the time required for the task. Also, the activity-based project had the active support and sponsorship of Steward's senior management, which both reduced the time required to gain commitment and also provided a strong stimulus to produce insights rapidly.

Four of the remaining projects (AMD, Slade, KRAFT, and Monarch) required between four and six months for completion. The four months at AMD and Slade represent the typical time required for developing an initial activity-based model. Both sites had strong internal project teams, with outside consultants playing a facilitating role during the project and helping to prepare analysis and recommendations for management. For example, at Slade the consultants, in addition to initial training of the project team, helped with the cost driver interviews and worked closely with the team to design the activity-based model architecture, such as the number and type of activity centers. KRAFT's project required more time than usual because of the limited internal and external resources available; Monarch's longer time scale was explained by management's desire to analyze completely two complex manufacturing sites plus perform a comprehensive market-segment profitability analysis. The first manufacturing site and market segment analysis required 5.5

months to develop and analyze; the second site required 3.5 months.

Farrall Corporation's model development and analysis took eight months. Two factors contributed to this extended time frame. First, activity-based models were developed at two sites, one in the United States and one in Europe. Second, and more important, the corporate controller (serving as project sponsor) did not want to release any information until he felt the numbers were correct and defensible. He stated, "As both projects were taking longer, I thought it best to take our time to get to the right numbers than try to pull something together in a rush. ... I think it's important to get to the right numbers quickly, but I think it's equally important to keep people aware of what's going on during the process."

Williams Brothers Metals' project took eight months to complete. The project scope expanded during the study, but the resources committed were not increased. Initially, only one site was to be analyzed, but the interactions among the primary and secondary distribution sites led the project manager to develop models for all five sites. He explained, "The original design for one site was too simplistic. But designing five sites also raised many questions. We went down a very complex path."

To summarize, a typical initial project to develop an activity-based model at a single site required about four months. This time is achievable with an internal commitment of about two full-time employees (FTEs) during the project's duration, plus assistance from outside (or internal) consultants to prepare and train people in the organization and help in the analysis and report presentation tasks. The four-month time can be reduced if the project scope is limited (as in ARCO Alaska and, to some extent, at Steward) to a subset of organizational expenses, or if consultants are used extensively to supplement internal project resources. Projects require more than four months when models at several sites and for multiple analyses (such as customer and market profitability analyses) are performed as part of the initial project. Also, if the project team is supplied limited resources (as at KRAFT), the model development will take longer. The time required to develop additional ABC models at new sites, after the internal project team had learned to do an activity-based model analysis, was significantly less than for the initial model development.

Project Resources: Data

Most of the sites reported some difficulty in obtaining data needed for the activity-based model, especially for the activity cost drivers.

Occasionally, the project team was surprised that data already existed in the company, but outside the financial system with which the team was most familiar. Several sites found that useful data existed in MRP, human resources, and sales order entry systems.

At Williams Brothers Metals, the project manager had assumed that much of the data needed for the activity-based model did not exist in the current databases and that the project would help to identify information that would need to be accumulated in the future. He was surprised that all the data required for the model existed and were accessible. He explained, "We had no idea that the original site was maintained on a transshipment record. The MIS group provided valuable assistance in extracting data from the existing systems. We were able to use data in new and relevant ways."

At the other extreme, the Monarch project group found that much of its cost driver data were not readily available. The team reported that extensive effort was required to collect cost driver information, involving a lot of off-line programming and manual data collection and entry.

Eventually, six of the eight sites collected hard, verifiable, activity cost driver data to use in their models. Only two sites, ARCO Alaska and Steward Brokerage, relied extensively on subjective management estimates ("soft" data) for their activity cost drivers. The use of hard versus soft data, however, seemed to have no impact on their use by management. Steward and ARCO Alaska both acted promptly and decisively from the information provided by their activity-based model, even with the extensive dependence on soft data. Many finance executives believe that management will not act on information unless it can be validated and reconciled back to the underlying financial transactions system. The experience at the eight sites did not support this hypothesis. Several sites, where great care, time and resources were committed to having the data be verifiable and traceable back to the organization's formal information systems, produced information that managers were slow to act upon. Conversely, the two organizations in which the data inputs were the most subjective took the quickest actions based on the numbers.

Obviously, the willingness to act depends on the traditions and culture of the organization, as well as on the pressures from outside competitive forces. Executives in the trading and brokerage business regularly take decisions within seconds on limited and incomplete information. ARCO Alaska's controller's department was forced by an externally mandated reduction-in-force directive to take immediate action. Its senior executives did not have the luxury of articulating all the activity-based numbers back to original transactions if they wanted to use the information in their immediate RIF decision.

Project Resources: Software

All of the sites used a PC-based software package that had been specifically developed for activity-based analysis. For the main analysis, none of the sites developed their own software, either on a mainframe or by using familiar spreadsheet or data base software programs such as Lotus 1-2-3, Excel, or dBase.[4] Nor did any of the eight companies attempt to implement their activity-based model using their mainframe computers and existing cost accounting packages. Data on expenses, product characteristics, and cost drivers were derived, when available, from existing databases on the company's systems and downloaded to the PC-based ABC software package. Data not available in machine-readable form were entered manually. The software package performed the mechanical tasks of driving resource expenses to activities and activity centers. Via activity cost drivers, it linked activity expenses to the products, customers, and account executives that had been identified as the cost objects for the study. Various reports on activity expenses, unit costs of activity cost drivers, expenses by cost hierarchy and value analysis, and product and customer profitability were produced from the software for management analyses and presentations.

All of the sites concentrated on defining and collecting data on activities and cost drivers, anticipating that these data could be brought together readily, without great work on their part, to obtain costs of activities, business processes, activity drivers, products, and customers. No modification was required to existing financial systems, and companies continued to run all of their existing systems in parallel with developing their new ABC models.

Some observers have questioned whether managers would find credible the numbers created "outside" of the official financial reporting system. This hypothetical concern never was expressed in any of the interviews conducted at the eight sites. If anything, managers found the numbers generated from the activity-based analysis to be more credible and relevant than the numbers generated from the official costing system. Basically, operating managers have become accustomed to their official financial systems not necessarily providing decision-relevant information. Most companies perform special studies to get information relevant for particular decisions. The operating executives tended to view their activity-based models as a more general "special study" that produced information to inform a wide variety of managerial decisions and actions.

In summary, one of the most important common characteristics across all eight sites is that no site viewed nor intended the activity-based model as a replacement to the organization's financial transaction system which, in all eight cases, continued to function as before and was expected to remain in the future. *The activity-based model was treated as a management information system, not as part of the accounting system.*

Summary

Managers at all the sites expressed interest in the newly revealed ABC information. The ABC effort was linked, in all five manufacturing sites, with the organization's formal quality and continuous improvement initiatives. At each site, managers gained considerable insights from the information revealed about:

- Activities and business processes,
- Cost drivers,
- Products and customers.

The activity and business process information was obtained relatively quickly and easily at all sites. The information was being used to target process improvement, process redesign, or process elimination activities, including using the ABC process cost information as a basis for outsourcing the activity entirely to an outside vendor.

Cost driver information was more difficult to obtain. Several companies had to make significant compromises either in the scope or the accuracy of their model because information on the most relevant cost driver was not readily available. Some companies (e.g., Monarch) reported considerable difficulty in accessing cost driver information from their diverse information systems while others (e.g., Williams Brothers Metals) expressed surprise that the cost driver information they wanted already existed in accessible databases. The cost driver information was being used to benchmark similar processes in other organizations and as targets for future performance improvements. Several companies felt that the cost drivers helped them to understand the quite different demands that different products, customers, or oil fields (for ARCO Alaska) placed on the support organization, and that this information would help future product design, product pricing, and managing customer relationships.

Information on the cost and profitability of products and customers yielded the usual ABC insights: a few products and customers accounted for the great bulk of profits, and several major product lines, customer groups, and market segments were revealed to be breakeven or incurring significant losses. The "bill of activities" available from the ABC product or customer costs explained to managers the reasons for the unexpectedly high costs of individual products and customers.

Several companies already had acted on the information. Decisions were being made on pricing (Slade), product mix (Steward, AMD, Slade), process improvements (Farrall, ARCO Alaska), and customer mix (Monarch, Slade). A few (Williams Brothers Metals, KRAFT) had yet even to begin to address the managerial implications. Most sites still were absorbing the messages, disseminating the message in the organization, re-estimating the model on newer data or in additional sites, and, most positively, discussing how the information likely would change their behavior or resource allocations within the next 12 months. In the next chapter, we will explain the reasons for the different reactions to the ABC information among the eight sites.

Notes

[1] We are using the word "model" in its general sense, "a description or analogy used to help visualize something that cannot be directly observed; a system of postulates, data and inferences presented as a mathematical description of an entity or state of affairs" (*Webster's New Collegiate Dictionary*). An ABC model refers to the description or representation of the organization's economics, not to the computer program or system used to estimate the model.

[2] The ABC cost hierarchy was developed by Robin Cooper in "Cost Classification in Unit-Based and Activity-Based Manufacturing Cost Systems," *Journal of Cost Management*, Fall 1990, pp. 4-14.

[3] At AMD, the limited scope of the initial ABC project, which encompassed only one part of the entire manufacturing process, likely limited the range of near-term management actions no matter how enthusiastic operating managers may have been, or how committed to the concept.

[4] Some of the companies used spreadsheets to develop activity information that subsequently was downloaded into the ABC software package. Two of the sites used spreadsheets for their customer and market profitability studies.

Chapter 13

Organizational Issues in ABC Projects

As described in the introduction to Chapter 12, activity-based cost management projects can be viewed as requiring two distinct processes:

1. Analysis: gain sponsorship, form a project team, get to the numbers, reveal hidden profits and losses;
2. Action: identify profit priorities, take action, get improvements to the bottom line.[1]

The previous chapter, and the extensive literature on activity-based costing that has emerged in the past five years, focused mainly on the analysis process, attempting to answer these questions: What is an activity-based cost model? How does it differ from a traditional cost system? What different insights does it provide from traditional systems? How does one estimate an ABC model?

Considerably less attention, however, has been paid to the vital second process—action—in which the insights from an ABC model are used to increase the profitability of the organization. A few of the case sites (Steward, ARCO Alaska, Slade) had taken actions based on the insights from their ABC models. Most of the other sites, however, had yet to make the transition from analysis to action. In these sites, one or more ABC models had been developed, the corporate sponsors and project leaders generally appreciated the insights revealed by the estimated models, but actions had yet to be taken based on the ABC analysis. In part, this pattern may have been due to the recency of the activity-based approach in the chosen companies. For most of the sites, the estimation of the ABC model was not completed until mid-1991. The time frame of this research study caused these sites to be visited while final estimation of the ABC model was still occurring or, at best, shortly after the final estimates had occurred. Senior management either had not been completely briefed on the findings or had insufficient time to establish their profit priorities for taking action. Given the radical change in thinking required by the ABC approach and the extended length of time for any new management decision and action to occur, the study may have captured companies at too early a stage to judge the efficacy of improved management actions from the newly created ABC information.

Organizational Barriers

But we feel that a more fundamental cause, inadequate preparation of the organization for changes in thinking and decision making, explains the delays in taking action. The delays at many of the sites in moving from a fully estimated and analyzed ABC model to actions that improve profits should concern corporate sponsors and finance managers who wish to have the output from their ABC models used productively. The most successful projects occurred when a specific *target* for change was identified early in the project. The target was the person or group whose decisions were expected to change as a consequence of the information revealed from the activity-based model. Also helpful was having a *sponsor* for the action stage, the senior person who wanted change to occur and who could authorize the actions to be taken by the target person or group.

If an explicit game plan does not exist to make the transition from analysis to action, including identifying both the sponsor and the target for the change, companies could find that their ABC project keeps cycling as a finance task; that is, the project team, most likely under the direction and sponsorship of people in the finance organization, will continue to refine the model, re-estimate it on new data (e.g., this year's actuals, next year's budget), and develop new models for different organizational sites. This pattern typically occurs when the project team has not identified the sponsor and the target for the action process. The danger of this pattern is that after several years of refinement, re-estimation, and extension, but no managerial decisions or actions, the ABC project becomes viewed as an initiative that concerns the finance group only but not one that has to be addressed, accepted, internalized, and acted upon by operating managers.

Sponsors and project managers of the analysis stage should recognize that a comprehensive ABC model is not an end in its own right. No organization ever made more money merely because it had a more accurate understanding of its economics. Only when understanding is translated into action is the potential for profit improvement unleashed. This chapter provides a structure for thinking about how to transform an ABC project from the analysis stage to the subsequent and vitally important action stage.

Management of the Change Process

To articulate the issues that arise when implementing projects and attempting to introduce change into organizations, we will analyze ABC projects as the two sequential processes described above: analysis and action. The analysis process requires good project management skills, the action process requires good skills in creating organizational change. The second process, creating organizational change, turns out to be much more difficult than the first process, the goal of which is to produce some new information for the organization.

Change is accomplished by people, not by systems, so we identify specific roles that must be played in the analysis and action processes.

Analysis Process
- Advocate: individual/group who *stimulates* the project.
- Sponsor: individual/group who *legitimates* the project.
- Project Manager: individual/group responsible for *implementing* the project.
- Target: individual/group expected to *change* based on the outcome of the project.

Action Process
- Advocate: individual/group who *wants* the change to occur.
- Sponsor: individual/group who *legitimates* the change.
- Change Agent: individual/group responsible for *implementing* the change.
- Target: individual/group who must actually *change*.

The advocate, sponsor, and project manager for the analysis process can function as advocates for the action process, but they cannot be the primary players for the action process. For making a successful change occur, the action process requires its own sponsor, change agent, and target. If the action process does not have a strong sponsor or a clearly identified target, the ABC project may fail to have an impact on the organization.

Based on the eight case studies (see Exhibit 13-1) plus our experiences with many other organizations that have built ABC models, the most likely failure occurs when the sponsor for the analysis stage, typically

Exhibit 13-1

PROFILE OF TARGETS AND SPONSORS

Site	Task	Advocate	Sponsor	Project Leader/ Change Agent	Target	Target Aware It is the Target?
Farrall	Analysis	Plant Controller & Division Controller	Corp. Controller	Plant Controller	Manufacturing Marketing & Sales	No No
	Action	Corp. Controller	—	—	—	—
KRAFT	Analysis	Controllers Group	—	Controllers Group	—	—
	Action	—	—	—	—	—
Steward	Analysis	CEO	CEO	CFO	Sr. Operating Mgmt.	Yes
	Action	CEO	CEO	Unclear	Sr. Operating Mgmt.	Yes
ARCO, Alaska	Analysis	R. Allaire, in Controllers Group	Corp. Controller	Controllers Group	Oil Field Mgrs. Marketing	No No
	Action	Company RIF	Corp. Controller	Corp. Controller	Controllers Group	Yes
AMD	Analysis	Group Controller	Finance Director, Far East Operations	Operations Head	Finance (transfer pricing) Operations	Yes Yes
	Action	Group Controller	—	—	—	—
Monarch	Analysis	CFO	CFO	CFO	Marketing Manufacturing	No No
	Action	CFO	—	—	—	—
WBM	Analysis	CFO	CFO	CFO	Sr. Operating Mgmt.	No
	Action	CFO	—	—	—	—
Slade	Analysis	Controller	Division Mgmt.	Division Controller	Plant Manager	Yes
	Action	Controller	Division Mgmt.	—	Division and Plant Mgmt.	Yes

someone in the finance organization, fails to identify both the sponsor for the action stage and the target—the individual or group whose behavior is expected to change as a result of the new ABC information. This pathology generally can be identified even at the start of the analysis stage. When the project advocate or sponsor of the analysis stage states that the purpose of the project is to provide a "proof of concept," or to generate "better transfer prices," or to reveal the hidden or unexpected profits and losses, or to "acquire better information"—the project has adopted analytic, not action, goals. The target for the better analysis or better information typically has not yet been identified. Even if the advocate or sponsor has some idea who the target might be, it is unlikely that the target knows that it has been selected for this role for the ABC project. The relevant question to ask is whether the target, such as the Marketing, Sales, or Engineering group, knows that it is the target and whether it has accepted the theory of the case that will soon be presented to it.[2]

This pattern by the project sponsor can be described as a "field of dreams" strategy: If I build it [the ABC model], they [an operating manager, somewhere] will come. Unfortunately, the field of dreams strategy is rarely successful, leading to frustration for the ABC project sponsor and perhaps a discrediting of the ABC concept caused by the failure to manage change effectively.

The alternative to the field of dreams strategy would have the project advocate or sponsor state at the outset that the goal of the project is to reprice products or customers, improve operating or design processes, improve product designs, change customer relationships, or to rationalize products, facilities, or selling channels. Clearly stated goals become even more compelling when they can be linked to an explicit corporate commitment to achieve demonstrable results—in financial performance, customer service, or internal business process improvement.[3]

Then the project sponsor can identify the targets, such as managers in charge of sales, operations, or logistics, at the outset of the project. The sponsor then should attempt to get the targets to agree with the potential action plan from the project. Otherwise, delays will occur before any action is contemplated, much less implemented.

For example, many ABC projects start by analyzing factory expenses and assigning them more accurately to products with the expectation that the new information will be used for pricing, product mix changes, and product redesigns. But if Sales & Marketing are not involved in this effort, no actions will be taken based on the more accurate product cost and profitability information. Significant delays will occur until Sales &

Marketing are brought into the process, learn the theory and estimates that underlie the newly produced information, analyze the implications, and start to take actions. Preferably, Sales & Marketing should be involved early in the analysis process, understand then that they are the primary target for the project, and perhaps even participate in the analysis phase of the ABC project, so that the transition between information generated and action taken will be swifter and smoother.

The finance organization can serve as advocate, sponsor, and project manager for the analysis process of an ABC project. But the finance organization must recognize, perhaps with difficulty and reluctance, that it can be neither the sponsor nor the change agent and certainly not the target for the action process in which operating managers make changes in the organization, strategy, and decision making based on information from the ABC model. If operating managers view ABC as an innovation for the finance department, then ultimately the organization will get little benefit from its initiative to generate the new sets of numbers (unless, of course, the finance organization is willing to define itself as the target and use the ABC information to downsize itself, as occurred in ARCO Alaska). To avoid this syndrome, the initial project sponsor should have clearly in mind who in the organization will take the insights from the ABC analysis and use the new information to establish the profit priorities for the organization. The target also must exploit the efficiencies gained through better use of resources either to increase the volume of business the organization handles or to reduce operating expenses. Only when the organization takes actions that lead ultimately to producing and selling more or spending less, will the insights from the ABC analysis have produced increased profits for the company.

ABC Project Management at the Case Sites

KRAFT

The KRAFT case provides a vivid illustration of an incomplete organizational change process. Jim Smith was a dedicated and capable advocate and project manager for the analysis process. He saw that an activity-based cost system had substantial potential benefit for his organization. He managed to generate modest funding for a pilot project by linking ABC to a more actively supported performance measurement project. This funding enabled him to get ABC models estimated in two food processing factories. But he had no sponsor, such as a senior person in the finance or operations hierarchy with a strong commitment to the

ABC innovation. In the midst of the turmoil created by the takeover by Philip Morris, and in the various TQM programs already underway, little organizational energy and few resources could be mustered for the ABC project. And, in addition to lacking a sponsor, the KRAFT ABC study also lacked a target. No person in Marketing or Operations had been identified who was supposed to change his or her way of doing business, either in pricing, process improvement, product design, or product rationalization. Consequently, the ABC models were developed, but no actions were taken or even contemplated. Only recently, with the possibility of sponsorship arising because of a new vice president, finance, and renewed interest from potential targets in Operations, was the ABC project revitalized.

Farrall

The Farrall site was a more typical example of an ABC project implementation. The advocates for the analysis process were Robert Spears and Carl Winecki, a plant controller and a divisional controller, who learned about ABC through articles and seminars. They believed that ABC would provide much better information for transfer pricing and for product and customer profitability analysis. Spears and Winecki brought their enthusiasm to Jay Hansen, corporate controller, who became the ABC project sponsor. Hansen already had been talking with the company president about the need and opportunity for improved cost measurement systems at Farrall.

In addition to the benefits identified by Spears and Winecki, Hansen was expecting ABC to provide better information to justify investment in advanced manufacturing equipment. Once Hansen had approved the project, Spears became the project manager at his Riverside plant, and his counterpart plant controller became the project manager at the division's U.K. plant in Southampton. The finance people—Spears, Winecki, and Hansen—expected the information generated from the ABC models to affect marketing and sales, manufacturing, and plant managers but had not identified any clear target among these operating managers in advance.

By the time of the site visit (summer 1991), the ABC project still was within the finance organization. Some plant managers, sales managers, and the director of worldwide operations had expressed degrees of enthusiasm for the ABC project, but none of them had taken ownership of the concept or was yet prepared to act on the information. The manufacturing manager at the Riverside plant was making some local process improvements based on the information, but, on a broader scale, no decisions on changing relations with customers, repricing or redesigning products, or changing product and customer mix had been taken or seemed about to be taken. The project now required that Hansen, the company controller, shift roles from being the project sponsor in the analysis process to becoming the advocate for the action process. But no sponsor for the action stage had yet emerged, and neither a change agent nor a specific target had been identified.

The finance function now was confined to being only a change advocate, and the project lacked a sponsor, a change agent, and a target for the action stage. Therefore, the ABC concept was proceeding slowly in affecting decisions in Operations, Sales & Marketing, and Product Engineering. The finance organization, in response, was returning to what it did best, updating the model with new data and looking for other organizational sites where it could estimate new ABC models. In effect, the finance function was cycling within the analysis process where it could have more control over the outcome. Note, however, that the company receives no benefit unless the project at some point moves out of an analysis process and into an action process, somewhere in the organization.

Steward

In contrast, one site, Steward, had a target well identified in advance. The company's CEO, Fred Benning, was the motivating force behind the ABC project.[4] Benning initiated the ABC project because of his concern with growing, and seemingly out-of-control, administrative and support costs. Thus Benning served in three roles in the analysis stage: advocate, sponsor, and target for the project. The target also encompassed people such as Larry Black, director and head of the company's core equity business, and other senior operating managers. With this strong sponsorship and target audience, immediate action was forthcoming even from the preliminary study, which had excluded two large support resources because of limited data availability. Major organizational changes were implemented and one product line was strongly de-emphasized.

Thus, Steward made a fairly rapid transition from the analysis process to the action process. When the CEO serves as project advocate and sponsor, and senior operating managers are the project targets, the transition between the analysis process—getting to the numbers—and the action process—making significant organizational or strategic changes—can be smooth and rapid. As shown in Exhibit 13-1, in this case, the key roles of sponsor and target remained the same at Steward for the analysis and the action processes, and the leadership and authority of the CEO enabled him to serve as the change agent for making sure that actions occurred.

Slade

At Slade, the ABC project was stimulated by the difficult financial situation in the parent company. Immediate action was needed to improve the profitability and cash flow of its large automotive components businesses. General awareness existed throughout the organization of the problems caused by the diverse, but inadequate, traditional costing systems. The Hudson Automotive Division of Slade proved to be a fortuitous choice because of a short-term need both to renegotiate a major parts contract with its largest Big 3 OEM customer and to stimulate cost-saving process improvements. Slade provides a good example of a situation in which the project aadvocates actively sought and involved line management to be both sponsor and target for the ABC project.

Bill Carlisle, Slade controller, and Larry Martin, newly hired controller of the Automotive Group, served as active aadvocates for an ABC project. They recognized the need for strong internal sponsorship but initially were rebuffed by the senior management group of the Hudson Automotive Division. Carlisle and Martin, with outside assistance, eventually convinced Hudson's president, Scott Springer, and his entire senior management group to sponsor the project and to serve on the project's steering committee.

Martin subsequently remarked on his good fortune in being able to revive the project, saying, "You rarely get a second chance to make a good first impression."

Carlisle and Martin made a formal presentation to Bud Cramer, plant manager of the Youngstown plant, who agreed to be the local (plant-level) sponsor and to function on both the steering committee and the project team. Cramer clearly was a target for the project. Cramer acknowledged the defects in Youngstown's existing standard cost system, which were contributing to the product and customer proliferation at the plant. Cramer was also aware that information from the standard cost system could not be relied on during the upcoming negotiations on a major contract extension with the plant's largest Big 3 automotive customer. Springer and Hudson Automotive's senior management team were also project targets. They recognized the need to improve profit and cash flow from the automotive businesses and the need to sustain and extend recent operating improvements in the plants. Larry Martin functioned as project manager at the Youngstown plant.

At the conclusion of the analysis phase, the project team presented its findings and recommendations to Cramer, Springer, and the Hudson management team. At this time, Martin could be the advocate for change but could not authorize new decisions or actions. Cramer and the Hudson Automotive management team, however, did act upon the recommendations. They negotiated with key customers to change ordering and delivery requirements that would lower the demands on Youngstown's activities. They pruned both the product line and customer base to eliminate low-volume, unprofitable operations. They bid strategically on an extension of a major product line that produced one year of sharply higher revenues but conceded considerable business in the subsequent two years. The loss of business was anticipated, however, and enabled the plant to reconfigure its resources and technology for a new generation in this product line.

In addition, the vice president of Sales & Marketing had incorporated the ABC information into a sophisticated quoting and bidding system. Cramer had used it in the Youngstown plant for cost-reducing process improvements in quality and maintenance activities. Thus, the sponsor for the action process was Springer, Hudson's president, who provided the authority for actions to be taken based on the ABC information. The action target included: (1) Cramer, as Youngstown plant manager; (2) the vice president of Sales & Marketing, who worked with customers to reduce their demands and who established a new bidding system using the ABC information; and (3) the entire senior management group, who now had the confidence to conduct a difficult negotiation with a large customer and to turn away business that the ABC analysis had revealed to be unprofitable.

ARCO Alaska

The ARCO Alaska site had all the symptoms of a project that was likely to fail. Initially, the study had limited organizational sponsorship. Only people in the controller's department were enthusiastic about the study—Dan Casey, corporate controller, became its sponsor. The study was to pilot ABC within his own organization and perhaps serve as a springboard for ABC projects elsewhere in the organization. Vague statements were made about having better cost data for negotiating with oil field co-owners and using the data to influence the demand for corporate services, but little apparent support existed for the ABC concept outside the controller's department. This had the classic "field of dreams" symptoms for an ABC project that would generate "better information" but no action. And one week into the project, Casey, the sponsor, was transferred to corporate headquarters and not replaced for three months.

At this time, the project had leadership (the project co-leaders and steering committee) but no sponsor and certainly no clear target. But the project had been initiated and was able to continue, likely because it had already been made a full-time assignment for two summer interns. Normally, when the ABC project had been completed at the end of the summer, managers would have looked at the numbers, expressed opinions on the validity of or insights from the study, and nothing further would have happened.

An apparently unexpected event occurred in the middle of the project that suddenly defined the target for the ABC study and mobilized the Controller's Group into action. In July 1991, faced with an oversupply of oil and falling prices, the corporate headquarters mandated a reduction-in-force (RIF) for all departments. This mandate led the ARCO Alaska finance managers to define their own organization as the target. The change that must occur was a headcount reduction without sacrificing existing services valued by external or internal customers. As described in Chapter 7, the ABC study was used to identify and eliminate low-value activities and to quantify the headcount savings that could occur once the activities themselves had been eliminated. One department manager stated:

> I always felt that some of our time spent in the policy support area was not as leveraging as the other areas within my group. I made a decision to reduce the amount of certain business policy activities, via headcount reduction of two people, choosing first the activity to reduce, then the individual. As a result, the overall time spent in the policy area is much more effective.

Another manager described the approach. "Our estimating process was always built from the bottom up. This caused a lot of effort. By using a top-down approach, at a higher level, we reduced headcount by two to three people overall, including one person in my own group, due to the ABA efforts."

A project co-leader summarized the actions taken. "We first looked at activities, then at people. We started with activities to eliminate, not just to drop by the RIF percentage. The activity-based data showed us where there were a lot of redundancies, especially in the review process."

While the RIF has been accomplished at ARCO Alaska, the interest in ABC remains strong. A new MBA has been hired to lead the effort on a full-time basis. If the effort is to be successful, however, sponsors and targets outside of the controller's group likely will be required.

The five projects already described span the range of successful change management: a project (KRAFT) that had neither a sponsor nor a target; a project (Farrall) where strong sponsorship existed for the analysis stage of the project but where the sponsor, change agent, and target for the action stage did not exist; a project (Steward) where the CEO served as sponsor and target for both the analysis and action stages; a project (Slade) where the initial advocates persisted to get line management to serve as sponsors and targets; and a project (ARCO) that initially had very limited internal sponsorship and project scope and no target. The ARCO project, however, suddenly became a high priority for the organization midway through the project because of a serendipitous event (for the project but not for the people who lost jobs) that defined the controller's group itself as the target.[5] The entries in Exhibit 13-1 suggest that project success will be highest when the sponsor and the target are the same person or organizational unit.

The remaining three sites were similar to the Farrall case study, with strong project advocacy and sponsorship but no clear target.

AMD

At AMD, the ABC project was expected to give "better" transfer prices from manufacturing to marketing, provide guidance to manage product design decisions, and encourage manufacturing efficiencies. As with Farrall, the project advocate and sponsor were in the finance organization (the group controller and financial director for Far East operations, respectively). The project leader, however, came from Operations. Other team members were drawn from Industrial Engineering, Product Engineering, Quality Analysis, and Cost Accounting. The project's steering committee included the plant director, the plant controller, and several departmental managers. Thus several operating managers played key roles in the ABC project.

Because of the limited scope of the project, however, encompassing only one factory in a manufacturing process that required products to pass through three separate facilities to produce a completed product, no action could be taken at the product or customer level based on the pilot study. This limitation was known in advance. Currently, ABC was being applied at a wafer fabrication plant in Austin, Texas, to gain more complete product costs for products that were transferred between Austin and Penang. Little evidence could be found, though, that even the manufacturing cost information for the Penang plant had led to significant changes in manufacturing operations, indicating that the transfer pricing aspects of ABC likely had been overemphasized relative to near-term process improvement opportunities.

Monarch Mirror Door

The project advocate and sponsor at Monarch Mirror Door was the company's finance director, Mike Laney, who learned of the potential value of ABC for his company through published articles. Laney kept promoting the concept within the company's senior management group and eventually got approval that allowed him to try an ABC project. Laney served as advocate, project sponsor, and project manager. He directly supervised the two project teams and coordinated the consultants' involvement with the project.

The target for the study was not clear, given senior management's lack of deep commitment to the concept. Monarch again exhibited the field of dreams recipe: a senior finance officer served as advocate, sponsor, and project leader to get an ABC model built but lacked a clear target, so that the impact of the project on managerial action was delayed. At the end of the project, senior executives were thinking about, but not yet acting on, the implications of the numbers they were seeing. The CEO speculated, "We need to use ABC as a pricing model, especially when determining discounts. ... I would like to someday see ABC predict price increases."

The vice president of sales also acknowledged the relevance of the information:

> We manufacture nationally and distribute nationally. Our competitors, however, are mostly regional distributors. We can see from ABC that our distribution costs vary greatly between markets and products. Should we be regional distributors? Or should we sell to regional distributors and stop trying to service our customers from a national base? ... Maybe we should consider selling our products to local contractors and let them do the install and service. What we do best is manufacture, let someone else worry about distribution and service.

The manufacturing manager saw the relevance of ABC for him. He stated, "I can use the data for certain make versus buy decisions. We are looking to bring in a new line. ... I would like to see ABC support that decision up front, let us know our costs before we get into them."

These quotes indicate acceptance and some support but no real action taken yet. The senior managers are speculating about some future decision or action, not acting upon the information already in hand. Laney, the chief financial officer, can be the advocate for change, but before any change occurs, a strong sponsor, change agent, and target for the action stage need to emerge.

Williams Brothers Metals

At Williams Brothers Metals, the advocate, sponsor, and agent for the analysis process also was the vice president, finance, Jim Curry. As at Monarch, Curry, the CFO, sponsored, funded, and actively managed the ABC effort. Curry launched the project with a two-day seminar that created awareness and expectations about ABC among project team members. The project lasted four months longer than initially anticipated, however, in order to develop models for the entire region rather than at a single site. As Curry commented, "The original design of one site was too simplistic. But designing five sites also raised many questions. We went down a very complex path."

Senior management liked the activity and business process analysis from the ABC study but did not accept the action implications. One owner/manager, whose two largest product classes turned out to be unprofitable under the ABC analysis, questioned the assumptions behind the analysis. Another owner/manager was disappointed that he was not supplied with a real-time order pricing and acceptance system. A third owner/manager didn't see the connection between the model output and the improved transfer pricing system he was expecting. The project targets for Williams Brothers were easy to identify: the three senior owner/managers. The transition to the action process, however, was blocked because each target had different expectations about the usable results from the ABC project, and these expectations differed from Jim Curry's, the project advocate and sponsor. Even though Curry had communicated monthly to the owner/managers about the project, the action implications had not been shared effectively. Each target (the senior owner/managers) found some shortcoming in the model that allowed him to reject the model's implications. Curry admitted that the long time span of the project may have contributed to this problem.

We should have come to the numbers quicker, even if they didn't reflect the economics of our transfers and transshipments. In the end, the business processes were a real hit. I could have showed that to them three months into the project.

People become stakeholders in projects like this. They naturally react when they see that the products they are responsible for are actually losing money. They read the last page in the mystery novel first and disregard the rest. In the end, one wrong cost driver, sales orders, threw every bit of credibility out the window.

Curry planned to update the model during 1992, using 1991 actual data. In addition to running the model with new financial numbers, Curry will involve more people in the organization (the targets) during the process. One owner/manager, asked if ABC had a future at Williams Brothers, stated, "Absolutely! We are just beginning to understand how we can use it. But more people need to be involved in the next phase."

As at Monarch, however, Curry will have to realize that he cannot replay his multiple analysis process roles of advocate, sponsor, and agent for the action process. At best, he can be only the change advocate. Therefore he needs to get the organization to identify and designate the action sponsor, change agent, and targets.

Change Agent in the Action Process

In the action process, the roles for the sponsor—the person or group who authorizes decisions and organizational changes—and the target—the person or group that is expected to change—should be fairly clear. Less clear is the role for the change agent—the person or group responsible for implementing the change. Ideally, the target, such as the vice president of operations who must implement the continuous improvement activities in operating processes, can serve as the change agent. In this case, the target has internalized the message from the sponsor and has taken ownership and responsibility for making sure the change occurs. For some change processes, however, the target may not have the requisite knowledge (e.g., on how to develop and implement a successful total quality management program) and therefore may require help from a knowledgeable person or group to facilitate the change.

A second possibility is for the sponsor to be the change agent. An active CEO or operating unit head can play the change agent role by continually examining the action process to make sure that it is on schedule and making progress. The authority of the sponsor gives that person or group the "decision rights" to obtain information about and continually intervene to ensure that action and change occur. This role, however, will require a considerable amount of time from the sponsor. Also, the sponsor may lack information about what changes are needed and how they should be implemented.

If neither the sponsor nor the target serves as change agent, then a third party must be identified to help the target make a successful change. Sometimes an internal person, serving as an internal consultant, can be the change agent. This situation occurs frequently in TQM programs, where, say, a vice president of quality improvement programs facilitates the continuous improvement programs in a target organization. While the target is ultimately responsible for the change happening in his or her organization, the change agent helps to make the change occur, within organizational constraints.

For the action process in an ABC implementation, senior finance executives can attempt to be the change agents, although unless they are truly viewed as business partners with operating managers, they will encounter difficulty. Historically, they have been viewed as "keepers of the numbers" and inhibitors of actions ("we can't afford that expenditure for that purpose"; "that investment has not been justified"). Many companies may not be prepared to think of their financial people as the ones who can or should stimulate operating people into action. Finance executives who appoint themselves as change agents during the action process may find, therefore, that the targets, and perhaps the sponsors, too, do not appreciate all the help that has been offered.

A final possibility is for outside consultants to serve as change agents for the organization. This role for outside consultants differs enormously from their role in aiding the analysis process. The analysis process has a known, determinable outcome: an estimated ABC model with analysis of the costs of activities, drivers, products, customers, and channels. In contrast, the outcome from the action process requires changes in organization, strategy, and operations. Consultants experienced in installing systems and helping in analytic studies may have limited skills for facilitating organizational change. Some consultants, however, specialize in implementation, a process that *starts* with the numbers or specific goals and does not stop until the organization changes in specific ways. The constant presence and prodding of experienced and knowledgeable consultants can effectively facilitate organizational change when sponsorship and targets exist but the knowledge or deep commitment to change is not available internally.

Summary: Organizational Resistance and Defensive Routines

We have identified two stages, analysis and action, that must be traversed successfully if an organization is to benefit from an ABC project. The experiences at the eight case sites and at numerous other sites indicate that the analysis stage now can be accomplished routinely in a relatively short amount of time in almost all organizations. As the experience at several of the sites showed, however, significant delays can occur before analysis is transformed into action. We have noted that such project delays are minimized when sponsors and targets for the action stage are identified, chosen, and involved early in the analysis stage. Even if this practice is followed, however, acceptance of ABC action implications still must overcome defensive routines deeply rooted in individual and organizational behavior. Such routines can attempt to maintain the status quo and undermine the process. Project sponsors may choose to bypass these personal and organizational defensive routines to avoid confrontation and personal embarrassment. But by not dealing openly and directly with the resistance, the project sponsor jeopardizes the transition from the analysis to the action stage.

Two factors can block the passage from analysis to action:

1. Complexity of understanding technical aspects of ABC,
2. Defensive behavior induced by embarrassment or threat of having to act on unfamiliar or new information.[6]

Activity-based cost projects can fail on either or both dimensions. Furthermore, the education required to overcome these two blocking factors must be targeted to the particular problem. The education to overcome technical ignorance of ABC concepts is quite different from the educational process to overcome defensive behavior that attempts to block organizational change.

On the technical side, ABC requires operating and finance managers to think differently about the cost behavior of their organizations. Some managers have become accustomed to make decisions using fully absorbed unit product costs, even when the unit costs include arbitrary allocations of overhead. These managers must come to understand that activity-based systems do not allocate overhead costs; they attempt to measure the cost of using resources to perform activities required by different outputs, for example, products, customers, business units, and services. Activities performed by indirect and support resources must be explicitly defined and activity cost drivers identified so that the cost of using these resources can be linked to the outputs produced.

At the other extreme, some finance and operating managers have recognized the essential arbitrariness of most full-cost allocations and have tended to make decisions based on what they believe to be short-run variable costs. These managers assume that the costs of most support resources will be fixed and unaffected by incremental decisions on individual products, services, and customers. With ABC, these managers have to learn that aggregating lots of short-run, apparently incremental decisions eventually leads to significant changes in the quantity of many resources that must be supplied or made available to perform activities. Moving from a focus on predicting changes in short-run spending, based on incremental decisions, to a focus on predicting aggregate, long-run demands for supply and spending on resources will be a major shift in thinking for these managers. ABC project advocates must successfully explain the new way of thinking and the type of actions required by line managers once the ABC information is supplied to them. If these technical aspects of the ABC approach are not communicated adequately, then management acceptance and willingness to act are unlikely.

Even beyond the technical issues involved in the new approach, however, any change is seen as threatening by many managers. ABC project advocates are usually analytic types, who are comfortable with the technical aspects of the approach. This fact just creates more resistance among some operating managers, who don't really understand what is being advocated. Project advocates and project managers often encountered statements such as, "We've never made decisions on this basis; I would rather fail using cost information I am familiar with than fail based on this ABC information," or "I'm too old to learn a new approach," or "Things aren't that bad around here; if it's not broke, why fix it?" Resisters classify the ABC advocates as people who "are talented, rigorous, and analytic but who don't really understand people and organizations. They don't understand how decisions are made around here."

This distrust is reciprocated by the ABC advocates who underestimate the human and organizational dynamic resistance to change and who may disparage the old-line finance managers or operating managers who are resisting the new approach, classifying them as not being technically rigorous in their thinking. Even attempting to bring the analytic and the organizational people together in a task force can fail. The two different ways of thinking and expressing ideas can create defensive behavior in both groups. For example, if the proposed target for the action stage becomes defensive in resisting change, then the target's main action will be to resist change and attempt to stop the ABC project. The "target" for this resisting action will be the ABC project advocate, likely a finance person or group, who is proposing the changes.

These complex organizational dynamics can be difficult even to recognize, much less overcome.[7] The resistance is less likely when the action target is involved actively in sponsoring the ABC project (see Steward and Slade cases). Lacking strong initial sponsorship or advocacy by the action target, the ABC project sponsor should attempt to identify potential action targets as early in the project as possible. The sponsor should strongly encourage the proposed targets to participate in the analytic stage. This participation can include designating a respected person in the target's functional area to be part of the project team and having the target serve on the analysis project's steering committee. This early participation and involvement can lead to commitment that will enable the action stage to be reached shortly after completion of the analysis stage. Without bringing the proposed action target into the analysis stage, considerable time may elapse before analysis becomes translated into action, and increased profits.

Conclusion

The study of eight diverse sites indicates that almost all organizations can sponsor, estimate, and interpret the results from an ABC model. While some of the ABC projects took longer than expected, all of them produced insights about the organization's economics that senior managers found significant and/or surprising. In a few of the companies, particularly those where a target existed or was created by an unexpected event, actions already had been taken on the basis of the new activity-based information. At most of the sites, however, senior operating managers still were contemplating the uses of the newly produced ABC numbers and had not yet acted upon them. In all these cases, the delay was caused by the project sponsor and team failing to get organizational targets committed in advance to the theory and action implications of the activity-based cost management project. A successful activity-based cost management project requires both strong project management skills for the analysis process and, even more important but more difficult, strong skills in managing organizational change processes if decisions and actions are to be taken.

Notes

[1]The importance of the action stage was highlighted in Robin Cooper and Robert S. Kaplan, "Profit Priorities from Activity-Based Costing," *Harvard Business Review*, May-June 1991, pp. 130-135.

[2]The failure to identify a target and a sponsor for the action stage may occur by design, not omission. The finance sponsor may anticipate difficulties in gaining strong sponsorship and acceptance for the action stage and therefore may bypass this important step so as not to subject himself or the project to a failure early in the ABC process. Later in this chapter, we will discuss the defensive reactions that arise to avoid personal embarrassment and threats when significant organizational change is contemplated.

[3]See Robert S. Kaplan and David P. Norton, "The Balanced Scorecard: Measures That Drive Performance," *Harvard Business Review*, January-February 1992, pp. 71-79, for a description of a performance measuring system designed to reveal whether the organization is achieving its explicitly stated goals.

[4]Not coincidentally, the Kanthal case (HBS case #9-190-007 and 008), which represents one of the more publicized success stories of an ABC implementation, also was motivated by the company's CEO, Carl-Erik Ridderstrale.

[5]The ARCO Alaska experience suggests that sponsorship is most important to launch the project (the project sponsor was transferred one week into the project), while the target need only be ready at the end of the project (the mid-project announcement of the mandated RIF created its own project target).

[6]See Chris Argyris, *Overcoming Organizational Defenses*, Needham, Massachusetts, Allyn-Bacon, 1990; and "The Dilemma of Implementing Controls: The Case of Management Accounting," *Accounting, Organizations, and Society*, Vol. 15, No. 6, 1990, pp. 503-511.

[7]See Chris Argyris, "Teaching Smart People How to Learn," *Harvard Business Review*, May-June 1991, pp. 99-109.

Bibliography

Anotos, John. "Activity-Based Management for Service, Not-for-Profit, and Governmental Organizations." *Journal of Cost Management,* Summer 1992, pp. 13-23.

Argyris, Chris. "The Dilemma of Implementing Controls: The Case of Management Accounting." *Accounting, Organizations, and Society*, Vol. 15, No. 6, 1990, pp. 503-511.

————. *Overcoming Organizational Defenses*. Needham, Mass., Allyn-Bacon, 1990.

————. "Teaching Smart People How to Learn." *Harvard Business Review*, May-June 1991, pp. 99-109.

Beaujon, George J., and Vinod R. Singhal. "Understanding the Activity Costs in an Activity-Based Cost System." *Journal of Cost Management*, Spring 1990, pp. 51-72.

Berliner, Callie, and James A. Brimson, eds. *Cost Management for Today's Advanced Manufacturing: The CAM-I Conceptual Design*. Boston, Harvard Business School Press, 1988.

Beynon, Roger. "Change Management as a Platform for Activity-Based Management. *Journal of Cost Management*, Summer 1992, pp. 24-30.

Borden, James P. "Review of Literature on Activity-Based Costing." *Journal of Cost Management*, Spring 1991, pp. 6-38.

Brimson, James A. *Activity Accounting: An Activity-Based Costing Approach*. New York, John Wiley & Sons, 1991.

Brinker, Barry J., ed. *Emerging Practices in Cost Management* [a compilation of 50 articles from the *Journal of Cost Management*, Spring 1987 to Fall 1990]. Boston, Warren, Gorham & Lamont, 1990.

Bruns, William J., Jr., and Robert S. Kaplan, eds. *Accounting & Management: Field Study Perspectives*. Boston, Harvard Business School Press, 1987.

Campi, John P. "It's Not as Easy as ABC." *Journal of Cost Management*, Summer 1992, pp. 5-11.

Committe, Bruce E., and D. Jacque Grinnell. "Predatory Pricing, the Price-Cost Test, and Activity-Based Costing." *Journal of Cost Management*, Fall 1992, pp. 52-58.

Cooper, Robin. "Cost Classification in Unit-Based and Activity-Based Manufacturing Cost Systems." *Journal of Cost Management*, Fall 1990, pp. 4-14.

————. "Does Your Company Need a New Cost System?" *Journal of Cost Management*, Spring 1987, pp. 45-49.

————. "Elements of Activity-Based Costing." In *Emerging Practices in Cost Management*, Barry J. Brinker, ed., pp. 3-23.

————. "Implementing an Activity-Based Cost System." *Journal of Cost Management*, Spring 1990, pp. 33-42.

————. "The Rise of Activity-Based Costing—Part One: What Is an Activity-Based Cost System?" *Journal of Cost Management*, Summer 1988, pp. 45-54.

————. "The Rise of Activity-Based Costing—Part Two: When Do I Need an Activity-Based Cost System?" *Journal of Cost Management*, Fall 1988, pp. 41-48.

————. "The Rise of Activity-Based Costing—Part Three: How Many Cost Drivers Do You Need, and How Do You Select Them?" *Journal of Cost Management*, Winter 1989, pp. 34-46.

————. "The Rise of Activity-Based Costing—Part Four: What Do Activity-Based Cost Systems Look Like?" *Journal of Cost Management*, Spring 1989, pp. 38-49.

————. "You Need a New Cost System When..." *Harvard Business Review*, January-February 1989, pp. 77-82.

Cooper, Robin, and Robert S. Kaplan. "Activity-Based Systems: Measuring the Cost of Resource Usage." *Accounting Horizons*, September 1992, pp. 1-13.

————. *The Design of Cost Management Systems: Text, Cases, and Readings*. Englewood Cliffs, N.J., Prentice-Hall, 1991.

————. "How Cost Accounting Systematically Distorts Product Costs." In *Accounting & Management: Field Study Perspectives*, William J. Bruns and Robert S. Kaplan, eds., pp. 204-228.

―――. "Measure Costs Right: Make the Right Decisions." *Harvard Business Review*, September-October 1988, pp. 96-103.

―――. "Profit Priorities from Activity-Based Costing." *Harvard Business Review*, May-June 1991, pp. 130-135.

Fisher, Steven A., et al. "Implementing Activity-Based Costing: Lessons from the Gencorp Experience." *Corporate Controller*, September/October 1990, pp. 15-20.

Foster, George, and Charles T. Horngren. "Cost Accounting and Cost Management in a JIT Environment." In *Emerging Practices in Cost Management*, Barry J. Brinker, ed., pp. 199-210.

―――. "Flexible Manufacturing Systems: Cost Management and Cost Accounting Implications." In *Emerging Practices in Cost Management*, Barry J. Brinker, ed., pp. 305-314.

Govindarajan, Vijay, and John K. Shank. "Strategic Cost Analysis: The Crown Cork and Seal Case." In *Emerging Practices in Cost Management*, Barry J. Brinker, ed., pp. 469-480.

Haedicke, Jack, and David Feil. "In a DOD Environment, Hughes Aircraft Sets the Standard for ABC." *Management Accounting*, February 1991, pp. 29-33.

Harvard Business School Case Series. John Deere Component Works A (187-107) and B (187-108). Boston, Harvard Business School Publishing Division, 1987.

―――. Kanthal case (9-190-007 and 9-190-008). Boston, Harvard Business School Publishing Division, 1990.

Hiromoto, Toshiro. "Another Hidden Edge—Japanese Management Accounting." *Harvard Business Review*, July-August 1988, pp. 22-26.

Howell, Robert A., and S.R. Soucy. "Cost Accounting in the New Manufacturing Environment." *Management Accounting*, August 1987, pp. 42-48.

Innes, J., and F. Mitchell. *Activity Based Cost Management: A Case Study of Development and Implementation.* London, England, The Chartered Institute of Management Accountants, 1991.

Johnson, H. Thomas. "Activity Management: Reviewing the Past and Future of Cost Management." In *Emerging Practices in Cost Management*, Barry J. Brinker, ed., pp. 145-148.

————. "Activity-Based Information: A Blueprint for World-Class Management." *Management Accounting*, June 1988, pp. 23-30.

————. "Beyond Product Costing: A Challenge to Cost Management's Conventional Wisdom." In *Emerging Practices in Cost Management*, Barry J. Brinker, ed., pp. 345-354.

————. "The Decline of Cost Management: A Reinterpretation of 20th Century Cost Accounting History." In *Emerging Practices in Cost Management*, Barry J. Brinker, ed., pp. 137-144.

————. "How Weyerhaeuser Manages Corporate Overhead Costs." *Management Accounting*, August 1987, pp. 20-26.

————. "It's Time to Stop Overselling Activity-Based Costing." *Management Accounting*, September 1992, pp. 26-35.

————. "Managing Costs Versus Managing Activities—Which Strategy Works?" *Financial Executive*, January/February 1990, pp. 32-36.

————. "Organizational Design Versus Strategic Information Procedures for Managing Corporate Overhead Cost: Weyerhaeuser Company, 1972-1986." In *Accounting & Management: Field Study Perspectives*, William J. Bruns and Robert S. Kaplan, eds., pp. 49-72.

————. "Performance Measurement for Competitive Excellence." In *Measures for Manufacturing Excellence*, Robert S. Kaplan, ed., pp. 63-90.

Kaplan, Robert S. "The Four-Stage Model of Cost Systems Design." *Management Accounting*, February 1990, pp. 22-26.

————. "Limitations of Cost Accounting in Advanced Manufacturing Environments." In *Measures for Manufacturing Excellence*, Robert S. Kaplan, ed., pp. 15-38.

————. "Management Accounting in Advanced Technological Environments." *Science*, August 25, 1989, pp. 819-823.

————. "One Cost System Isn't Enough." *Harvard Business Review*, January-February 1988, pp. 61-66.

————, ed. *Measures for Manufacturing Excellence*. Boston, Harvard Business School Press, 1990.

Kaplan, Robert S., and David P. Norton. "The Balanced Scorecard: Measures That Drive Performance." *Harvard Business Review*, January-February 1992, pp. 71-79.

King, Alfred. "The Current Status of Activity-Based Costing: An Interview with Robin Cooper and Robert S. Kaplan." *Management Accounting*, September 1991, pp. 22-26.

Lewis, Ronald J. "Activity-Based Costing for Marketing." *Management Accounting*, November 1991, pp. 33-38.

MacArthur, John B. "Activity-Based Costing: How Many Cost Drivers Do You Want?" *Journal of Cost Management*, Fall 1992, pp. 37-41.

Maisel, Lawrence S. "Performance Measurement: The Balanced Scorecard Approach." *Journal of Cost Management*, Summer 1992, pp. 47-52.

Ostrenga, Michael R. "Activities: The Focal Point of Total Cost Management." *Management Accounting*, February 1990, pp. 44-49.

Rotch, William. "Activity-Based Costing in Service Industries." *Journal of Cost Management*, Summer 1990, pp. 4-14.

Roth, Howard P., and A. Faye Borthick. "Are You Distorting Costs by Violating ABC Assumptions?" *Management Accounting*, November 1991, pp. 39-42.

Sakurai, Michiharu. "Target Costing and How to Use It." *Journal of Cost Management*, Summer 1989, pp. 39-50.

Shank, John K., and Vijay Govindarajan. *Strategic Cost Analysis: The Evolution from Managerial to Strategic Accounting*. Homewood, Ill., Dow Jones-Irwin, 1989.

Shields, Michael D., and S. Mark Young. "A Behavioral Model for Implementing Cost Management Systems." *Journal of Cost Management*, Winter 1989, pp. 17-27.

Steedle, Lamont F. *World-Class Accounting for World-Class Manufacturing*. Montvale, N.J., Institute of Management Accountants (formerly the National Association of Accountants), 1990.

Turney, Peter B.B. *Common Cents: The ABC Performance Breakthrough*. Hillsboro, Or., Cost Technology, 1991.

Turney, Peter B.B., and James M. Reeve. "The Impact of Continuous

Improvement on the Design of Activity-Based Cost Systems." *Journal of Cost Management*, Summer 1990, pp. 43-50.

Turney, Peter B.B., and Alan J. Stratton. "Using ABC to Support Continuous Improvement." *Management Accounting*, September 1992, pp. 46-50.

Utzig, Larry. "Reconciling the Two Views of Quality." In *Emerging Practices in Cost Management*, Barry J. Brinker, ed., pp. 365-368.

Appendix

Fundamental Implementation Steps

This appendix is intended to provide an approach that has been used successfully to implement activity-based costing in a variety of industries. The approach assumes that a computer software package is being utilized as part of the implementation. If it is not, the approach and terminology may vary to a certain degree but will remain largely the same. This appendix assumes the reader has an understanding of ABC and the related ABC terminology. The approach includes 12 basic steps, which are covered below:

1. *Determine the scope, timing, and objectives of the project.* What buildings, employees, product lines, and so forth are to be included in the study? What period of time is the study going to cover and what are the start and completion dates? What are the key business issues? What kind of information does the company want generated by the project?

- A static product costing model of all end products/services;
- Value analysis of activities;
- Cost of quality information;
- A dynamic model with "what if" capabilities for business expansion/contraction;
- Cost information on serving certain customers or distribution channels.

2. *Fact find.* Before launching an ABC project, it is important to understand how the business is functioning currently in order to form the basis for a solid project plan and successful implementation. Knowledge about the current material and information flow can be acquired from available flow charts, organization charts, P&L statements, interviews, and current cost system and other information systems-related documentation.

3. *Develop a project team and work plan.* A cross-functional team should be placed in charge and be held responsible for completing the project. Team members should include representatives of at least the financial, operations, and information systems areas. A detailed project work plan should be created, covering the tasks, timing for completing the tasks, and person(s) responsible for completing them.

4. *Carry out training.* Training will be required at various intervals throughout the project:

- Executive and related staff training is required before the project is launched to gain and maintain top-down support;
- Project kickoff training is required for department heads at the start of the project;
- Implementation training for the project team usually is done during each new phase of the project;
- Applications training is performed during and after implementation to get employees making operational changes to the business as information is made available.

5. *Capture activity-related information.* Determine the activities performed by all the employees included in the study. Use an activity dictionary (an extensive listing of precoded and defined activities by industry) wherever possible to avoid extensive interviewing. Capture employee time by activity for the time period included in the study. This can be done by a number of different methods but normally is done by estimating time.

6. *Do value-added coding of activities.* Some companies want to make process improvements and/or reduce costs without sacrificing customer service. An ideal way to understand where opportunities exist is coding activities using a value-added coding scheme. There are a variety of such schemes; companies should pick one that meets the objectives of the business.

7. *Create activity centers.* Depending on the ABC software, it may be possible to segment activities within or across departments into activity centers. Activity centers provide another means of capturing information for the objectives and business issues identified at the beginning of the project. Activity centers allow activities to be captured along business processes rather than functional departments if so desired to provide additional insight to the business. Activities usually are driven to activity centers using a first-stage driver such as percentage allocation or number of occurrences.

8. *Code payroll-related expenses into hierarchy categories.* Payroll activities should be coded to hierarchy categories (unit, batch, product-sustaining, facility-sustaining, and administrative if desired). This segregation will enable the company to understand better the impact of making certain changes to the business. For example, what the impact will be of increasing volume 20%; what expenses could and should go away if a product line is phased out.

9. *Split and code nonpayroll-related expenses.* Like payroll-related expenses, nonpayroll-related expenses (activities) need to be split into logical activity centers and coded to hierarchy categories (unit, batch, product-sustaining, facility-sustaining, and administrative if used). For example, unit-related expenses most likely will be related to the production department and should be placed in a production activity center and coded as unit-sustaining expenses. The same process should be used to scrutinize batch, process, facility-sustaining, and administrative expenses.

10. *Identify and capture cost driver information.* Each individual activity needs to have a link to an end product/service(s). This link normally is made through a second-stage cost driver that is measurable and identifiable to a component or end product/service. Interviews normally are conducted with informed persons to review the activities performed so as to determine the ideal and surrogate second-stage cost drivers. Companies that have captured second-stage driver quantities at the component level will need to create or download a bill of materials into the ABC model to get the associated cost to the end products defined in the model.

11. *Load the model.* Expenses from the general ledger should be loaded into the model at the line item level. The steps carried out above will allow the expenses to be split into activities and driven to activity centers using first-stage drivers. Where indicated, second-stage drivers then will take activities to the products. Product identification numbers need to be loaded into the model to allow this process to happen. Inputting hierarchy codes and value-added codes by activity should be performed as part of loading the model.

12. *Run the model and generate reports.* Model output reports can be generated once input data are in the model and validation routines have been performed to ensure data integrity. A variety of output reports can be generated depending on the information needs of the user, some of which have been included in the eight ABC case studies included in this research project. Data also can be downloaded to a Lotus 1-2-3/graphics file for further analysis by the user.

As a final step, *analyze the results*. If the ABC project has been structured properly, most of the objectives and business issues identified or established at the beginning of the project should now be addressed, based on the data collected and reports generated. Additional analysis may be required to interpret the results and provide the basis for recommendations going forward.